Mark Woods has covered national and international stories for the UK's premier news agency, the Press Association, as well as playing a part in helping a TV company lose and Comic Relief raise a billion pounds each. He lives in south-west London with his wife and three children.

Also by Mark Woods

Pregnancy for Men (White Ladder, 2010, 2018)
Babies & Toddlers for Men (White Ladder, 2012)
Planet Parent (White Ladder, 2012)

Pregnancy, Babies & Toddlers for Men

Mark Woods

white
LADDER

First published in Great Britain in 2024 by White Ladder
An imprint of Hodder & Stoughton
An Hachette UK company

Parts of this book were originally published as *Pregnancy for Men*
(2010, 2018) and *Babies & Toddlers for Men* (2012).

1

A CIP catalogue record for this title is available from the British Library

Trade Paperback ISBN 9781399720830
ebook ISBN 9781399720847

Typeset in Bembo MT by Hewer Text UK Ltd, Edinburgh
Printed and bound in Great Britain by Clays Ltd, Elcograf S.p.A.

Hodder & Stoughton policy is to use papers that are natural, renewable
and recyclable products and made from wood grown in sustainable forests.
The logging and manufacturing processes are expected to conform
to the environmental regulations of the country of origin.

Hodder & Stoughton Ltd
Carmelite House
50 Victoria Embankment
London EC4Y 0DZ

www.hodder.co.uk

Sarah, Stan, Louis and Nancy, with love.

ACKNOWLEDGEMENTS

I owe a huge debt of gratitude not only to all the dads who contributed to this book, but to the mums too. Your honesty, and in many cases bravery, will not go unrecorded in the annals of parental history. I salute you.

Many thanks also to the fantastic teams at Crimson Publishing and Hachette.

Thanks to Rebecca Winfield for the sage advice, Caroline Millar for her invaluable research, Sara Warren for casting an experienced midwife's eye over the detail, and my mum and dad for deciding that six kids just weren't enough.

But mainly, thank you to my amazing wife Sarah for the three beautiful children she has miraculously made happen and for only very occasionally letting the fact that I take notes more often than I take the rubbish out get on her nerves.

CONTENTS

Introduction   xi

Month 1: Is there anybody there?   1

Month 2: Say hello to my little friend   22

Month 3: Show and tell   40

Month 4: I see you baby   51

Month 5: Scans, flans and holiday plans   67

Month 6: Move over Dad   85

Month 7: Brace yourselves   115

Month 8: Last orders please   148

Month 9+: It's showtime   167

First days: What happens in the hospital?   219

0–3 Months: The first day of the rest of your life   237

4–6 Months: Getting down to business   277

7–9 Months: The fog begins to lift   295

10–12 Months: You've come a long way, baby   314

13–16 Months: Your baby: the information junkie   336

17–20 Months: Getting away from it all   366

21–24 Months: The twos: just how terrible are they?   393

25–30 Months: Fancy another?   422

31–36 Months: Bye bye, baby   449

Index   467

INTRODUCTION

A generation or two ago you were more likely to see a fully grown llama attending a birth than the father of the child.

Now, something like 90% of deliveries have the dad-to-be in attendance. That's a profound change, not least for llamas who no longer get much of a look-in. With this shift has also come what feels like a seismic shift in the involvement of the father in the pregnancy, birth and early years of their children's lives.

In the main, it's fair to say that this change has been welcomed by modern man; as the nature of relationships has changed for the better, so has the desire of many new dads to be involved in almost certainly the most important event that a couple can share together.

Preparing for such a momentous period isn't easy. All pregnancies, births, and parenting rides are different, but despite this, over the years some excellent books have been put together to give women the blow-by-blow information they need on carrying, delivering and caring for their baby.

Of course, the central characters of any book on pregnancy are always going to be the main protagonists in the drama, the mother and the child – and quite right, too. But with the increasing role of the father, having a book that looks at things from their perspective felt like it might be mildly useful – and that was all the lukewarm encouragement I needed to write one.

Judging by the reviews of earlier editions of my books there is a distinct possibility that this is being purchased by a woman for a man, most likely her partner – sometimes even to announce that you are both expecting. If you happen to be a woman, hello; you are most welcome and please rest assured that within these pages you are held in the highest regard, revered in fact, for what you go through to produce and nurture a baby. You may even find the way the information is communicated here a refreshing alternative to the many pregnancy guides you have no doubt got stacked beside your bed at this very moment. Or you may have been thoroughly put off already. Either way, thank you.

If you're a same-sex couple you are incredibly welcome too and not just because you might buy a copy each, but because in my experience for what it's worth you do an extraordinarily good job. There are, no doubt, much better books out there which hone in on your particular journey, but if you've ended up with this one I hope it's useful or entertaining and hopefully both.

As in every other facet of life, things don't fall neatly into designated time frames throughout pregnancy and early parenthood, but I've done my very best to ensure that most of what is contained within each section is roughly relevant to that part of the journey.

To avoid confusion, I refer to the baby as 'he' in the pregnancy section of this book and 'she' in the post-birth section. Or is that more confusing? I'm not sure but that's what I've done and it feels right that it's all square.

I really hope you enjoy reading *Pregnancy, Babies and Toddlers for Men* and find it useful. I loved researching it, interviewing other dads for it and writing it.

Most of all, though, I love being a dad and I'm absolutely certain you will, too.

IS THERE ANYBODY THERE?

(1–6 weeks)

You've done it. You have played a not insubstantial part in the creation of a new life. The chances of you doing something more profound, more impactful, more 'God-like' during the entirety of the rest of your life are zero. Making a baby is an extraordinary thing to do.

Yet everyone's at it, aren't they? Every tired face you see on a Zoom, every football fan in a packed ground, every chippy teenager on the back seat of the bus – they were all conceived, carried and delivered in one way or another. In fact, every single second that ticks by sees around four women give birth to a baby somewhere on the planet. It's no big deal.

And that's the pregnancy paradox you are about to enter into; this most natural of happenings, this most common of occurrences, will utterly rock your world in spectacular fashion.

Of course people close to you will take a lot of interest (mainly those who have already been through it) but, all in all, the nine months of your first pregnancy are a time when you and your partner are in the most beautiful of bubbles.

It's not all back rubs and belly laughs, for sure; the whole experience is laced with an unspeakable fear, the dread that something could go wrong. But as you stand at Month 1, make a little promise to yourself that you'll do your very best to savour every day – because it'll be gone before you know it.

CONCEPTION – IN THE BEGINNING WAS THE WORM . . .

If I was to ask you to tell me how conception works – actually what happens from the moment of ejaculation to the precise point when you have a new life on your hands, would you be able to tell me?

The scores of dads I've spoken to in the course of writing this book were, to a man-jack, pretty hopeless on that one – and I was the worst of the lot. Most started off confidently talking about the cervix, took a wrong turn at the uterus and ended up saying the word fallopian a lot, but not much else.

Now, it's entirely possible that I have a particularly uninformed set of friends and acquaintances and, if you knew me, you'd say that was a stone-cold certainty. But I suspect a lot of people, like me, don't really have a clue what happens when a baby is actually conceived – but the details become very important as you navigate the nervy first few months.

How it actually happens

The ovaries – two small organs on either side of the womb (aka the uterus) – are the egg warehouses of the female body. The vast majority of baby girls are born with up to 450,000 eggs in their ovaries, many of which begin dying off as soon as she enters the world. And there is a steady decrease in number as time goes on. During a woman's fertile years she'll probably release about 400 eggs, beginning with her first period and ending with the menopause.

So far, so double biology.

Every month – usually during the middle of the menstrual cycle – between one and three eggs start to reach maturity in one of the ovaries. The ripest, juiciest, most prime egg out of the three is then released and in a flash is sucked up by the opening of the nearest fallopian tube – the channel that leads from each ovary to the womb.

This, my friend, is ovulation.

Your average egg survives and can be fertilised for about 12–24 hours after it's released. If it's lucky enough to meet up with a sperm in that time, the two can hook up and make a baby. Ahhhh. If not, it ends its journey at the womb, where it disintegrates and is expelled during a period. Better luck next time.

Meanwhile, in a scrunched-up scrotum near you, sperm is being produced at a fantastical rate – millions of the microscopic miracles flow off a 24/7 production line, and with 300 million sperm liberated with each ejaculation you can see why your little testicles need to put in the overtime big style.

Working conditions for the heroic duo have to be pretty much spot on and the testicles hang outside your body because they're quite sensitive to temperature. To produce healthy sperm they have to stay at around 34°C (94°F); that's about 4°C (39°F) cooler than normal body temperature so at some point in evolution they built their own external ball park.

Once sperm is created, it's stored in a coiled tube in the testicle called the epididymis, which if unfurled would measure 12m (40ft).

When the erection alarm bells start ringing as an ejaculation is approaching, the sperm are scooped up and mixed with semen, which helps them travel. They are now ready to have their one and only crack at achieving the goal they were made for – fertilising an egg.

So, having acquainted ourselves with the stars of the show, let's fast forward to curtain up – what happens when you have sex? In men, orgasm sends sperm-rich semen shooting into the vagina and towards the cervix at about 10 miles per hour, giving them a good send-off as they embark on their long and hazardous journey.

Inside your partner, millions of your sperm are beginning their quest to find an egg. Tragically, though, the scene in there resembles the first 15 minutes of *Saving Private Ryan*. If it's not the acid in the vagina out to burn them alive, it's the cervical mucus that hauls them back like quicksand. Out of the millions who began the trip, only a few dozen will make it to the egg, the majority getting trapped, fried, lost or, one would imagine, just plain depressed at the scale of the task they have been asked to perform.

It's carnage in there.

Only the very best swimmers make it the 18cm (seven inches) from the cervix through the uterus to the fallopian tubes, with the real athletes arriving in as little as 45 minutes and the knackered old war horses limping in up to 12 hours later. But no matter how long it takes them, what the sperm are all desperate to find on arrival is an egg. If they don't find what they're looking for immediately, all is not necessarily lost – the sperm can wait there in a resting stage for 12–24 hours. Conversation between the tense sperm must be quite awkward at this stage, I'd imagine, but the line 'Do you come here often?' must be too hard to resist, surely?

Once a sperm does meet an egg, it then has to find the energy for one final push to get inside it before any of the others do. The very instant one is successful, the egg effectively clamps down a protective shield around itself so that no other sperm can get inside.

Now that the race is over, the real work can begin as the genetic material in the sperm combines with the genetic material in the egg to create a new cell that starts to divide rapidly.

Technically, pregnancy begins when that bundle of new cells, known as a zygote, and then an embryo, travels the rest of the way down the fallopian tube and attaches itself to the wall of the womb and bang, you're both expecting!

PREGNANCY TEST – FINDING OUT AND KEEPING QUIET

Such is the gravity of discovering that you have actually made another person – created a member of the most complex and profound species on the entire planet – that it's a wonder the news isn't accompanied by the sound of heavenly trumpets, rather than the tinkle of wee onto plastic.

Now and then

The home pregnancy test is of course a standard piece of kit in the modern world. In fact so sophisticated are the latest models that they have done away with the blue line appearing – no, no, that was way too confusing. Nowadays you get tests that don't leave anything to chance and flash up the words 'pregnant' or 'not pregnant'. But that's not all: they tell you how many weeks gone you are, too.

5

The vast majority of home pregnancy tests work by detecting the hormone human chorionic gonadotrophin (hCG), which is secreted by the placenta into both the bloodstream and into the urine after passing through the kidneys, right after a fertilised egg implants in the uterus. Most tests offer a percentage accuracy rate well into the high 90s.

It wasn't until the 1980s that pregnancy tests as we now know them started to appear, though. Before that there were some really quite disturbing methods of detecting if there was a little person knocking around. The ancient Egyptians were the first ones to focus in on urine as the best place to start looking. But mixing wee with different grains to see if they germinated was where the smart thinking stopped, mind you. The quacks of the Middle Ages kept on sniffing around urine too, but their idea was to mix it with wine or whatever alcohol was lying about the place. Does this taste corked or conceived to you?

It wasn't until a century ago, when scientists were uncovering the secret world of the hormone, that the modern pregnancy test really began to take shape. This milestone was bad news for baby rabbits though – the *méthode du jour* of detection to find out if a woman was pregnant was to inject a urine sample from her into a little fluffy bunny. The only drawback was that in 100% of cases the procedure meant that the bunny died. As if that wasn't bad enough, the results themselves weren't even accurate! Happily, this wretched method didn't catch on and by the late 1970s a woman could test her own urine at home. But my God what a palaver it was: mixing with various solutions in a range of test tubes was required – a kind of baby home-brew kit. But the home test was here and pretty soon it had turned into what we recognise today and will almost certainly be the way you find out that you're a father-to-be.

Be ready for the emotional rollercoaster

Congratulations, you're about to enter a world full of words you've never heard before, sights you've not seen before and emotions so new to you that they will knock you flat on your back.

For many men, the very moment they discovered the news is indelibly marked in the consciousness forever, a kind of JFK moment without the grassy knoll. Some are on the end of the phone; some are standing right there with their partner waiting for the test to do its thing; some no doubt find out on WhatsApp, some may even be lucky enough to find out by being presented with a book just like this one – good on you!

But no matter where or how you discover the news, you'll probably be hit by an emotional triple whammy. Firstly, there's the joy hearing for the first time that you've managed to make a baby is a blast of the pure good stuff, you and your partner are superstars!

The second emotion that almost all the dads I have spoken to admit to feeling is relief. Secretly, it seems, many of us fear that we'll have problems right up until we get the ultimate confirmation that it's not blanks we're firing.

Then, finally, you worry. A new kind of worry that in truth never ever stops for as long as you're a parent. But there's absolutely nothing you can do to stop it so, you know, don't worry about it.

And now it's time to tell your friends and relatives the amazing news.

Except you can't.

That's right, the news that you've created the beginnings of a completely new life, a totally new person – the biggest thing you've ever had to tell anyone ever – you have to keep between the two of you.

Spreading the joy

If ever you wanted to tell someone something, it's this. God knows we have enough bad news to impart over the course of our lives – so let's ring out the bells, take out a page in the paper and let everyone know how clever we are.

But that's not the way it works, is it? Modern wisdom dictates that you don't spread the word until you reach the three-month mark. The three-month silence is a far from universal or uniform practice, though. Many people choose to tell parents or very close friends as much to gain early support in the tough first few weeks as out of a desire to spread the joy. There is no right or wrong way of doing it, just what suits you and the mother of your child best.

Around the world things differ somewhat too. In Java, pregnancy is announced right from the off and celebrated with ceremonial feasts and rejoicings – which sounds lovely, doesn't it? Then again, in several other cultures the whole thing is kept secret for a belt-bursting seven months to avoid various superstitious ills.

Of course, there are very sound reasons why the vast majority of people choose to keep quiet until the first trimester is out of the way – and almost all of them centre on miscarriage. As we are about to discover, almost 98% of miscarriages happen within the first 13 weeks of pregnancy, so it's easy to see why many couples choose to keep the news close to their chests.

Words from your fellow man:

Tom, 34, father of two: *We were in bed at my wife's sister's house and Jane said she thought she was late, had sore boobs and had been sick. Years* of avid Colombo-watching led me to conclude we needed to purchase a pregnancy test.

The next day on the way to her parents we stopped off at Tesco Extra and Jane bought one there and then, leaving me to the shopping. With a knowing look from the till lady she headed straight to the toilets, past a security guard who had clearly seen it all before.

Meanwhile my shopping continued and I came across cans of Napolina chopped tomatoes on buy one get one free. As I loaded my 11th and 12th tins into the trolley, I saw Jane at the opposite end of the aisle. A smile, a nod, small tears of joy and we were expecting our first baby.

After a long embrace, the trolley was emptied of all tinned goods and I headed straight for the organic veg aisle.

Enzo, 36, father of one: My wife bought me a book entitled Conception, Pregnancy and Birth in the hope that I would read between the lines and discover that she was pregnant.

I didn't.

I simply focused on the word 'conception' and thought to myself, 'Here we go; she is going to get me to eat lentils for the next six months to boost my fertility . . .'. In the end, she had no choice but to show me the two positive test results and shout 'I AM PREGNANT'.

MISCARRIAGE – THE M WORD

A fair chunk of your partner's time – and therefore your time – will be used worrying about miscarriage across the first months of pregnancy. The fretting and the nervousness is relatively unavoidable, I'm afraid, and the sad fact is that miscarriage is not an uncommon occurrence.

The often-quoted figure is that around 20% of all pregnancies end in miscarriage, but this is increasingly being seen as a conservative estimate. Many miscarriages can and do happen without women even realising they were pregnant, and putting the episode down to a heavier than usual period. With that taken into account, the miscarriage rate is thought to be more like 40% or 50% – with some experts going as far as to say that almost every sexually active woman will have one at some point in her life, whether she is aware of it or not.

Whatever the true figure is, what's for sure is that miscarriage lurks around the first three months of pregnancy like a menacing playground bully; unlikely to strike, but always carrying a threat.

With that in mind, it's worth getting clued up on the real facts and figures around miscarriage, rather than listening to some of the more widely held myths and scare stories – that way you can sleep a little more easily, and, more importantly, you can help the mother of your child navigate through what are often choppy early waters.

What is a miscarriage?

The word miscarriage itself refers to the loss of a developing pregnancy until the 20th week of gestation. Medical terminology, in all its clumsy clinical glory, labels this event a spontaneous abortion. Not surprisingly, most women who miscarry would react pretty badly to hearing that phrase at such a traumatic time, but it is worth noting that 'abortion' merely means the loss of a pregnancy – it doesn't assume that the pregnancy ended out of choice.

There are three types of miscarriage:

- **Complete miscarriage:** This means that the woman's body expels all the tissue. Symptoms include the passage of all pregnancy tissue and a closed cervix.
- **Incomplete miscarriage:** This occurs when the body expels part of the pregnancy, with portions of the foetus, amniotic sac or placenta being retained. Symptoms can include cramping, and the discharge of blood and foetal matter.
- **Missed miscarriage:** This means that the woman's body doesn't get rid of the dead foetus itself. Missed miscarriages may go unnoticed for weeks and symptoms may include a lack of feeling pregnant. However, because of the high hormone levels, some women go through this awful experience even while experiencing a wide range of pregnancy symptoms.

Management of miscarriages that are missed or incomplete often includes dilation and curettage (usually referred to as a D&C). In this procedure, doctors manually open the cervix and get rid of what's inside the uterus.

What causes a miscarriage?

Although this is somewhat of a grey area, it seems pretty certain that foetuses that have some kind of abnormality tend to miscarry. For instance, it's thought that around half of all first trimester miscarriages are the result of chromosomal abnormalities that prevent the foetus from developing as it should.

Another cause is that the foetus did not implant, or bury itself, into the womb lining properly – again, down to bad luck rather than carelessness or bad decision-making.

Maternal age can be a factor, though. For women younger than

35, the miscarriage rate is 6.4%; for those aged 35–40 it is 14.7%; and for mothers-to-be over 40 it's 23.1%. A woman is also at a higher risk of miscarriage if she has had more than one miscarriage already.

There is also thought to be a link with the use of certain pain-killers. The use of some nonsteroidal anti-inflammatory drugs (NSAID), including popular pain relievers such as ibuprofen and naproxen, has been shown by a 2011 study of 52,000 pregnant Canadian women to be potentially associated with an increased risk of miscarriage. These results, together with earlier studies that suggest a similar link, cause many women to avoid aspirin and ibuprofen altogether and stick with paracetamol as their pregnancy painkiller of choice. There has been no link found whatsoever between paracetamol and miscarriage.

In 2017, another substantial Canadian study suggested some antibiotics could double the risk of miscarriage if taken during early pregnancy. While the major risk highlighted by the study is for women prescribed antibiotics who do not yet know they are pregnant, caution and a medical consultation are certainly advisable before any antibiotics are taken.

The warning signs

The most obvious signs of miscarriage are period-like pains and heavy bleeding, but your partner could miscarry without even knowing, especially very early in pregnancy.

The sight of blood during early pregnancy doesn't always signal a miscarriage. Often called spotting, light bleeding is fairly common and it's estimated that about 15%–25% of women experience some sort of bleeding in the first trimester. Although in many cases it turns out to be nothing, the medical advice is unanimous – at the first sight of bleeding during pregnancy, no matter how light, contact your doctor, midwife or hospital straight away for advice, even if the bleeding soon stops. Don't take any chances.

The aftermath

Losing a baby is a tragedy, no matter how early in pregnancy it takes place. Like almost every other emotional event in our lives, everyone's feelings vary. You and your partner may want to start trying to get pregnant again straight away, or you may differ on that score. A degree of apprehension and anxiety at the thought of going for it again is almost unavoidable. Medically, most doctors advise waiting until your partner has had at least one period before trying again, but emotionally it's much more difficult to put a generic time frame on it.

The sense of loss you both feel may be similar or poles apart. It may also be linked with the type of miscarriage you had; later or missed miscarriage, which involve medical intervention, may obviously cause a great deal more emotional and physical upheaval.

The knowledge that early miscarriages, in particular, could well be nature's way of stopping something that isn't quite right before it really starts, does sometimes help people to rationalise what has happened – and can give our brains the capacity to move on. No matter what the circumstances, though, getting over a miscarriage, especially for the mother-to-be, is never to be underestimated.

But however awful your experience may be, or however deep your sense of loss, take some heart in the fact that the vast majority of couples come together, help each other get over it in their own time and go on to have a happy and healthy baby.

Words from your fellow man:

Chris, 34, father of one: *Since we had our first we've suffered two miscarriages. The first was because of a condition called trisomy 13 – the baby forms and is alive but its brain doesn't form as it should, there's no face, too many digits – it's horrific. Most die in the womb before birth, a few make it but die very shortly afterwards.*

We were gutted to say the least and it hit my wife particularly hard and she was in meltdown for a long time. We were told, however, that there was no lasting damage and that we could try again. So we did.

This time we were soon told we had identical twins. I had a good feeling about this one, but my wife was understandably nervous as hell leading up to the three-month scan.

As a vet, she can pretty much 'read' the screen of the scan. I can't. As I was staring at it trying to find the image of a baby, my wife just looked at the doctor in terror – and he just said, 'I'm sorry' – we'd lost them. Then all hell broke loose. Talk about raw human emotion flooding out. We cried for days.

Levi, 36, father of two: *When our first child was nearly two, my wife had a miscarriage at about eight weeks. She bled heavily for two weeks and felt very poorly. Her next period, maybe two months later, was a mixed bag of emotions for her – she was sad that it was definitely the end of the pregnancy, even though she had rationalised it well up to then.*

I was upset but without a doubt, my wife suffered more. But it's something we could get through, and was not the end of our world. I think the reason we managed it OK was through her strength of character. We agreed we would try for a baby as soon as she felt OK again. As it happens, it took a little longer than we thought for her to get her head round things, but we managed to conceive again about four months later.

Ectopic pregnancies

While we're under this dark but necessary cloud, it's probably worth getting ectopic pregnancies dealt with too. Given the relative rarity with which they occur – it happens in about one in every 100 pregnancies in the UK – this complication certainly punches above its weight in the scare-the-living-daylights-out-of-you stakes.

What is an ectopic pregnancy?

This condition is essentially a pregnancy that develops outside the womb (ectopic means 'in the wrong place'). It can occur in several places: the ovary, the abdomen, the cervix, at the join between the tube and the womb; all over the place, but by far the most common area is within the fallopian tube itself.

As the pregnancy grows, it causes pain and bleeding and, if not recognised, the tube can rupture, causing internal bleeding. It's not pretty and unless treated quickly, it can be fatal. No matter where it occurs and how it's treated, the pregnancy itself never makes it – it has to be completely removed.

Most commonly found between the fourth and tenth week of pregnancy, the most common reason for an ectopic pregnancy is thought to be a blockage or narrowing of the fallopian tube, which stops the egg from making its way to the womb. Instead, it implants where it can.

How to spot an ectopic pregnancy

Generally they show themselves in two ways:

• A missed period and positive pregnancy test accompanied by some abdominal pain, quite often on one side, and some irregular bleeding. This is by far the most common way of discovering something is wrong.

- As a full-on medical emergency. Without warning the woman becomes deeply unwell, collapses and is taken to hospital. A positive pregnancy test is found and she is transferred to theatre there and then, and a ruptured ectopic is found bleeding into the abdomen.

Now you can see why this particular complication has developed a very bad name for itself.

How is it treated?

In a small number of cases ectopics will not rupture and will be naturally absorbed back into the body. Another small percentage of cases can be treated with a drug that makes the pregnancy shrink away by stopping the cells from dividing.

But the vast majority of instances will require either keyhole surgery or more traditional open surgery. Whichever of these routes is taken, two courses of action are open to the surgeon, either to open up the tube and remove the pregnancy, or remove the tube altogether.

Around 65% of all women who have an ectopic conceive again within 18 months, but for many other women, their fertility can be affected – and possibly affected badly, depending on the damage done to one or both of the tubes.

The aftermath

Given the drama and danger that goes with an ectopic pregnancy, it can be easy to forget that as a couple you have also lost a very much wanted pregnancy and that, just as with a miscarriage, the grieving process may well take time. If your partner is unfortunate enough to go through this time, tenderness and support from an organisation such as the Ectopic Pregnancy Trust will be needed in spades.

PROGRESS – MONTH BY MONTH

Someone once said that a week was a long time in politics. It won't surprise you in the slightest to learn that (i) the person in question was himself a politician and (ii) that he didn't know how easy he had it given Brexit was still decades away.

If you want to experience weeks where truly momentous things happen, though, things like growing a heart from scratch, or creating not one, but two eyes out of a bag of gunk, then the womb is the place to be. As well as the often blistering pace that your soon-to-be son or daughter sets when it comes to growing and changing, your partner doesn't hang about either in these very early days.

These little progress reports will give you a bite-sized rundown of everything you need to know about the changes the two most important people in your life are going through month by month.

The age of your baby

In order for us to take this information on board in palatable monthly chunks, rather than week by week, we need to do a bit of nifty maths at this stage.

Your baby's age can be determined by counting the first day of your partner's last menstrual cycle as day one. Although she wasn't actually pregnant on that day, this is the system – the gestational age method – that most doctors use in determining due date and therefore how old your very wee one actually is.

This means that we add in the extra two weeks (it can obviously be a few days either way, but 14 days is used as a standard measurement) that it takes to get back to the first day of the last period. See the Month 9 chapter for more on due dates if you dare.

All that adds up to mean that month one for the baby is counted as running from the first week to the sixth week. Don't worry if that has made your nose bleed, pretty much every other month is just your standard four weeks long, so month two is from the seventh week to the 10th week and so on.

PROGRESS REPORT, MONTH 1

Your baby at 1–6 weeks

Your little one is on fire. At the end of this month your baby will be about the size of a raisin, but what a sun-ripened chocolate-coated little belter of a raisin it is!

Once the fertilised egg is embedded in the lining of the uterus, it multiplies and grows at a truly astonishing rate. What was originally a sperm/egg combo is now officially a blastocyst (fluid-filled ball) comprising several hundred cells. Pretty soon, though, this blastocyst divides into two.

The half still attached to the womb will become the placenta – unlucky. The other half will become your baby – jackpot.

The baby section then divides into three layers which will go on to form your baby's body. The innermost layer will later develop into the thyroid gland, pancreas, lungs, liver, urinary tract and bladder. That's quite a layer you'll be thinking, but wait.

The middle layer will become the entire skeleton, all the muscles (including those in the heart), testes or ovaries, spleen, blood vessels, blood cells, kidneys and the dermis, the deepest layer of skin.

And the outer layer pulls its weight too – this will provide the hair, nails, tooth enamel, the lenses of the eyes, epidermis, sweat glands and nipples.

By the end of the first month, the beginnings of the spinal cord are in place and there's even a rudimentary, but very much beating, heart – and all this while your partner may well just be thinking that she has a bad case of wind, rather than a microscopic miracle taking place inside her.

Your partner

For most first-month mothers-to-be there is a distinct lack of symptoms. Your partner may feel slightly premenstrual and she may pass urine more often than usual or have sore breasts. Some women may even get the first knockings of morning sickness. But compared with later months the first handful of weeks can be a veritable breeze.

But that doesn't mean there isn't stuff happening to her. The hormone progesterone is busy making her cervical mucus thicker and more gloopy, eventually forming a plug. This, as the name suggests, is nature's way of putting a big, snotty bouncer on the door to stop anything getting in or out.

MUST-DOS OF MONTH 1

You'll love 'being pregnant' as you will now find yourself saying. But don't let me give you the impression it's a doddle. Your partner is about to go through a series of physical and psychological changes of gargantuan proportions. What's more, you, yes you, will need to become her masseuse, her counsellor, her bag carrier and her punch bag – all while trying to get your own head around becoming a dad.

It's far from easy, but to help you navigate your way through, here are three little things you can do this month that will help make your partner happy and you feel you're chipping in practically as well as emotionally.

Mum's the word

Sounds simple this, but worth a mention for sure; if you've agreed with your partner not to tell anyone your big news until the three-month scan, for Christ's sake don't blurt it out to your mate, your mum or your boss. No news travels like pregnancy news.

Testing time

Make no mistake: your reaction to the positive pregnancy test result will be remembered, regurgitated and requoted for decades to come.

For the love of God don't let any fear or anxiety you may be feeling turn into words at that precise moment. If you're feeling like the contents of your stomach have divided equally and are heading to both your north and south orifices, keep it to yourself and tell her later after the initial moment has passed.

It's an overwhelming thing to find out that you are on your way to being a dad and it has the potential to mess with your head for a second or two even if you are nothing but thrilled, but be positive and warm; she's almost certainly twice as apprehensive as you are beneath all the joy. Besides, there's plenty of time to worry yourself sick later – just enjoy this moment.

A spot of bother

It's startling how easy it is to worry yourself into sheer blind panic once you're expecting. The urge to protect the tiny life is a trigger-happy little blighter and can, if you're not careful, lead to you making situations a whole lot worse rather than better.

A typical example of where a cool, calm head is needed, is vaginal bleeding, or spotting. Around 25% of all pregnant women suffer some sort of bleeding in the first trimester, with more than half of them going on to give birth to a healthy baby at full term.

Bleeding doesn't necessarily mean miscarriage; it doesn't necessarily mean anything is wrong at all in fact. In many cases it is down to break-through bleeding – the hormones that control the menstrual cycle can cause bleeding when your partner's period would have been due.

Another innocent explanation could be implantation bleeding – when the fertilised egg attaches itself to the wall of the uterus causing spots of blood to appear in your partner's underwear.

At this point, screeching, 'Blood, blood, there's blood,' isn't what's called for. Your partner will be petrified with fear as it is and your calm reassuring presence will work wonders.

If your partner does experience any level of bleeding whatsoever at any point in the pregnancy, the thing to do is call your midwife, doctor or hospital straight away to get it checked out.

SAY HELLO TO MY LITTLE FRIEND

(7–10 weeks)

For many women the first month of pregnancy is a bit of a non-event in terms of the physical impact it has on them. For a minority it's the first of many months of nausea or even deeply disruptive sickness.

All in all, though, the tiny little bag of cells buried deep inside a woman's tummy doesn't really make its presence felt in the first few weeks in the way it most certainly does later on in proceedings. It quietly goes about its business, dividing and growing, growing and dividing, feathering its nest for the long journey ahead. But once it has got its newly formed feet under the table by around the second month, it often makes a surprisingly large impact for one so small.

Let's tackle the little blighters one at a time, shall we?

EARLY PREGNANCY SYMPTOMS – MORNING SICKNESS AND CO

Morning sickness

First things first: morning sickness doesn't just happen in the morning. Whoever named it patently got bored waiting around and chipped off for lunch thinking they'd seen enough. Nausea and sickness can and do strike pregnant women at any time of the day or night.

It's reckoned around eight out of 10 mothers-to-be feel sick at some point, with half of them actually vomiting. Symptoms vary wildly from woman to woman. The lucky ones will get the odd bout of mild queasiness, whereas others will be struck down by the severest, truly debilitating, form of the complaint called hyperemesis gravidarum. If your partner is struck down by this, you are both in for a tough time. She will be vomiting morning, noon and night, unable to eat and drink properly, and even losing weight when she should be putting it on.

Make no mistake, this can be serious and many women who get chronic nausea and vomiting in pregnancy (NVP), to give it its clinical name, often feel like no one takes their plight seriously or understands the magnitude of what they are going through – which can lead to depression.

Why morning sickness occurs is a bit of a mystery. One theory is that the changes in hormone levels during the early stages of pregnancy may cause short-term nausea and vomiting. The pregnancy hormone human chorionic gonadotropin (hCG) is thought by many to be the culprit – which is why those women expecting twins often suffer from worse morning sickness because they are producing more hCG. Oestrogen levels also rocket during the first three months, coinciding with the time that morning sickness is at the peak of its puke-inducing powers. Rising levels of oestrogen may heighten the sense of smell too, which may explain why certain pongs can trigger the onset of symptoms.

The second predominant theory is that it's all Darwin's fault. Many scientists believe that NVP is an evolutionary adaptation to ward women off potentially dodgy food.

You'd have thought that some kind of pamphlet would have sufficed.

The theory goes that morning sickness often puts women off eating foods that can potentially become contaminated, such as meat, poultry and eggs, and nudges them towards preferring foods that have a low risk for transmitting infections.

It's certainly true that pregnant women often develop a sense of smell that puts them on a par with police drugs dogs. That tuna melt you had at lunch will soon have your bloodhound partner running screaming out of the back door the moment you walk in through the front. It's also been suggested that substances such as alcohol can set off a bout of sickness. NVP often acts as nature's very own prosecco-prevention officer, too, rendering hitherto desirable tipples utterly vomit-inducing for many a mother-to-be in the early weeks.

As with many facets of pregnancy, there are also 101 – for clarity, let's say more challenging – theories as to the cause of morning sickness. My favourite is that it's the result of the mother-to-be's loathing of her partner; the subconscious manifestation of which is a desire to abort the foetus through vomiting.

Take a bow Sigmund Freud for that belter.

One thing there is agreement on is that, on the whole, morning sickness does no harm to the baby at all provided crucially that the mother-to-be can keep some food and fluid down – if the frequency of vomiting starts to go much beyond twice a day and dehydration is a worry then a visit to the GP or midwife is a smart move.

Recent thinking sees morning sickness more as a sign of a healthy pregnancy, signifying that the female sex hormones that keep the placenta implanted in the womb are plentiful. But I seriously wouldn't try to float that cheery piece of news by your partner as you are holding her hair back for her in a Costa toilet.

In most pregnant women, NVP starts to ease off between the third and fourth month mark, but for some it lasts longer and for a cursed few it stays with them for the entire pregnancy.

What can you do to help?

One thing you shouldn't do is try to insist that your partner continues to force down a healthy balanced diet if it makes her hurl. A spell of eating little else but grapes, the middle bit of a sausage roll and the salt off Tuc crackers isn't the end of the world – and if that's all your partner can keep down then that's what's for dinner.

Luckily the mother-to-be's liver stores a lot of the nutrients the baby needs to keep on track, so a spot of weird eating doesn't do any damage (lots of fluid and a folic acid supplement are a must, though).

A few other tips are:

- Avoid drinks that are cold, tart, or sweet.
- Drink little and often, rather than in large amounts.
- Eat small, frequent meals that are high in carbohydrate and low in fat.
- Eat some plain biscuits 20 minutes before getting up. This one seems to get passed on from generation to generation and is, if nothing else, a good excuse to snack in bed – you're on de-crumb duty, by the way.
- Avoid piping hot meals – clever little one this. Cold food doesn't give off as much of a smell as hot food.

Sore breasts

Two words that are well worth remembering.

Particularly during early pregnancy many women have extremely sensitive and sore breasts – really, really sore.

As their body gets ready for the months of pregnancy to come, they produce the hormones oestrogen and progesterone and it's these two that are the main culprits behind what can be a pretty troublesome pregnancy symptom. As well as the hefty hormone surge, your partner's breasts are also beginning to store fat and increase in size as milk glands start to appear ready for the big feed once the baby arrives.

The worst of this phase has usually passed by the end of the third month, but not always, so steer well clear.

Hurting hooter

Before we move on from soreness, one pregnancy ailment that doesn't get much of a look-in but can cause nagging discomfort is something called rhinitis of pregnancy.

Our old friend oestrogen basically makes the inside of the nose swell and can even trigger the production of more mucus – leading to a constant runny or stuffy nose for around 20–30% of pregnant women.

Constipation

Women who suffer from chronic constipation during pregnancy are often truly plagued. Irregular bowel movements and sluggish, turgid intestines can make their lives, well, shit, really. And when constipation's sidekick from hell – haemorrhoids – pops up, or out as the case may be, then things really can turn nasty.

And who's behind this anal Armageddon? That's right; it's those dastardly hormones again. This time they are causing the muscles in the bowels to relax on the job. There is at least a decent reason for this particular disruption: the general go-slow means that food stays around longer so more nutrients are absorbed for both mother and baby.

All is not lost though; here are three key ways you can help your partner avoid a major and painful log jam.

- Fibre is your best buddy in the fight against constipation. Plenty of fresh fruit and vegetables, wholegrain cereals and breads, legumes and dried fruit all help to get things moving. But for the sake of the neighbours, jumping right in to a fibre-rich diet if it's a departure from the norm can bring on wind and bloating like you would not believe.
- Eating six mini-meals a day rather than three full-blown ones can make a significant difference.
- Water, fruit and vegetable juices not only get things moving, but soften the stool so when it does finally make an appearance it's not like passing a pinecone.

Heartburn

This is an all-too-common pregnancy complaint and can cause real and prolonged discomfort for the whole nine months.

Progesterone slows down the movement of the gastrointestinal tract, essentially causing food to just sit in the stomach. Not content with that, it also softens the oesophagus and lessens its pressure, which allows stomach acid to head north rather than staying in the depths where it belongs.

Get this, though: the opening in the diaphragm that the oesophagus passes through from the chest into the abdomen can widen during pregnancy. This delightful scenario is for all intents and purposes a hiatal hernia, and if a portion of your partner's stomach slides up through this gap, it can cause havoc with stomach acid going back down. This type of heartburn is worse when lying flat so often strikes at night.

The good news is that most women who suffer from heartburn during pregnancy get a form that can be dealt with by using a normal antacid.

The important tip here is for your partner to take the medicine about 15 minutes before she eats – otherwise she is just pouring it over the semi-digested food like some hellish custard, rather than letting her stomach lining absorb it.

Exhaustion

Imagine – your body is hard at work on every level creating, housing and nourishing a new life. Your sleep patterns are shot to buggery because you're uncomfortable, weeing every 35 seconds or being doubled up with heartburn. You've spent half the day vomiting and the other half worrying about miscarriages. And, oh yeah, your hormones are doing their bit to keep your bowels nice and clogged too.

Unsurprisingly, with all this going on pregnant women get very, very, very tired. Even former dirty stop-outs who thought nothing of a 3 a.m. finish on a school night soon fail to make it through the very beginnings of a box set. The best way to cope is simple. Give in.

That sounds straightforward, but of course it isn't. If your partner loves her job or can't bear to miss out on what her friends are up to, she may well fight it for a while, but both work and social engagements eventually have to come second to the relentless waves of exhaustion that early pregnancy can bring.

You can help here in a big way by toning down your own social activity, stocking the fridge with healthy ready meals and treats to make a night in that little bit more attractive, and making it possible for her to fit in a daily nap – perhaps by swapping a few Zooms for zzzzzz's. It would also be considerate to try and make weekends an oasis of tranquillity and peace. Although it's different for everyone, the chances are that she will begin to feel like her old self during the second trimester, before coming to a grinding halt at about eight months.

It's also worth bearing in mind that once the baby is born you will be begging on hands and knees for just four hours of continuous sleep – so the pair of you should make hay and kip like nobody's business while still you can.

Mood swings

As we've seen, it's fair to say that pregnancy brings with it an eruption of hormonal activity on a volcanic scale. Almost every symptom, every change, is driven by a heady cocktail of chemicals – the word hormone itself means to 'spur on' and you can see why.

This potent pregnancy pina colada unsurprisingly also leads to mood swings and heightened emotions of all types for the mother-to-be. Of course, this is all played out against a backdrop of the whole gambit of feelings that having a baby throws up, too – joy, fear, worry, excitement. They are all there in spades, so pour on a bucketful of hectic hormones too and it's little wonder that the odd tear is often shed.

And that's just by you.

Many women find that their mood fluctuations flare up at around the month 2 mark, reduce in the second trimester, before reappearing to stir things up a bit ahead of labour.

Your role within all this is key. It's easy to find yourself fretting that you aren't reading the right books (although of course you are at the moment), buying the right kit (of which there is more in the Month 6 chapter) or generally worrying whether you will be able to cope. Although you may well be all at sea too, you are fortunate enough not to be drunk on hormones, so trying to instil an air of calm and confidence could well bring things down a notch or two.

Physically, your partner's body is changing as well and she may be starting to feel less body-confident, or even that she is putting on too much weight. Again, keeping an eye out for these feelings and riding to the rescue with a few chosen words or a cuddle can really work wonders.

Then of course there are arguments. Even though it's really, really hard at times to avoid a row with someone who is joyfully weeping openly at the weather forecast one minute and having a full-blown slanging match with Alexa the next, the onus is on you to take one for the team, swallow the bitter pill of righteousness and end any rifts quickly. Think of the children, man, think of the children. Good luck.

Words from your fellow man:

Colin, 33, father of one: From about six to 15 weeks my wife was sick three to four times a day, every day, without fail.

Everything from detergent to chewing gum set her off and she ended up having to take medication as she was getting really ill. Morning sickness has a bit of a jokey reputation, but when it's bad, it's a real curse.

Levi, 36, father of two: My wife has a tremendous sense of smell at the worst of times, but I would quite often be sent to the spare room if I had eaten something smelly or done something unspeakable in bed. Quite right too.

While alcohol was out of the picture a new brew took its place in my wife's life – Gaviscon. She was getting through a bottle a day at the height of her habit. I was boozing for two at this stage, so we clung to each other for comfort like a crack fiend befriending a heroin addict.

There were also more tears at adverts than normal. Soap operas were often washed down with a good cry too.

But my wife remained calm throughout. Only joking. She was a nightmare.

Once, on a long car journey when I was driving at 80mph down the motorway, she just said, 'I have an overwhelming urge to hit you.' She managed to hold off, at that point anyway.

SEX AND PREGNANCY – THE FULL INS AND OUTS

Now then. There's a fair bit of rubbish trotted out about what pregnancy does to a couple's sex life – the main lazy stereotype that masquerades as fact is that women get pregnant and completely go off sex, turning men into walking, talking gonads, driven to distraction and much worse, as they hump the nearest chair leg in a bid to satiate their unfulfilled sexual needs. While that may happen to some, the picture is far more complex than the 1970s sitcom model of pestered wife and groping husband suggests.

Before we delve headlong into what really goes on when three-in-a-bed finally becomes a reality in your relationship – let's look at the facts around sex and pregnancy.

First things first. With a normal pregnancy, having sex is safe right until your partner's waters break. Unless you have a traffic cone for a penis there is no way you can hit, prod, nudge or poke your baby. Surrounded by amniotic fluid, shielded by a drawbridge-like cervix and sealed in with a mucus plug, your offspring is incredibly well protected and an ample but limited appendage like the one we all carry around with us just doesn't have what it takes to gatecrash the pregnancy party.

As we will see later, though, those reassuring words count for absolutely nothing once you are actually in situ. There isn't a father-to-be alive who hasn't let the proximity of his angry penis to that of his tiny baby's soft little head cross his mind at the most inopportune of moments.

There's also no link whatsoever between having sex while pregnant and either early miscarriage or premature birth.

There are, though, certain circumstances that can make sex during pregnancy unsafe. Women who have any of these health complications should seek medical advice before doing the deed:

- a previous premature birth
- leaking amniotic fluid
- a history or high risk of miscarriage
- unexplained vaginal bleeding, discharge or cramping
- placenta praevia (a condition in which the placenta is low and covers the cervix)

- incompetent cervix (when the cervix is weakened and opens too soon).

So if none of the above applies to your partner you are home and dry. Of course, there are certain things you should avoid – inserting any objects into the vagina that could cause injury or infection for one, but you two wouldn't do that, would you? If your sexual technique involves blowing air into your partner's vagina, not only do I have an inflatable dinghy I'd like you to have a go at, but you need to avoid doing that, too, because it can force a potentially fatal air bubble into her bloodstream. Nipple stimulation also needs to be removed from your repertoire as it releases the hormone oxytocin, which can cause contractions – and as we all know there's nothing like a contraction to put a dampener on things sexually.

But generally the message from the world of medicine is that as long as your partner is having a straightforward pregnancy and you're not a colossal pervert, you can have sex as much as you like.

But will either of you fancy it?

Feeling up for it?

After talking to many, many fathers and mothers about how their sex lives were affected during pregnancy, it's clear that there is a wide range of scenarios that play out around sex, with different months heralding different feelings and libido levels for both partners.

But despite this fluctuation, for the majority of couples, a rough pattern does seem to emerge of how sex life changes through the pregnancy.

First trimester

The first trimester, with its vomiting, heartburn and constipation, funnily enough sees many women relegating sex to somewhere just below 'get toenails pulled out' on their priority list. But plenty of men don't exactly feel rampant at this stage either, and the often-cited reason for a lowering of the libido is the Darwinian feeling that somehow the job has already been done.

As ever, there are exceptions to this – more than a few men said that they enjoyed wilder, more passionate, sex with their partner in the first few months of pregnancy than they ever had before. Some said this was down to feeling a new, closer bond with their partner, others that they were still testosterone-fuelled after having their masculinity confirmed by the positive test result, while a few said that the freedom of not using contraception was what spurred them on to new pleasurable heights.

For the most part, though, sex seems to be put on the back-burner for the majority of couples during the early throws of pregnancy.

Second trimester

Once the fierce initial pregnancy symptoms die down for women, the second trimester can usher in some serious how's-your-father-to-be, it seems.

This midway sauciness is down to more than just a lack of morning sickness, though, because our old friends the hormones can contrive to make some women feel super-sexy and super-sensitive, with increased blood flow to the pelvic area meaning all sorts of receptors are switching on to wooooooahhhhh mode. So much so, in fact, that some women find the increased blood flow also increases their ability to have an orgasm – or two, or three.

Add to this the increased voluptuousness, sexy curves and general gorgeous glow that many women start to exhibit at this stage of proceedings and you've got one hot nearly mama on your hands, who you may well struggle to keep up with.

Of course for some women the exact opposite is true. Many find sex during pregnancy painful, others have huge self-image issues as their body changes and others even pay for their multi-orgasmic state by feeling abdominal cramps during or after they climax, which can even set off a wave of mini-contractions.

Third trimester

As the due date nears, sex can often fall away again as the now-sizeable bump becomes a physical and – especially for many men – a psychological barrier to getting intimate.

Being kicked by your own child when having sex with its mother is perhaps one of the oddest things that can ever happen to you. The notion of your penis being inches away from a living, breathing baby in itself has the power to dismantle an erection in seconds. Throw in the fact that your child can actually hear you grunting and groaning at this stage, too, and round it all off with actually seeing or feeling him move while you are at it – and it's easy to see why for some men the final trimester signals a real slow-down in sexual desire.

Then, of course, there's the logistics of it all. A huge great tummy with a huge great baby in it does get in the way somewhat, so some lateral thinking on the positional front is needed.

A Netmums survey found that 39% of women said the second trimester had definitely seen them have a sexual surge. However, the same survey also found that when given a list of options and asked, 'Which of these would you prefer?', although a relatively healthy 27% went for 'uninterrupted sex with your partner', 38% said 'a good night's sleep' – a choice you will come to understand and empathise with very soon. So it seems that how you and your partner deal with sex during pregnancy really has as much to do with your individual personalities and the state of your sex life before conception as it does with any standard pregnancy horniness template.

You and your partner will find what works for you, which could mean experimenting with different positions, having the time of your lives during the second trimester, or ditching intercourse completely and focusing on less intrusive ways of getting intimate. Whatever you both decide to do, as long as you keep talking and touching you won't go far wrong – and of course never underestimate the power of a kiss and a cuddle.

Words from your fellow man:

Peter, 33, father of one: It never really appealed to either of us, we were only going to give it a go for the novelty value. If I'm being honest I was pleased to have the rest.

Levi, 36, father of two: Sex was infrequent throughout, to say the least. It was useful towards the end when we found out at an antenatal class that there's something in sperm that can bring on labour. I had to fight hard to resist the temptation to ask the instructor if it could be taken orally, mind you.

Colin, 33, father of one: Sex wasn't a massive issue, although we did try a few times – I'm not sure what it was but there was a physical and psychological barrier there for both of us. Oh yes, I remember, it was a baby.

Jim, 34, father of one: The regularity stayed much the same and if anything it was a bit more romantic, a little more sensual. Once the bump arrived it became more sensual still, slower.

PROGRESS REPORT, MONTH 2

Your baby (7–10 weeks)

By the end of this month, your baby will be four times the size it was at the start of it. That is quite some growth spurt by anyone's standards. Having said that, even after expanding at such an indecent rate, the little fella is still about the length of a fun-sized Mars bar.

Your baby's head is also growing at an alarming pace to make way for its relatively gigantic brain. A neck is also beginning to develop, and the primeval tail, which has momentarily developed at the base of the spine, will be reabsorbed back into the body. Probably for the best, that.

All major organs develop in this intense period and the heart, although no bigger than a peppercorn, begins to beat strongly. Wrists and fingers begin to appear on the end of the still-forming arms, and legs start to develop with, amazingly, tiny little toes already appearing on the ends.

Under the baby's paper-thin skin its face starts to take shape too; bones fuse, the beginning of a nose is formed and the outlines of the cheeks and a jaw can be seen. Inside his mouth sits a minute tongue.

Genitals have even begun to develop. All this on a mini Mars bar. It might be happening at this very moment in thousands of wombs across the planet, but it is still an amazing feat of genetic engineering.

Your partner

As we've seen, for many women this is the month when junior and his hoard of hormonal henchmen announce their arrival on the scene in a big way.

As well as the symptoms outlined earlier, your wife's metabolic rate starts to increase and she will begin to take in more protein, more calories and often an inordinate amount of Rich Tea biscuits. All of this is fine and best not mentioned.

Although she won't look pregnant yet, her uterus has actually doubled in size since conception and that could result in a tighter waistband, which, as we all know, can bring with it a fair amount of upset in itself – so be prepared to lavish compliments from now on.

Finally, the blood supply to your partner's vagina and vulva increases in a big way from now on and they both tend to turn a rich purple colour. So please don't be alarmed.

MUST-DOS OF MONTH 2

Tuck her in

Changing bed linen is a job with a very high pain-in-the-arse rating – every man knows that. Every man also knows just how much better you sleep on lovely, cool, new sheets. Chances are your partner is more exhausted right now than she has ever been in her life. You know what to do.

The cat's done a whoopsy

Cat crap can pose a very real danger to your pregnant partner. A horridbug called Toxoplasma gondii lurks in cat faeces, as well as in unwashed fruit and veg. If caught by a pregnant woman it can be transferred from her via the placenta to her baby. The infection has the potential to cause miscarriage, blindness in the foetus or damage to its nervous system.

Read the next chapter now

The three-month mark sees the first scan being done and all the joy, nerves and occasional heartache that can bring.

Knowing what's going on ahead of time will help reassure you and your partner so you know what to expect and not put yourselves through any undue worry.

She will also see you as a frankly fabulous father-to-be as a result – which of course you are.

SHOW AND TELL
(11–14 weeks)

In a lot of ways this is one of the toughest months of all. Morning sickness and its outriders of early pregnancy misery are often in full force; the fear of miscarriage hangs around like the smell of a damp dog on a blanket; and the time comes to do two joyful and simultaneously scary things.

First up, we have what for most people is the first set of ultrasound scans. On one hand it's a time of almost overwhelming wonderment to be able to see your baby for the very first time – or a map of a particularly bad storm over the Orkneys, depending on how good your sonographer is – but it's also a moment of worry. Lots and lots of worry.

Second, once you've negotiated that little emotional minefield it's time to break the peaceful pod you and your partner have been living in for the past 12 weeks and tell your news to the cruel, cruel world. Again, for many it's a joyous time, for others a proper pain in the arse full of underwhelmed mates and overwhelmed family members, or vice versa.

So then, with your tube of gel at the ready, let's have a close look at what you'll be mainly watching this month. Your baby.

THE EARLY SCANS – THE JOY AND FEAR

Not that long ago the scanning of babies in the UK was far from a uniform science. Like bin collections, council tax and two-to-a-bed graveyard plots, it all depended on where you lived. Things have improved enormously over the past few years, but it's still a bit of a hotchpotch, especially given the advent of screening blood tests on top of ultrasound scans, some of which are available on the NHS, some only privately.

While a decent amount of research is advised, one thing is for sure: your growing baby has never been more looked after than it is now. Given that just a couple of generations ago scanning babies was basically science fiction, we've come an awfully long way in a very short space of time.

Although it may go without saying nowadays that ultrasound scans have an exemplary safety record, with no side effects being found whatsoever, there was a time in their infancy when they were viewed with suspicion. They work by sending high-frequency sound waves through the womb, which bounce off your baby before being turned into an image on a screen – which when put like that must have sounded pretty bizarre to the first parents to be offered them.

Hard tissues such as bone reflect the biggest echoes and show up white, with soft tissues coming out grey. Fluids, such as the amniotic fluid that your baby lies in, come up black as the echoes pass right through them.

Your sonographer – presumably calling them a scanner felt a bit too Tesco – will interpret these images or, failing that, take an educated guess. Apart from the gel being a little chilly on her tummy, the only real discomfort caused to your partner is down to the curious fact that to obtain a better picture her bladder needs to be full during the scan. Just what a wee-machine with a growing baby nudging her bladder needs.

The dating scan

All pregnant women should be offered a dating scan when they are between 10 and 14 weeks pregnant. As the name suggests, this primarily is to nail down exactly how pregnant your partner is in a bid to avoid her going full term in Caffé Nero when she actually thinks she still has a month to go. Also, because hormones vary at different stages of pregnancy, pinning down exactly what stage she is at is vital for future tests to be valid.

That isn't all the scan does though. It can check that your baby has a regular heartbeat and is developing normally. Your baby's head, hands, feet and limbs can all be seen after a fashion and even some organs can be viewed. Depending on the quality of the equipment, any major limb abnormalities can be picked up at this stage but the main major news you could find out is that you are expecting twins, triplets or more.

If you have recently discovered that you are expecting a multiple birth, put this book down immediately, you lunatic. You've got no time for reading – you should be out there hunting for that crucial third job, or at least just be asleep in a vain attempt to bank some glorious shut-eye.

All right, it might not be quite that bad, but man alive, it must be the test of all tests. Although they are on the increase, thanks to higher instances of in vitro fertilisation (IVF) treatment, multiple births are still rarer than you might imagine, having risen from

9 per 1,000 births globally in the 1980s to roughly 12 per 1,000 today.

Listen to the beat

There's a good chance that this scan will be the first chance you get to actually hear your baby's heartbeat, as well as see it on screen.

If you're lucky and the sonographer or midwife can find it using the hand-held instrument, you'll hear a noise that resembles someone bouncing a basketball in a wind tunnel – a frighteningly quick boom, boom, boom accompanied by a shedload of crackling and white noise.

Despite the static there's no mistaking that this is a strong sound; in fact, it's hard to imagine a more resounding confirmation that there's a separate life taking shape than the thumping and relentless pound of a baby's heart in its mother's tummy.

The picture

There's something iconic, almost Warholesque, about traditional baby-scan pictures: the moody shade and light; the somehow comfortingly shaky detail; the tantalising first glimpse of a new life.

There are new kids on the pictorial block available – three- and four-dimension scans that you can fork out for from the five-month mark to have your baby turned into something resembling Jabba the Hutt covered in caramel.

The scan of my eldest son Stanley is still on the heaving notice board above me as I write this, curled and a little faded even, but looking back, his perfect little profile really did give us a peak at how beautiful he would be – just as your baby will be too.

Or is that a takeaway menu I'm looking at? Either way, whether you tweet it, Instagram it or take out a full-page ad in your local paper for it, your first baby scan picture is a thing of wonder forever.

The Classic Scan. Yet more snow forecast for the Grampians.
Buddha takes a nap.

The nuchal translucency scan

This bit of the scan isn't half as much fun.

Nuchal translucency (NT) is the name given to a build-up of fluid under the back of a baby's neck. All babies have some of this fluid, but many babies with Down's syndrome have an enlarged amount.

To be effective the scan must be performed between 11 and 14 weeks and almost always happens at the same time as the dating scan – any earlier than this and it's too hard to perform, any later and the excess fluid can be absorbed by the baby. Recently the NT scan has been renamed 'the combined test' and is offered in England, Scotland and Wales for free on the NHS. However, if you're in Northern Ireland, you'll need to pay to have it done privately.

Using ultrasound, the NT scan measures this area of the neck and the results give a likelihood, but crucially not a definitive diagnosis, of a baby having Down's. The image is often poor, and the way of measuring on the screen is startlingly crude, but as you and your partner look on with a strange feeling in your stomach, time stands still. The results of this, your child's first-ever test, could have a profound effect on all of your lives.

As well as the scan described above, this procedure also includes a blood test, which checks for the hormone human chorionic gonadotrophin (hCG), as well as pregnancy-associated plasma protein (PAPP-A). The results of the scan and blood test are combined with factors such as the mother's age to determine how likely it is that you're expecting a baby with a chromosomal abnormality such as Down's, Edwards' or Patau's syndromes, as well as assessing the risk of your baby having a congenital heart condition.

If the results show your pregnancy is low risk, as the vast majority are, then you hug, kiss and move on to the next milestone.

If the risk is found to be high, further diagnostic tests may be offered, such as chorionic villus sampling (CVS) or amniocentesis, which can provide a definitive diagnosis but carry a small risk of miscarriage.

Alternatively, some women may be offered a Non-Invasive Prenatal Test (NIPT) which is a blood test that can be done from 10 weeks of pregnancy.

This ingenious test analyses fragments of the baby's DNA in the mother's blood to detect the presence of any extra chromosomes that may be associated with Down's syndrome. NIPT is more accurate than the Combined Test and has a lower risk of miscarriage than invasive diagnostic tests.

Words from your fellow man:

Chris, 34, father of one: I was pretty nervous at the three-month scan stage. My wife is very medically minded, being a veterinarian, so was the researcher from hell in terms of what could go wrong – glass is half empty – whereas I am a glass half full merchant, so I just assume by default that everything will be all right.

The Down's syndrome scan was my first indication that there are actually a multitude of things that can go wrong and often do. It also started discussions about the 'what ifs', which makes you question some very big moral values as a couple.

Enzo, 36, father of one: We failed the general screening and decided to go with one of the two invasive Down's syndrome detection tests.

TELLING PEOPLE – SPREADING THE WORD

By the time the choppy waters leading up to the first scans have been navigated through, some couples are bursting at the seams to tell all and sundry their news; one of them almost literally.

Many others, though, have come to love the little bubble they have constructed around themselves. Despite the vomit, the heartburn, the tears (and of course whatever the mother-to-be may have been through, too), they have become a real unit, the two of them and their tiny little baby. And now they've got to spoil it all by saying something stupid like 'I'm pregnant'.

Of course you've got no choice; pretty soon your partner will give the game away in a quite spectacular abdominal fashion and besides, telling everyone often turns out to be a fantastic time and means you and, especially, your partner can talk about what you're going through with other people who've been there.

If they don't already know, parents are usually first on the list, and depending on your circumstances their reaction can range from hyperventilating joy and the immediate drawing up of a list of things to buy, through to cardiac arrest and the immediate re-drawing of wills. Hopefully, though, both your folks and your in-laws will be nicely placed nearer the shopping-list end.

Look out, though, for a muted response at best from couples

who, perhaps unbeknown to you, have been trying unsuccessfully to conceive for a good while. It might sound like a random thing to mention, but it's almost certain that someone you know has some sort of fertility worries, even if it's just being miffed they haven't got there yet themselves.

Crucially, if more mundanely, your partner doesn't need to tell her employers about the news until 15 weeks out from the big day – or if for some reason that isn't possible, i.e. they've not known they are pregnant until after that point, employment law states employers must be told as soon as is possible.

Words from your fellow man:

Donald, 34, father of two: We used the most foolproof broadcasting method there is when we wanted to get the news of our pregnancy out there – we told my sister.

Tom, 34, father of two: We decided to tell close family only, until the three-month scan was out of the way. Unfortunately for my wife, though, any lack of drinking was deemed so completely and utterly out of character that people were guessing left, right and centre.

PROGRESS REPORT, MONTH 3

Your baby (11–14 weeks)

By the end of this month your baby is fully formed. Job done, the show's over, move along, nothing more to see here.

Well not quite. All he needs to do now is grow. Not that he's been hanging around on that front for the past four weeks either – lengthwise he's gone from a mini Mars bar to pretty much the full-blown version. That's a lot of work, very little rest and next to no play at all.

All your baby's major organs have formed and his intestines have even been packed away neatly in his abdomen. He has nails on his toes and fingers, and could even have some hair.

The little champ has even started drinking. Not being able to get out much, it's more of a quiet one at home swallowing amniotic fluid and weeing it out like a good 'un. Inside his miniature little mouth there are even tooth buds.

There's some serious movement going on now as well – knee jerks, back twists and the odd all-body hiccup – not that your partner will be able to feel any of that yet. Oh, and your baby can also smile, frown and suck his tiny thumb too – you've already got a genius on your hands!

All of this awesome development means that from now on your baby will be at less risk because the critical phase of growth has passed. You can breathe a little easier from now on.

Your partner

For most women these are the final few weeks of morning sickness and a range of other rather annoying early pregnancy symptoms. From now on, though, as your baby and his entourage of support systems begin to expand at a greater rate, your partner will too. As well as the to-be-expected expanding waistline, it will also see her making even more trips to the loo than before, if that's possible. Hormone levels will start to settle down from now on, too, and that, coupled with less worry about miscarriage, means that if the atmosphere in your household has been a little tense thus far things could well begin to lighten.

A trivial but welcome little bedtime bonus is that if, pre-pregnancy, your partner had ice-block hands and feet at night-time, they'll miraculously find them nice and toasty from now on in. To help lower blood pressure to cope with the extra strain being caused by the baby, your partner's arteries and veins relax, warming up the extremities – drop that little fact in tonight like the pregnancy sage you are fast becoming.

MUST-DOS OF MONTH 3

The light of my wife

There's going to be a lot of late-night weeing going on in your house from now on. Put a small light in the path of your partner's route to the loo so she can see where she is going. Sweeping the route before you go to bed for any dangerous items she might trip over is a good idea too.

Take her away from it all

The beginning of this month can be a brute for your partner; little or no let-up in symptoms, scans on the horizon and six more months to go. Booking a night away in a quiet hotel will go down a treat, or if money is tight, a candlelit night in with you waiting on her hand and foot before making time to talk about any worries she might have, will be long remembered.

Class act

This one is a blinder. Not only is it a very good idea, but I swear to you, if you do this, you'll be in clover.

Antenatal classes might seem a long way off in the seventh month or so, but the best ones get booked up way ahead of time. The sessions run by the National Childbirth Trust (NCT) get snapped up especially quickly and have – rightly or wrongly – more of a reputation for forging long-lasting friendships among parents than some of the NHS-run ones.

Get online, get on the phone, find out the details and watch the mother-to-be of your child melt in admiration as you tell her you've been doing a bit of research into classes.

MONTH 4

I SEE YOU BABY

(15–18 weeks)

For many of us the moment we see our child on the scan screen, or hold the fuzzy but precious picture in our hands, is when we truly believe.

I'm not for one moment suggesting, of course, that until this point we suspect our pregnant partners of fabricating violent bouts of sickness, molten lava-like heartburn and a bladder of quite extraordinary weakness; we know she has a baby in there – but there's nothing quite like seeing it for yourself, is there?

This moment of tangible proof, together with the start of the second trimester and its more physical signs of motherhood, can have quite an effect on a new father-to-be. In many cases it cranks up the level of interest in both the mother-to-be and baby to new, dizzying heights – which while generally welcomed, can, if not tempered, become as one medical professional put it, a right ball-ache for your partner.

Of course you're not going to constantly question your partner about everything she eats, how much exercise she is or isn't taking, or whether she should really rest her iPhone on her growing bump.

You're a sensitive and well-balanced individual who will keep his concerns and fears in check, while trusting his partner's judgement implicitly. Just to be on the safe side though, here's a quick list of pregnancy dos and don'ts for you to have in your pocket, should your overactive worry gland get the better of you.

WHAT'S SAFE AND WHAT'S NOT – THE LONG LIST OF DOS AND DON'TS

Food and drink

The big one. From people at work helpfully enquiring, 'Should you be eating that?' of your partner, to your well-intentioned mother saying that in her day raw egg was seen as a maternity superfood and guzzled down by the half dozen, there's a fairly bewildering array of advice to be had on what is and isn't safe to eat as a pregnant woman.

Here's a rundown that should help clear up a few common worries, or alternatively turn you into the food police.

- Oily fish is good for both mother-to-be and the developing baby, but there is a risk of high levels of pollutants, especially mercury. It's best to have no more than two portions a week of the likes of mackerel, trout and sardines, so all the benefits are reaped without chancing overexposure to any nasties. The old cupboard staple of tuna should be limited to no more than four medium-size cans or two tuna steaks a week. Swordfish, marlin and shark should be off the menu altogether – both eating them and swimming with them. While it is usually safe to eat sushi and other raw fish dishes when you're pregnant, certain fish used would have to have been frozen to reduce the risk of it carrying delightful parasitic worms that could cause problems for mothers-to-be. Finding that level of detail out during a 30-second lunch-break dash to the supermarket is very tricky, so avoiding them altogether is often advised.

- Pâté is a no-no I'm afraid, no matter what it's made from, where it's been made or how you pronounce it.
- The threat of listeria means that soft blue cheese such as Danish Blue or other soft cheese that are mould-ripened, such as Brie or Camembert, are out. Unpasteurised soft cheeses, such as those made from sheep and goat's milk, should also be consigned to 'the first thing I'm going to have when it's out' list. Recently, though, the NHS has advised that Stilton is back on the menu so go crackers (within reason).
- As well as being vile, raw or uncooked eggs are off limits. Supermarket salad dressings and most everyday mayonnaise brands are made from pasteurised egg and are safe, though. Hurray.
- Unpasteurised milk and any dairy products made with it can lead to food poisoning, meaning they should be history for nine months, too.
- Eating meat is fine, but make sure it's well cooked with no pink or red bits. Take special care when eating barbecued food. Cured meat products, such as salami, are also best avoided.

Alcohol

Hmm, alcohol and pregnancy. The advice on this seems to change on a daily basis but what's for sure is that no one really knows what a safe level of alcohol consumption is for a pregnant woman. The most comprehensively safe course of action is for your partner to go on the wagon for the whole nine months. Not only is there no known safe amount of alcohol use during pregnancy, there's also no safe time for its use either.

The mixed messages on this issue continue unabated, though; so much so that within the same week in September 2017 the media reported both a hard-hitting campaign launched by NHS Scotland to avoid alcohol altogether, and a University of Bristol study showing that the evidence against light drinking in pregnancy is flimsy at best.

But despite these odd media moments it feels pretty clear that alcohol and pregnancy just don't mix, with a long list of negative impacts such as miscarriage, premature birth, low birth-weight and even Foetal Alcohol Syndrome Disorder being linked to its use.

Exercise and pregnancy

You'd imagine being pregnant is as good a reason as anyone is ever going to get to not do any exercise. I'm afraid not.

Exercising in the right way during pregnancy is a very good idea indeed. Not only does it build muscle tone, strength and stamina (all of which can help your partner's body cope with the weight gained during pregnancy), keeping active can also make it easier to regain pre-pregnancy fitness levels after the birth and can even help to reduce constipation and tiredness, as well as circulation problems.

What's more, the Active Pregnancy Foundation, an organisation set up to champion the physical activity needs of women throughout their childbearing years, say that only 1 in 4 women meet guidelines for activity throughout pregnancy, 64% of pregnant or new mums have experienced nervousness or anxiety about being active and a third of healthcare professionals rarely or never talk about being active with pregnant women.

Of course, taking up hammer-throwing or kick boxing wouldn't be the brightest move, but following a fairly straightforward list of dos and don'ts should see your partner get all the benefit without any of the risk that exercise, if done in the wrong way, can pose to a pregnant woman.

If you can help her to remember the following, she won't go far wrong:

- Exercise doesn't have to be strenuous to be beneficial – that walk to the shops counts, too. As long as it's not the chip shop.
- The appropriate level of exercise will depend on how fit your partner was before she became pregnant. Tragically your semen has not turned her into an Olympic athlete.
- She should drink plenty of fluids when exercising.
- It's also wise to take a gentle approach to exercise that doesn't put strain on her joints and ligaments.
- Exercising during pregnancy isn't about losing weight.
- She shouldn't exercise flat on her back, particularly after 16 weeks, because her bump presses on the big blood vessels, which isn't a good idea at all.
- Don't use saunas or steam rooms because they put too much pressure on an already overtaxed circulatory system.

It almost goes without saying, but not quite, that any activity that puts your partner at risk of falling has got to be in serious doubt during pregnancy, too. That doesn't just mean the obvious ones such as skiing and tightrope-walking either; tennis and cycling, for instance, have to be done with extreme caution, especially as your partner's sense of balance may be more than a bit wonky thanks to the bowling ball she is carrying around with her.

Scuba diving and other sports that run the risk of planting a potentially deadly air bubble in her blood stream are out, too. Walking and swimming seem to be the favourite choices of a lot of mothers-to-be, with pregnancy yoga coming up on the rails.

Is it safe to fly during pregnancy?

In the first and second trimesters, pretty much yes. The third trimester is more dicey because not even the most accommodating of flight attendants wants to deliver a baby using a plastic spoon and the whistle from a lifejacket. Some airlines actually have specific policies regarding flying when pregnant so it's always worth checking. Besides, wedging a woman in her ninth month into a plane seat isn't good for anyone concerned.

Be warned, too, that ticket agents don't tend to ask if you're pregnant when you book your seats, the little blighters, but there's a good chance your partner could be questioned about her due date at check-in – and airlines are well within their rights to bar you from travel if they think there's a chance there might be an extra passenger on board by the time they land.

Once you are past week 28, to confirm it's safe for you to fly it's smart to get written permission from your doctor if you can. If your pregnancy is complicated by medical problems you would do well to check with your GP before travelling at any stage.

Flying during pregnancy can slightly increase your partner's risk of thrombosis, but wearing support stockings will help keep her circulation flowing. Pregnant women should give small planes that don't have pressurised cabins a miss, too. As well as the air-pressure issue, small planes (in my slightly panicky experience) are almost always bowel-squeezingly scary and wobble around like a 1950s washing machine.

Hair colour

Hair colour? Yes, hair colour! It might not seem like a big deal to you, but what seems like thousands of online message boards hum with the white-hot chat of whether dying your hair is bad for your baby. Annoyingly no one has enough information to say with absolute cast-iron certainty that using a lovely rusty red or mahogany brown during pregnancy is completely and utterly safe.

With all this unsatisfactory information about, it's no wonder this issue always turns up like a bad penny. The consensus at the moment, however, is that if the dyes are applied safely, using gloves in a well-ventilated room, and if solutions are not left on for any great length of time, it probably is safe. While a handful of studies have found that very high doses of the chemicals in hair dyes may cause harm, in reality the amount of chemicals that a woman is exposed to when colouring her hair is very low. For some people, though, that just isn't good enough and many women use alternative routes such as using vegetable dyes like henna while they are expecting.

Is it OK to wax during pregnancy?

As hair growth tends to increase for some women during pregnancy, this is another one that comes up more than you'd imagine. There's no evidence to show that waxing is unsafe during pregnancy and if, like I did, you are wondering if the baby feels an agonising shock as the strips are removed – apparently they don't, so rest easy. Your partner, on the other hand, could well be in for a rougher ride than usual because her skin may become even more sensitive in pregnancy.

Is it safe to have dental work during pregnancy?

Not only is it safe, there are two very good reasons why your partner should go and see the dentist while she is pregnant.

Firstly, the hormones cascading through your partner's body can wreak havoc with her gums, and, secondly, in the UK, dental care for pregnant women is free, free I tell you, right from the moment when pregnancy is confirmed, through to the little one's first birthday. That makes this the single solitary time when having a baby might actually save you some money.

Root canal, anyone?

Is it safe to paint during pregnancy?

Watercolours? You're fine as long as you take it nice and easel.

Painting the new nursery? No one really knows. There's no doubt that painting does expose you to some pretty nasty chemicals, but because it's next to impossible to measure how much the body absorbs, calculating the risks is equally tricky.

There is some evidence, though, that exposure to the type of chemical solvents found in paint does increase the chances of birth defects. The study found that the risk of having a baby born with gastroschisis (a nasty and potentially fatal abnormality where the baby's intestines protrude through a hole in its abdomen) was up to four times higher. There are guidelines for those women who do choose to paint, such as limiting the amount of time you spend doing it, keeping the windows open and wearing long garments to protect the skin, but by far the simplest and safest answer is for your partner to let someone else do the painting. That means you, by the way.

Are mobile phones safe to use during pregnancy?

Are mobile phones safe to use full stop? Who knows.

There has to be a chance, no matter how slim, that in 50 years' time when the first people to have had a phone stuck to the side of their heads for their entire lives start to reach their dotage, we may just start to realise that placing an electronic device next to your brain for long periods of the day isn't the smartest thing we've ever done as a species. Having said that, current research suggests that there is no risk whatsoever to health from mobile phones in the short term.

While two related studies have found a possible connection between unborn babies exposed to mobile phones and behavioural problems during childhood, other, follow-up studies found no link whatsoever to behavioural problems. They also found no evidence of developmental delays in children at six and 18 months of age.

If you're especially worried about your partner's mobile usage during pregnancy, though, a good tip is that unbeknown to the majority of us, every single mobile phone is rated according to the levels of electromagnetic radiation that it emits. The SAR (specific absorption rate) value reflects the maximum amount of energy which can be absorbed by your body when you're using the phone. The higher your phone's SAR, the more radiation you are absorbing.

Google 'SAR values' and you'll find websites that will tell you the SAR of every handset on the market, as well as a whole load of scary information you'll probably wish you'd not read.

PHANTOM PREGNANCY – I'M SUFFERING TOO YOU KNOW

The concept of the phantom pregnancy, of hairy-arsed blokes clutching their backs or feeling a bit sick in support of their heavily laden but perfectly calm wives, is a comedy staple.

Only two of the multitude of new fathers I spoke to in the writing of this book were brave enough to admit to having shadowed any of their partner's symptoms.

It's fairly easy to see why the whole idea is met with such ridicule. When researchers at St George's University, London, carried out a study of 282 fathers-to-be in 2007, one of the men who admitted to being affected by the phenomenon came out with this little gem: 'I was constantly hungry all the time and had an unstoppable craving for chicken kormas and poppadoms. Even in the early hours of the morning I would get up and prepare myself one. It was strange to say the least.' By that definition I have been suffering from secondary pregnancy symptoms for the whole of my adult life.

However, recent research is beginning to paint a very different picture.

Couvade syndrome, as this phenomenon has been coined (it's from the French word meaning 'to hatch') has been documented throughout the ages and some studies put the number of expectant dads who suffer from it in some shape or form as high as 65%. The condition presents itself in men with symptoms such as nausea, vomiting, stomach pain, back pain, toothache and exhaustion. For many, the symptoms are pretty subtle, a spot of weight gain here, an unexplained ache or pain there. Other men, though, have full-blown mirror pregnancies, having exactly the same symptoms at exactly the same time as their wives.

A pair of heavy duty, bone fide studies carried out in Canada and the US have found what may well be a genuine physiological rather than psychological cause for these symptoms: hormones.

Yes, those pesky hormones, the very same ones that make your partner's life a misery during pregnancy, can also give you a damn good going over, too.

The studies, conducted at Memorial University and Queen's University in Canada and in 2014 at the University of Michigan, took blood or saliva samples from couples at different stages of pregnancy, as well as shortly after birth, and monitored specific hormones because of their links to nurturing behaviour.

First up there's cortisol, which is seen as a good indicator of a mother's attachment to her baby. New mums who are found to have high cortisol levels can detect their own infant by odour more successfully than those with lower levels, for instance. The Canadian tests found that in expectant fathers, cortisol was twice as high in the three weeks before birth than earlier in the pregnancy.

Then there's prolactin, which among other things has been shown to bring on parental behaviour in a number of birds and mammals. The studies discovered that prolactin levels rise too, by around 20%, in men during the weeks before their partner gives birth.

That's not all, either; the clever Canadians also discovered that fathers-to-be had elevated levels of oestrogen, of all things, many weeks before and after birth. Best known as a female sex hormone, oestrogen exists in small quantities in men, too, and animal studies show that it can turn males into super-sensitive fathers.

Then there's the biggie – testosterone. When sweet little birdies who have just become dads are given testosterone, rather than looking after their new offspring, they strut around defending their territory and even mate with other females, the dirty birds. In humans, research has shown that males experience a surge in the levels of this hormone when they win sporting events and other competitions. It's probably fair to say then that testosterone isn't conducive to producing the most caring dad the world has ever seen.

Guess what? The studies found that testosterone levels dropped by a third in new dads during the first three weeks after the baby arrived. So essentially mother (or father) nature has found a way to engineer it so that the chemical that makes you such a chest-beater reduces dramatically just at the very time that you need to bond and coo over your newborn baby.

So . . . what's going on?

There's a potential clue in that these hormonal changes in men closely parallel those of their pregnant partners. Although far from a scientific certainty, the smart money among scientists is that intimate contact and communication between partners is what brings on these changes.

In other words, spending time with a mother-to-be turns you into a father-to-be. Not (necessarily) in a psychological, 'Look at me, look at me, my waters have just broken too,' kind of way, but in a very real physiological way. The same chemical forces that make your partner throw up for three months are essentially at work turning you into a more caring dad.

Exactly how this hormonal osmosis takes place isn't known, but the transmission of pheromones looks to be a very likely candidate. Pheromones are mysterious, little-understood but seemingly extremely potent chemical wafts that we animals constantly give off through our skin or sweat to stimulate other animals – usually in the 'I'm feeling horny' sense of the word. It's believed that pubic hair aids the transmission of pheromones, which is why, it's thought, we have kept hold of our underarm and pubic furriness while losing the rest of our body hair.

If women living in close proximity can synchronise their menstrual cycles via pheromones, as has been proved, then it's really not that inconceivable that a pregnant woman lying next to her partner in bed could send a few chemical cocktails to start the process of turning him into a doting dad. This intimacy effect, and the hormonal alterations it may cause, could also be the reason why many men experience pregnancy-like symptoms too. So as well as the umbilical cord attached to the baby, your pregnant partner also has an invisible, but powerful, link with you, too.

Perhaps the best way to view this strange phenomenon, though, isn't that we men are being held in some sort of hormonal hypnosis by our pregnant partners, but rather that with a little help from them, nurture really is part of our nature.

It's still not enough to blame for craving a curry seven days a week, though.

Words from your fellow man:

Jim, 34, father of one: I definitely showed signs of a sympathetic pregnancy. I had headaches during the first few months and became exhausted on doing the slightest thing. That has continued after the birth too, but that's probably more to do with being actually knackered all the time than any phantom response. I also had dreams of having a baby, physically. Not sure if that is phantom or just weird.

David, 34, father of one: I've always thought this is a load of rubbish cooked up by blokes to try and get out of doing stuff – but I felt seriously sick for the second and third months. I've no idea what else it could have been.

PROGRESS REPORT, MONTH 4

Your baby (15–18 weeks)

Be warned, your baby can now hear what you are saying. Fair enough, it might not be able to make any sense out of it, but thanks to his hardening inner ear bones, the little fella has begun to pick up his first sounds – which at this stage are mainly your partner's soothing heartbeat, rumbling digestion and all-important voice.

Despite still being only around 14cm (5.5inches) in length and weighing in at not much more than 190g (7oz) by the end of this month, complex pieces of kit such as taste buds are already starting to develop. Crucially, lung development is steaming ahead, too. Your baby is essentially doing breathing exercises, ready for the big moment when he will take his first breath once the umbilical cord has been cut. As these exercises happen, your little one's chest rises and falls as his lungs begin to exhale amniotic fluid. Not to be left behind, the tiny heart is now capable of pumping as much as 24 litres (42 pints) of blood a day, too.

Your baby is also going nuts on the workout front, twisting, turning, wriggling, punching, kicking and generally seeing what his amazing new body is capable of within the confined space he finds himself in.

You'll also be pleased to know that your baby's eyes aren't miles apart anymore either, which is nice.

Your partner

All things being equal, your partner should be over the worst of her sickness and exhaustion and may well be feeling, if not full of beans, at least able to eat them.

Although your partner may not have gained a whole load of weight yet, in other, less conspicuous areas her pregnancy really is motoring along now. Her nipples are darkening in colour, and down the centre of her abdomen she may well be developing a dark line, called the linea nigra, as the growing baby pushes her uterus out of its normal home in the pelvic area.

Her heart is now working twice as hard as it was before she conceived, with six litres (10.5 pints) of blood per minute being pumped around her body to feed the long list of vital organs that are being pressed into action to keep your baby growing.

Given the baby's gymnastics there's a good chance that towards the end of this month your partner (but not you) will be able to feel the baby moving for the first time – not the thumping great kicks that will boot you out of the bed in months to come, but a fluttering sensation that's been likened to having a flock of butterflies flying around in your stomach or, alternatively, wind.

MUST-DOS OF MONTH 4

Me Tarzan

During the second and third trimesters the slightest fall for your partner can lead to some pretty serious problems. It sounds obvious, but gently suggest that you are now the chief lifter and mover in the household.

Dear diary

As the baby starts to move it's not a bad idea for your partner to keep a rough record of what she feels when. Buying her a journal that she can use to do just that is a good move and once baby is born she can use it to keep a track of feeds, sleeps, poos and, crucially, who has done the early shift most times each week.

And relax

Pregnancy yoga is fast becoming a very popular part of the pregnancy routine for many mums-to-be – and with good reason. As well as being a gentle way to relax as her body goes through its myriad changes, it's also a great way for your partner to meet other women who are going through the same thing.

Get yourself online and research a few courses in your area – she'll love you for it.

SCANS, FLANS AND HOLIDAY PLANS

(19–22 weeks)

For some reason 'five months pregnant' sounds an awful lot closer to 'nine months pregnant' than 'four months pregnant' does, if you see what I mean.

Although you are still basking gloriously in the mid-trimester sunshine, with all its non-nausea and even a spot of sex to pass the time, too, within the wonderful world of pregnancy there's something to worry about just around the corner.

In this case it's the anomaly scan, a brutally named ultrasound check to see if everything is as it should be with your rapidly developing baby. With a long list of deformities and complaints to search for, this is another squeaky-bum moment on your journey to fatherhood, but as ever the nervousness comes hand in sweaty hand with the wonderment of seeing your now very baby-like baby up on screen and even, should you so desire, finding out if it's a boy or a girl.

Once what is almost certainly your final big scan before the birth is behind you, many couples take advantage of the mid-pregnancy lull and go on what will be their last-ever holiday as a childless couple. Given the delicate nature of your partner's physical state, these little before-the-baby breaks, be they a swanky getaway or an Airbnb round the corner, aren't always totally devoid of stress, but in general they are a fantastic, not-to-be-missed chance, if you can afford it, to spend some time together before all hell breaks loose. In a nice way of course.

I wouldn't want you to get the impression, though, that this month represents time off for your partner, a kind of commercial break in the middle of her personal pregnancy nine-part boxset. Far from it. Just when she is giving a two-fingered farewell to the symptoms of early pregnancy, another bunch ride into town, including the crazy world of cravings.

THE ANOMALY SCAN – MORE FEAR, MORE JOY

Although it only takes around 20 minutes to perform, this scan covers an awful lot of ground. Most sonographers begin by show-ing you and your partner the baby's heartbeat and quickly pointing out parts of the tiny body before getting down to the serious business.

If at this point the screen is turned away from you, don't panic like I did; it's standard practice in many hospitals. The baby's head is often examined first, with shape and structure thoroughly checked. Although thankfully rare, many severe brain problems can be visible at this stage as well as the presence of a cleft lip, but not cleft palates which are hard to see.

Next up, your baby's spine is looked at to ensure that all the bones are in the right place and that the entire area is covered in skin. The heart is then given its MOT, with size and valve movement under scrutiny; the stomach gets a once over too, as do the kidneys. If your baby's bladder happens to be empty, the chances are it should fill up during the scan as it downs another gulp of that scrumptious amniotic fluid.

The position of the placenta is then checked to ensure it's not low-lying, a condition called placenta praevia, and the umbilical cord will also be looked at; the final box to be ticked is that the little mite has enough fluid to comfortably move around in.

Now the tape measure comes out, or at least an onscreen version, and your baby's head circumference and diameter are measured, as well as the size of his abdominal area and length of the thigh bone, bringing the nuts and bolts of the scan to an end.

This exhaustive list of checks can highlight about half of all major problems that could be lurking at this stage of pregnancy – remember though, we are talking about rare problems here. The Royal College of Obstetricians and Gynaecologists helpfully and somewhat scarily lists the chances of these abnormalities being picked up during this scan, should they be present, as:

- spina bifida (open spinal cord): 90%
- anencephaly (absence of the top of the head): 99%
- hydrocephalus (excess fluid within the brain): 60%
- major heart problems (defects of chambers, valves or vessels): 25%
- diaphragmatic hernia (hole in the muscle separating chest and abdomen): 60%
- exomphalos/gastroschisis (defects of the abdominal wall): 90%
- major kidney problems: 85%
- major limb abnormalities: 90%

Not a nice list.

If a problem is discovered, and again the chances are that none will be, you'll be told straight away. You should be given an appointment for a scan with a fetal medicine specialist within days. A repeat scan doesn't necessarily mean the worst though. Most problems that need repeat-scanning are not serious. About 15% of scans will be done again and most reasons are not found to lead to complications.

If, though, the second scan does indeed reveal a serious problem, you'll be given support to guide you through all the options, none of which, of course, are easy.

Hamburger or turtle?

As with all scans, everything will go swimmingly for the vast majority of couples and the biggest dilemma they will face is whether to find out if they are having a boy or a girl.

While it's true that some health authorities don't give you the option because of fears over wrong gender terminations, most will, and the 20-week scan is predominantly the time when people choose to find out.

Not that it's a cut and dried case of 'Where's the winkle?' for the sonographer, you understand – oh no, they can and do get it wrong. There are scores of stories of people being told they are expecting one to be handed what is quite obviously another a few months later.

The problem is that even by Month 5, the boy bits and the girl bits don't look all that different. An experienced sonographer will be on the lookout for one of two signs if you ask them to tell you the sex of your baby. In a girl the three lines that make up the clitoris surrounded by the labia are often charmingly referred to as the hamburger sign. In a boy it's the turtle sign they are watching out for, where the tip of the penis just peeks out from the testicles. It could just as well have been called the walnut whip.

Rather than putting your faith in modern medicine you can, of course, indulge in a spot of homespun gender detective work. There are countless ways of determining what you are having, with every country seemingly having its own methods. Here's just a selection of the most scientifically robust ones:

You're more likely to be having a boy if . . .

- your partner's right breast is bigger than her left
- your partner's pillow faces north when she sleeps
- your partner is asked to show her hands and she presents them palms down
- your partner's age at conception combined with the number of the month in which she conceived results in an even number.

You're more likely to be having a girl if . . .

- the exact opposite to the complete load of rubbish above happens.

Words from your fellow man:

Nick, 35, father of two: They go very quiet in between taking measurements, which is understandable I suppose given they are concentrating so hard, but you end up waiting for a noise or listening to their breathing for clues. The thing that stood out was that after the scan it became apparent that this was the last time they were going to check on the baby until the birth, which felt as though we were going freestyle – alone for a long time.

Chris, 34, father of one: Before our daughter came along I, like many, just assumed it's all a natural and straightforward process where the majority sail through easily. As it happens there's always something dramatic around the corner, or at least the threat of it.

Levi, 36, father of two: I was amazed by the virtual check-up the baby had at the 20-week stage. It's a real MOT before they are even born and I was stunned by what the scanner could see on screen.

THE BABYMOON – GETTING AWAY FROM IT ALL

Travelling is never the same once your child arrives – and by travelling I mean anything that involves going out of the front door. Travel cots, baths, nappies, sterilisers, the dreaded baby bag and more toys than you ever knew existed, will turn a weekend away into a military operation with the potential to claim a casualty or two, namely your back and sense of humour.

Across the land dads can be seen packing and unpacking cars like demented worker bees and if you watch carefully you'll notice that once they have expertly jammed the boot to its absolute capacity, the realisation dawns that they have left the three-tonne pushchair/pram/travel system combo unit on the pavement.

And that's just for three days in Devon.

For those brave enough to contemplate flying, packing the motor is just the beginning. The mumbling and grumbling of other passengers on the flight as your beloved tot starts to kick off is bad enough, but two hours in when the first 10 rows have got a petition together to hand to the pilot, you will dream of being somewhere, anywhere, else.

Things get easier as your family gets older and can be readily bribed with iPhones, iPads or, if you're lucky, eye masks. But for the foreseeable future the wanderlust you once had will be put on the backburner, on the spare gas ring next to your friends, lazy Saturday morning breakfasts and any semblance of a savings account.

But of course, you'll never have felt love like it so every challenge is worth it.

Bearing all that in mind, getting away in the second trimester if you possibly can is a smart idea on all sorts of fronts. With the risk of miscarriage and the bouts of sickness of the early months now hopefully in the past – and the third trimester a no-no for soon to be very obvious abdominal reasons – the second trimester holiday has become something of a well-trodden path in recent years.

Where not to go

While many women may experience an energy burst in mid-pregnancy, this quite obviously doesn't represent a green light to climb a mountain or book yourselves into that residential trampolining weekend you've heard so many good things about.

If you do venture overseas, try to avoid anywhere with a huge time difference. And if ever your partner deserved a comfy bed and a fluffy towel rather than a backpackers' hostel, it's now.

The level of hygiene of your destination is also a key factor. Many vaccines are off limits and in the case of areas with a high risk of malaria, pregnant women need to think very hard before they travel, as they are especially vulnerable to the killer disease. Pregnancy makes women more susceptible to malaria infection and increases the risk of illness, severe anaemia and even death. For the unborn child, maternal malaria increases the risk of spontaneous abortion, stillbirth, premature delivery and low birth weight. It's not to be messed with.

Zika virus is another disease that has also made headlines – for all the wrong reasons – and is something you should absolutely look into before you travel if you are pregnant or trying to become so. Like malaria, the Zika virus is mainly spread by mosquitoes and, for most people, is a very mild infection and not harmful; however, for pregnant women it can cause severe birth defects – in particular, abnormally small heads, a condition called microcephaly.

While Zika doesn't naturally occur in the UK, outbreaks have been reported in the Pacific Islands, South and Central America, the Caribbean, Africa and parts of South and South East Asia. If you plan to travel somewhere you even half suspect might be at risk, seek specific travel health advice before your trip.

Exposure to the sun obviously needs to be carefully controlled, too – and not just for the obvious reasons. Some pregnant women are particularly susceptible to a skin condition called melasma, otherwise known as (to be said in throaty film trailer voice) the mask of pregnancy. Melasma, which causes patches on the face, is believed to be connected to the female sex hormones oestrogen and progesterone – hence the link to pregnancy, and is made worse by exposure to the sun.

Those few factors aside, the world is, as someone once very nearly said, your lobster.

Family Traveller, the magazine and website dedicated, funnily enough, to all things family travel, say that the babymoon market, originating as it did in the USA, is now very big business in the UK too. So much so that hotels at home and overseas are now providing bespoke packages to cater for what for them is a year-round evergreen market. So if you fancy a pre-baby break get searching. Having said that . . .

No surprises please

For many couples, the mid-pregnancy break lingers in the memory for years and can take on a real second honeymoon air as you take some time out to enjoy each other's company and talk about the momentous changes that are about to happen to you both. With the stresses and strains of labour and the early days of being parents just around the corner, it is time fabulously well spent.

For the love of God though, don't try to book it as a surprise. Despite her current mild-mannered appearance, your partner is still a pregnant woman and as such the chances of you taking every one of her many, many worries, fears and random thoughts into account and correctly choosing a destination are infinitesimally small. But bless you for thinking of it.

MORE SYMPTOMS – EARTH, WIND AND FORGETFULNESS

It really is quite staggering what carrying a baby can do to a woman's body and her mind doesn't get off scot-free either of course. After the early raft of symptoms have hopefully all but subsided, another band of shysters often appears to take their place. While admittedly they tend not to be as unremittingly awful as vomiting every single day for three months, these new pretenders are worth knowing about because each of them has the potential to have a big impact on your partner and therefore you too.

Cravings

When one survey asked more than 2,000 women if they craved a certain food stuff or taste while they were expecting, more than 75% said they had. That's a lot of women eating a lot of cheese flan with ice cream. What's more, half a century ago the figure was at about 30%. So what's going on? In short, no one really has a clue.

In recent years the notion that craving something represented your body crying out for whatever vitamin or mineral that particular foodstuff was rich in, really took hold and has been quoted by some pretty eminent pregnancy experts. A craving for chocolate for instance is put down to a shortage of B vitamins and red meat cravers were secretly in need of a protein boost. Currently, though, that nice, neat explanation has taken something of a scientific kicking and given our culture's seemingly inexorable march towards mass obesity, it's not hard to see why.

If the 'cravings tell you what you need' theory holds water, as our bloated and enormous frames consume more and more beige, Captain Craving should kick in at some stage and send us sprinting to the nearest greengrocers to smash down the doors and devour every green vegetable we can get our hands on.

So, with that theory losing ground, what is responsible for cravings and the desire for odd flavour combinations in pregnant women?

The hormonal upheaval brought on by pregnancy definitely has the power to turn what was once a despised item into an adored one – and vice versa – and the need for strange textures has been cited as being behind why a lot of mothers-to-be crave ice. But no one really knows what's behind the phenomenon in truth, which makes dealing with it a bit tricky.

For most women, their particular craving causes no real health problems, other than the psychological trauma of being stared at by fellow shoppers as she puts 98 courgettes on the check-out at Sainsbury's.

Things can start to get serious if a condition called pica raises its head though. Named after the magpie, because of the bird's tendency to consume some pretty horrible stuff, pica is an eating disorder that causes craving for non-food items such as coal, earth, soap, washing powder, hair and cigarette butts.

The causes of this strange condition are pretty woolly too, but what's certain is that it can affect pregnant women and that emptying the ashtray into your mouth isn't recommended. If your partner develops a taste for Persil non-bio, gently suggest that she talks to the midwife or health visitor about it sharpish – and then put her on a spin setting.

Aside from the peculiar world of pica, though, most food-based cravings are harmless and if it's what she wants, she's the one carrying the bowling ball around in her stomach so it's her call.

Words from your fellow man:

Peter, 33, father of one: My wife decided to forgo prawns, blue cheese and white wine – and of course all three immediately became obsessions – but she held out. Nothing bizarre was eaten, but mountains of chocolate and cakes were consumed. Her pregnancy lipstick seemed to be a permanent dark shade of Galaxy brown.

Nick, 35, father of two: Scotch eggs and cereal were the big winners on our weekly shop as my wife went through a lot of both – although thankfully not at the same time.

Chris, 34, father of one: My wife didn't have cravings, rather a complete aversion to pretty much all food, except for yoghurt, fruit and a white, it had to be white, buttered, it had to be butter, roll for lunch.

Levi, 36, father of two: Gin and tonic was the (largely) unrequited craving of choice for my wife.

Wind

There's no easy way to tell you this, but your partner will almost certainly pass more wind from both ends during her pregnancy than you hitherto dreamed possible. The reason for this often sudden increase in gas, as our American brethren are wont to call it, isn't because she can no longer be bothered to pretend she's saintly in that direction, it's actually down to two separate little wind-generating factors.

Firstly, the hormone progesterone, which surges around your partner during pregnancy, relaxes the smooth muscle tissue through-out her body – which sounds lovely, doesn't it? Unfortunately it includes her gastrointestinal tract in this smoothing out process, which slows down digestion and generates bloating and lots and lots of wind.

Secondly, around Month 5, as the baby slowly starts to crowd your partner's insides, her digestive system takes another pounding as it gets squeezed and manoeuvred about something rotten, leading to even slower digestion and an even higher food-to-fart ratio. Oh dear.

Helping her to reduce this troublesome gas, which can bring with it painful cramps, isn't all that easy. Part of the problem is that a lot of the foods that she has quite likely taken to eating to improve her diet are the biggest culprits of all. The old classics such as beans, Brussels sprouts, broccoli, cabbage and cauliflower all contain a fantastically named substance called raffinose, which is pretty much as near to fart juice as you are ever likely to get. Then there are certain starches, such as pasta and potatoes, which can bring on a bout of belching and worse, too, not to mention fibre-rich foods such as oat bran and a fair few fruits that can also stoke things up.

So if totally avoiding the foods that cause wind is all but out, what else can be done to stem the flow? Eating several small meals a day rather than one or two feasts is a good start, as is avoiding eating or drinking while scrunched up or lying on the couch. Other than that it's selective deafness and 'more tea vicar?' for you from now on.

Getting its kicks

It's around now that mothers begin to feel the first fluttering of movement from the baby. Sometimes called 'quickening', which sounds very *Game of Thrones* somehow, it's described as feeling like the flapping of butterfly wings by those who presumably have spent some quality time with a red admiral on their arm.

From the fifth month onwards, many women start to feel the

baby hiccupping as it necks pint after pint of its favourite amniotic brew. The time women feel these flutters can vary dramatically, from as early as 18 weeks to past 23. So don't worry if your baby is taking his time. As the weeks roll on, the frequency and type of movements increase dramatically, as does their brute force.

Waking up startled and realising that your unborn child has just booted you is one of life's more surreal experiences. In fact, if ever there's a moment when you realise this tiny thing means business, and will undoubtedly rule your entire life in a matter of months, it's when you also come to on the floor, having been kicked clean out of bed by the little blighter.

In the final few weeks, the baby assumes the position, hopefully head down, limiting himself to the odd punch and kick to the ribs as he waits for disembarkation. In the final trimester, your partner may be asked to 'count the kicks' by her midwife, monitoring how many she feels on average per day.

Wondering if your baby is kicking enough can cause a fair bit of angst, especially for your partner, who is tuned into the baby channel 24 hours a day. The truth is that there are times when the baby wants to rest and times when he wants to play. Studies show that every baby has his own individual pattern of waking and sleeping in the womb. You'll undoubtedly be told by someone that if the baby sleeps during the day and is awake at night you're in for a tough time when he's born, as he will follow the same pattern.

Not only is there no specific scientific evidence to back up that theory, you are also 100% guaranteed to be in a sleepless living hell for at least the first few weeks of parenthood whatever happens, so don't bother worrying about it at this stage and just go to bed while you still can.

PROGRESS REPORT, MONTH 5

Your baby (19–22 weeks)

After weeks of relentless growth, once your baby reaches the five-month stage and is roughly 19cm (7.5 inches) long, his rate of expansion reduces somewhat (although his weight gain doesn't) and he focuses on other crucial areas of his development – like growing brain cells.

At the centre of his new little brain an area called the germinal matrix is busy manufacturing cells at an almighty rate. The production line stops before birth, but actually your baby's brain will keep on expanding until around the age of five years.

As nerve fibres get connected up and muscles get switched on like Christmas tree lights, your baby embarks on an ever-more-elaborate gymnastics programme designed to improve motor skills and strengthen bones.

A thick white greasy substance, not unlike cottage cheese in appearance and – who knows? – maybe even taste, is starting to cover your baby's body. Called vernix, it acts as a waterproof barrier to prevent his skin from becoming waterlogged in the sea of amniotic fluid he finds himself floating in. If only he had a stick of celery or carrot baton in there he could have himself his first-ever snack, too. Alas.

Down at the sex organ department, things are coming along very nicely, too. If you're having a daughter her ovaries will already contain about seven million eggs, which will reduce to about two million at birth. In boys, primitive sperm have already formed in the testes, ready for the whole process to start again for them both in years to come. If they want children that is. No pressure, kids.

A little welcome gift of baby's first ever poo is also progressing beautifully, as a delightful tar-like substance called meconium begins to accumulate in his bowels. You'll be seeing, and indeed smelling, more of that later.

Your partner

The single biggest thing that this month represents for the majority of women is the high-water mark of wellness in the pregnancy. Your partner should be not too sick, not too sore and not too big, but just right – a healthy and glowing mother-to-be in her prime. Of course, although your partner may be feeling as well as she has for a good long while, there's still plenty of tough stuff going on, too, as she moves ever closer to the big day. As well as the cravings, chronic wind and having the turning circle of a Fiat 500, your partner's gums may well become spongy and she is probably sweating more heavily than usual as her thyroid gland becomes more active.

Unfeasibly early as it sounds, your partner's breasts may also have begun to leak colostrum, the substance that will constitute your baby's first meal should breastfeeding be the way you go.

But despite the farting, sweating, leaky-breasted picture this chapter has painted, your partner is almost certainly looking unfeasibly beautiful at the moment.

Go on, tell her.

MUST-DOS OF MONTH 5

Magic hands

A spot of smart forward-planning. In the coming weeks, various parts of your partner's body are going to ache, creak, lumber and throb like never before as the strain of carrying round a small person in her abdomen starts to really crank up. Be warned, you will be called upon, on a regular basis, to massage said body.

If, like most of us, your idea of a massage is 15 seconds of dough-like kneading followed by a few karate chops, it might be a good idea to do some YouTube research on a few gentle but effective massage techniques.

Dirty cash

As the halfway mark of the pregnancy is reached it's not uncommon for many men to be struck down with a severe dose of the 'How are we going to afford this?' flu. It's a nasty affliction which often strikes at night, rendering the bowels permanently open.

If you find yourself suffering from this, don't panic.

As tempting as it may be to push for a promotion, take on more responsibility at work or get your old paper round back, a year down the line time will be the resource you crave the most, so stay cool, read the section in the next chapter on buying kit for the new arrival and rest assured that given the choice of seeing your face in the evening or having a cot that doubles up as an all-in-one 3D printer at the push of a button, your baby and its mum would much rather have the former.

Eau my God

The vast majority of us are dehydrated, according to research. Drinking enough water is something almost everyone in almost every developed country is spectacularly and ironically pisspoor at. While this is bad news for us all, as a pregnant woman it's to be addressed straight away as water helps to carry nutrients to the baby and also helps to prevent infections, constipation and the dreaded piles.

To help your partner drink the three pints of fluid she needs (coffee, tea and pop don't really count I'm afraid, as they make you wee more out than they put in), make up jugs of water with wedges of lemon or lime in to help her overcome water boredom.

MOVE OVER DAD

(23–26 weeks)

There's now more of the pregnancy behind you than there is still to come. Scary, but bloody exciting!

It probably doesn't feel much more than half an hour ago that you had a plastic stick covered in urine placed lovingly under your nose and the whole thing began. Since then you and your partner have almost certainly already been through two scans, a handful of scares and hundreds of night-time wees and morning-time hurls. You'll have cried, laughed and argued in hopefully relatively equal measure and the excitement, together with a dash of apprehension, will be starting to build in a big way now.

Although you've seen the baby on screen and he has made his presence very much felt via his gang of hormonal heavies, the chances are the introduction of a fledgling third person in your relationship has so far pulled you and your partner closer together rather than making you feel less of a unit.

In a very physical sense though, the sixth month marks the beginning of a new chapter when you will be moved gently (at first) away from the mother-to-be of your child. Inch by inch your baby will announce its arrival in your household, your bed and your relationship, by creating its own rotund calling card. The bump is well and truly on its way.

There's no getting away from it (and soon no getting around it either): there's an ever-expanding person inside your loved one and it's had the very first announcement from the pilot in the sky to prepare for landing. Before you know where you are, it will be seatbelts on, doors to manual and cross-check.

As the bump arrives, so can three other jolting realisations:

- Pretty soon you are both going to have to pay for this person and all its paraphernalia.
- You are going to have to come up with a name for it that neither you nor your partner detests.
- You are going to be a dad, just like your dad and his dad before him.

BUMPS AND BRAXTON – SHOWING

Does my bump look big in this?

If you are glancing nervously at your partner as you read this think-ing, 'She hasn't got much of a bump,' keep that thought firmly in your head and out of your mouth. The shape, size and position of each bump is as unique as the baby inside it, but that doesn't stop some pretty fierce comparisons taking place between mums-to-be, or even with the odd nosy random pitching in to give their tummy-two-pence as well.

It's also worth forewarning you that the moment your partner begins to show any sign of a bump – that entire area of her body turns into a mobile petting zoo. Old women on buses, old men in trusses, anyone and everyone feels like they can have a little touch. On one level it's quite endearing of course, a very real sign of the shared joy and interest that many of our species still take in the upcoming birth of another of our already numerous clan. It's easy for me to take that philosophical view of course; it's not my stomach being molested in Wagamama, is it?

In terms of advice about the size and shape of the bump, though, the only person who is worth listening to about this outward sign of the inward baby is your partner's midwife.

The number of antenatal check-ups differs from woman to woman, but at each one, the midwife will examine the area by starting under the breastbone and moving down until she feels the top of the womb, an area rather magnificently called the fundus. A measurement is then taken from the top of the pubic bone to the aforementioned fundus and, as a rule of thumb, the number of weeks pregnant should roughly correspond to the number of centimetres measured, so at 26 weeks, the bumpage should come in at around 26cm (10 inches). Some areas of the UK have begun to use a new, customised bump measurement chart, which takes into account factors such as age, body mass index and ethnicity, the idea being that these factors will affect how big/small a baby should be, and lead to a better detection of babies smaller than they should be.

If the midwife has any worries whatsoever, she'll get an ultrasound scan jacked up sharpish to check that the baby's growth is normal and put your mind at rest.

The most common factors that could affect bump size are:

• High blood pressure: This causes blood vessels in the placenta to tighten and cuts down on the oxygen that the baby receives. This unsurprisingly sends the little mite into red alert mode and it diverts the available oxygen to its two most important organs – the heart and brain – meaning the rest of the body loses out and can remain small.

- Too much fluid: Too much amniotic fluid could make your bump seem unfeasibly large.
- Not enough fluid: Too little and it appears on the small side.
- Smoking: Smoking reduces the amount of oxygen reaching your baby and women who smoke are three times more likely to have a low birth-weight baby.

Smoking in pregnancy is a disaster all round.

But, of course, what's really key to the size of the bump is the size of the baby and the shape of the mummy.

Bump measurement aside, the thing to really keep a close eye on is the baby's movements, and get your partner to contact her midwife should she notice them lessening. If at any point you or your partner become worried about a lack of movement contact your midwife or GP and put your mind at rest.

This is your father speaking

There was a time, not all that long ago, when leaning into your partner's tummy and talking to your unborn baby was seen as being sweet but kooky, a kind of pleasing but pointless gesture. Now though, scientists are pretty convinced that at around this stage of the pregnancy the baby is capable of learning to recognise the voice of not only his mother-to- be, but his soon-to-be father, too, as well as pieces of often-repeated music.

A BBC project found that playing the same tune every day for the last trimester of the pregnancy resulted in the baby still recognising the music (and no doubt being thoroughly sick of it) on hearing it again a year later. Even more astonishing was that an opera singer who took part in the research recounted that she was performing *Aida* while five months pregnant, meaning her unborn son would have heard it non-stop. When, five years later, she was in a production of *Aida* again, her son came to watch her and sat mesmerised through the entire three-hour performance. A five-year-old sitting for three hours at an opera, or indeed anywhere else on the planet, is a feat so unlikely that you can only draw the conclusion, as indeed she did, that somehow he had remembered the music.

Or she'd given him her iPhone.

So get chatting to your child right now; it's never too early to start the indoctrination process toward your football club or odd sense of humour – tragically, it can only be a matter of time, though, before uterine French lessons spring up, with a vocab test taking place five minutes after delivery.

Braxton Hicks – the contraction comedian

You'd imagine the last thing a woman needs as she approaches the great unknown of labour for the very first time is her body sending her a few pretend contractions just to keep her on her toes. But that's pretty much what happens in the shape of Braxton Hicks. These are named after John Braxton Hicks, an English doctor who first documented this most cruel of all the practical jokes in the late 19th century.

Towards the middle of the pregnancy, or sometimes even earlier, your partner may well start to notice the muscles of her uterus tightening for up to a minute or two. Usually painless, this can cause the abdomen to become hard and even contorted, and as the delivery date draws closer they helpfully become more frequent, more intense and more like real contractions, just to really scare the bejesus out of you both. Some women don't get them at all, while some poor souls can have them come on several times an hour.

As for why they happen in the first place and what purpose they serve, opinion is divided. Some experts describe them as being a training exercise, a kind of boot camp for the womb, getting it ready for the big push ahead and helping to 'ripen' the cervix so it can go on proper manoeuvres when it's required. Others, though, struggle to see how these false contractions, as they are sometimes called, achieve much real physiological value at all.

Just to top it all off, if your partner asks a midwife or a mother how you can tell the difference between Braxton Hicks and the real deal, the answer will invariably be 'You'll know the difference, don't you worry about that.'

What's annoying is that it's true. Labour contractions last longer, are more regular and increase in frequency, as well as hurting like no other hurt, as my wife once put it. A good barometer is that if your partner hasn't told you to rot in hell and never, ever, come anywhere near her again, it's probably a Braxton Hicks.

Of course, if you are worried that it might be something more, or the tightness is accompanied by any kind of discharge or lower back pain, get on the blower to your midwife or doctor pronto.

Counting those kicks

By this stage of pregnancy most women are feeling a regular pattern of kicks coming from the little one with the seemingly big feet.

Recently, a simple but smart campaign has been launched to encourage pregnant women to if not exactly count every single kick then certainly begin to recognise the pattern of their baby's movement and, if it should change, alert their midwife or doctor.

While there's no set number of kicks to be felt or indeed a set time to feel them, by becoming tuned in to when their little bundle likes to do their womb walkabout, mothers-to-be can try and notice any prolonged periods of inactivity and get things checked out.

Words from your fellow man:

Donald, 34, father of two: I got on quite well with the bump, spoke to it, played music to it, touched it. But I wasn't big on touching what was apparently an arm or a leg as it felt a bit awkward, a bit intrusive. My wife was much more confident with poking body parts . . . but it was in her body after all.

Stuart, 37, father of two: The bump made me feel a bit scared to be honest, made the whole thing seem a lot more real and nearby. I talked to it a lot and rubbed the stretch mark cream in quite a bit so I wasn't disengaged from it – I was just very aware of what it meant!

Levi, 36, father of two: I stroked the bump but felt a proper berk talking to it. I had no such problems the second time around of course, as fatherhood robs you of your dignity anyway.

FINANCING THE FAMILY – MONEY AND LOTS OF IT

Are you sitting down? Good. Here's what's coming.

According to research carried out by the Child Poverty Action

Group in 2022 the cost of raising a child to the age of 18 for a couple is £160,000.

Luckily, though, you don't have to pay upfront.

But then it's the real kicker of higher education costs, with the average 18- to 21-year-old receiving £149 a month from their parents according to a survey by Save the Student.

But those university challenges are miles away from you now and besides, our kids will almost certainly be taught everything they need to know by an AI called Clive whose level of knowledge is only bettered by the depths of its sarcasm, so banish those worries from your already furrowed brow.

So, it's not cheap then, this parenting carry-on. In fact if you were to stare at those figures for too long you'd probably get under the bed and pray to the Almighty that your little one isn't so much born with a silver spoon in its mouth as a diamond-encrusted shovel.

There are, of course, many ways of keeping costs to a minimum, without resorting to having your baby sleep in a drawer or train as a chimney sweep. Forgive me, but I've presumed that you aren't the type to take a pair of fabric scissors to an old sheet and snip it down to a perfect cot size, or make a crib out of papier mâché and old lentil packets. Thought not; so here's some of the most useful and least time-consuming ways to avoid baby bankruptcy.

The big bad buggy

You may be the kind of man whose right index finger has actually taken on the shape of an Allen key. You may be the kind of man who hides the Screwfix catalogue inside a copy of *Razzle* on the train to avoid any embarrassment. You may even be the kind of man who not only knows which drawer the key to bleed the radiators is in, but also how and when to use it with optimum efficiency.

I'm not that kind of man at all and I'll go as far as to say that, far from being an unfortunate and unusual specimen, there are many hundreds of thousands of men like me across Britain. For some reason the line of knowledge about how to put a new blade on the lawnmower, rather than throwing the whole thing away (into the correct skip at the recycling plant of course) has met with a fatal roadblock at our generation. Were we not listening, or could our fathers just not be bothered to tell us? Mine certainly did but somehow I became almost allergic to screwdrivers. The tools, not the drinks.

Who knows what's happened but what's for sure though is that for many of us, phrases like 'tongue and groove' conjure up altogether different images than DIY.

Of course, for most of us this doesn't impact on our lives in any great way; we go about our daily business without the need to read an instruction manual, or construct anything more complex than an outrageously overloaded dishwasher. Then, just as you are beginning to tackle the not insubstantial issue of your impending fatherhood, the baby buggy looms into view.

I don't want to scare you, I really don't, but this is a world the like of which you will have hitherto never seen. To give you a glimpse behind the wipe-clean curtain of doom, here is a list of just some of the choices that await you when you begin the quest to buy what used to be simply called a pram:

- three-in-one pram and pushchair combination
- two-in-one pram and pushchair combination

- pushchair
- traditional-style perambulator
- three-wheeler pushchair
- travel system
- pramette pushchair
- all-terrain system
- buggy
- stroller
- tandem
- double buggy

I could have included the wonderful worlds of car seats and carry-cots into the list above but the risk of giving you a nosebleed, with the different weight factors, attachment systems and basing units, would be too much for me to cope with, especially with you just about to become a dad and all.

Once you enter this stroller solar system, there really is no extracting yourself. Initially I tried to avoid the whole thing by desperately clutching to a few choice baby-kit facts and deploying them randomly in the hope of deflecting attention away from my crippling lack of expertise. My most successful weapon of mass distraction was: 'The man who came up with the light-weight baby buggy – a Mr Owen Finlay Maclaren – was inspired by one of his previous inventions, the under-carriage for the Spitfire.'

If that failed to derail the conversation I'd unfurl: 'The woman credited with making the Tommee Tippee baby accessory empire the success it is today was sentenced to eight years in prison in 2007 for plotting to kill her former partner and his wife.'

Not bad, are they? And true as well. But in all honesty they only really put off the inevitable for a short while and at some point soon you are going to have to go there too.

If you're waiting for me to tell you which one of these child chariots is best, you are out of luck I'm afraid. If I were to point the finger and even gently criticise any one of the main players, I'd be bundled into the back of a Transit van within hours as the axis of pushchair evil unleashed its foldaway wrath on me for daring to cast aspersions on one of its members.

What I am prepared to say is this.

- Ask your friends who have already been there and get their advice – or even a secondhand buggy!
- Newborn babies need to lie back flat, as their malleable spines can be damaged if they are kept curved for any great length of time, so take that into account.
- Think about where your baby is going to sleep as this may affect what you buy.
- If you live in a flat, have a normal sized car, get the bus or train every now and then, or don't happen to have biceps the size of Anglesey, then seriously, seriously think about the size and weight of what you buy. Both you and your partner will have backache aplenty thanks to rocking your baby back and forth without having to fold and unfold an armoured personnel carrier five times a day too.

What all of these little pointers amount to is a roundabout way of saying that despite the tedium, the overblown marketing and the colour schemes from hell, it really is worth taking your time over this purchase because with some of the bells and whistles versions coming in at more than £1,000 a pop, this is the single biggest buy you'll make. The number of couples who go through two or even three different versions within the first year alone would make you weep and your virtual bank manager swing for you, if they had arms.

The essentials

Where babies are concerned there are a few items, and only a few, other than the dreaded pushchair, that you'll find in every single house that has just taken delivery of a new delivery.

The bed

If you're not careful you can start off with a Moses basket, move on to a carrycot, then a fully blown cot before then realising you need a cot bed for your ever-expanding youngster.

Moses baskets are lovely but only useful for a month or two. If you can borrow one, great, and there are some cool ones that attach to your bed so you can scoop your nipper up in the middle of the night if that's your thing. Whatever your preferences early doors, buying a cot that will transform into a small bed is a smart move (called a cot bed). It might seem a long way off, but before you know where you are your defenceless little baby will be vaulting out of their caged pen like a pyjamas-clad gymnast.

The bath

To a newborn baby, being lowered backwards into an adult-sized bathtub is akin to us plucking our eyebrows with a hedge trimmer. The sheer scale of it all often sends the tiny little beauties into the first real fits of fear you'll have witnessed from them. All of which means baby baths are worth buying – but remember, it's a plastic bowl that's used to hold water, so the varieties that describe themselves as the ultimate in bathtime pleasure and relaxation for your most precious creation, are probably trying to justify the 50 quid they have lumped onto the price.

The changing mat

Stops your house getting covered in poo – £10 well spent in anyone's book. Having one both downstairs and upstairs if you live on two floors is, and I can't overstate this, a monumentally brilliant idea.

Nappies

You'll spend some serious cash on nappies in the first two years or so. While there's no doubt that the environmental impact of disposable nappies is vast – the latest figures say that eight million are thrown away in the UK each day – there are brands out there marketed as being more environmentally friendly.

Or of course you can try washable nappies. There are a lot of options out there, all taking various levels of commitment, so it's worth looking into.

Muslins

This is an absorbent square of cloth usually worn over the shoulder as a badge of honour and used to wipe up all sorts of sticky messes. It has been scientifically proven for it to be impossible to have too many of these in the house. You will have bought three quarters of a million and have every one of them stashed around your home but it'll be a cast-iron certainty that at the precise moment when you so desperately need one to scoop up a gobbet of milky sick, they will all gather together under the sofa and laugh at you.

Clothes

Babies grow. Babies really grow. In the time it takes for you to bend down to pick up one of those disappearing muslins, your child can have grown out of an entire wardrobe full of vests and little socks. It's that fast.

In the first six months, if anyone asks what you need, say baby clothes, practical, usable baby clothes. It might be dull, but for every cuddly crocodile you get given as a gift, you'll wish your friends had spent the spondooliks on two short-sleeved babygrows and a pair of mittens to stop your baby scratching himself to smithereens in the night – which also get in on the growing act in quite spectacular fashion.

The real thing to remember is that someone you know will have a bin liner full of baby clothes in the loft; just take a little moment to think about it and you will hit romper suit gold. The baby clothes merry-go-round is a modern-day institution: make sure you get in on it and you'll save yourself a fortune. And if you don't know anyone with a loftful, get onto Freecycle or the million baby-sharing apps where you can see what people in your neighbourhood are giving away for free, to a good home.

The nappy bin

While not strictly essential, the following item has become a firm favourite in a relatively short space of time and deserves a mention in dispatches.

Nappy bins are plastic tubs which house a cartridge in the top that contains a roll of scented nappy bags. Stuff the dirty nappy into the hole, turn the handle and the smelly article has been sealed and can be forgotten about until the bin is full. No trips outside in the middle of the night; no reeking kitchen bin and no leaving them on the stairs for a week.

Be warned. Once your baby starts to eat solids like a grown-up they also start to poo like a grown-up and the nappy bin begins to struggle to contain its ultra-toxic contents. Eventually the poor bin, after months of sterling service, has to be retired from action and a new plan of attack formulated.

Words from your fellow man:

Suki, 34, father of two: The best piece of kit we bought was the travel system. If you can get one with the carrier that goes straight from the car into the pushchair without waking the baby you will begin to love it like a brother. On the downside, the breast pump didn't work very well – but that's obviously second-hand information. Honest.

Nick, 35, father of two: We employed a one-stop-shop strategy in terms of getting all the baby stuff. We wrote a long list compiled from talking to a lot of people who'd been there and then went to a baby warehouse where they have everything under one roof. Done and dusted in one go, except for the things that we forgot – which was almost everything. The one piece of advice I'd give a soon-to-be dad is never attempt anything without a muslin. It takes me all my might not to take one to work with me nowadays.

Enzo, 36, father of one: I found the whole buying for baby thing pretty stressful and very expensive. The marketing people at baby shops are extremely clever. They know parents – particularly the ones who would rather cut both their arms off than scrimp on stuff for their kids – so they screw you for every penny.

Our very first trip to Mothercare cost us £900 and we only went for a catalogue.

Peter, 33, father of one: The process of buying all the baby paraphernalia highlights the male/female divide in all its glory. My wife wanted to buy everything and all of it the most expensive. I wanted to try and get bargains. Bottom line in all these arguments was 'she who bears wins'.

Paternity leave

The paternity leave situation has brightened up somewhat in recent years, but it's still not great. You can take up to two weeks of 'ordinary' paternity leave immediately after your baby is born, or any time within the following eight weeks in blocks of at least one week.

Statutory paternity leave is paid at the same rate as statutory maternity pay – £151.20 per week or 90% of your average weekly earnings, whichever is lower. So, you know, it's hardly a golden hello to being a dad but just about better than nothing. It's worth checking your employment contract to see if your employer offers its own range of paternity benefits – if you get lucky you could have a considerably better package.

Whatever you are due it's advised that you let your employer know that you're taking paternity leave at least 15 weeks before your baby is due, which you can work out by finding the Sunday of the week your baby's due and counting back 15 weeks. Shoes and socks off.

If your baby is born early, you can take paternity leave straight away after the birth, or up to eight weeks after the original due date, but if you have twins, triplets or more your time off doesn't double or triple, unfortunately.

The reason this is labelled 'ordinary paternity leave' is because now you can often qualify for shared parental leave.

By law, your partner can't work for the first two weeks after your baby's born, but once this is up she can either return to work or take up to a further 50 weeks of maternity leave – all or some of which can now be shared with you.

If your partner returns to work before the 50 weeks are up, you can take the remaining weeks of her maternity leave as 'shared parental leave'. Or, if you prefer, you and your partner can split her leave between you, sharing the responsibility of caring for your baby. You can even both be off work at the same time if you can afford it. You may also qualify for statutory shared parental pay, which is paid for up to 39 weeks at the same rate as maternity pay and paternity pay. If you take time off together, you will both be paid. Bear in mind that the pay entitlements are also shared. This means that you have 37 weeks of pay between you, not each; it's not a lottery win.

There are plenty of options to chew over, and any flexibility which recognises the millions of households where the bigger wage is being earned by Mum and not Dad is a smart move.

THE NAME GAME – WHAT TO CALL YOUR BABY

There are three questions you'll get asked in the immediate aftermath of your child being born and they almost always come in the same order:

1. boy or girl?
2. what did he weigh?
3. what are you going to call him?

The first two require little thought; a tale and a scale will tell you all you need to know.

What to name your baby, though, now there is a real belter of a question and there's a pretty good chance it will have been one that you started arguing over at around this time of the beginning of the pregnancy. It used to be pretty simple of course; you had a bank of boring but solid names to choose from and choose from them you did. For instance, the top five British boys' names in 1940 were:

1. James
2. Robert
3. John
4. William
5. Richard

In 1950 the list was:

1. James
2. Robert
3. John
4. Michael
5. David

Not what you'd call seismic change over the course of a decade. Of course the war had just ended and people had better things to do than wonder whether 'Powdered Egg' would sound good as the name of their third daughter.

In many ways we have now gone full circle through the Kylies and the Ethans, and a time when celebrities seemingly arrived at their children's names by picking up the first inanimate object they saw and tarting it up a bit – Plunger Moonlove, Remote Control Angeltears – to a place where, in 2021, the names Olivia and Oliver are consistently near the top of the annual most popular name lists for girls and boys. What a creative lot we are!

These days, what most of us are searching for when we name our offspring is a middle ground of something that doesn't have 15 people in the class shouting 'Yes Miss!', when it's called out at registration, but also won't prove be a source of lifelong shame and embarrassment for its incumbent. Tricky.

But does it really matter? Do names really make much of a difference to the life your little one will lead? There's a fair bit of research that suggests the answer could well be yes.

Firstly, a group of 80 experienced teachers were each given four essays, all of similar quality, and asked to mark them. The only identification on them was a first name and a false last initial. The names used were David, Elmer, Hubert and Michael. Before starting their experiment the researchers predicted that the essays 'written' by the children with common, popular names would be graded higher – and their prediction proved to be spot on. The Davids were given the highest marks; the papers by Michael the second highest; those by Elmer the third highest; and poor old Hubert was given the dunce's hat and made to stand in the corner. Poor Hubert.

This study was quickly followed up by another experiment, which asked a group of teachers to rate boys' names as desirable or undesirable.

The academic achievement scores for the group with desirable names were then compared with the group with undesirable names, and guess what? The average score for the Jameses was almost twice as high as that of the Arbuthnots – all of which suggests a merry-go-round of inherent and subconscious name-related bias from the teachers and debilitating self-consciousness from the unusually named students.

To put a tin lid on it, there's a slew of research, old and new, that shows pretty conclusively that what a child is called really is quite important. One study found that teachers identify troublemakers before they even so much as step foot in the classroom, just by looking down the register. Jacks were considered potential problems, which given the number of them out there doesn't bode well for the nation's educational well-being, as were boys called Callum and Connor. Alexander and Adam on the other hand were seen as names more likely to belong to the swots. As for the girls, pupils called Chelsea, Courtney and Chardonnay were seen as a potential handful by teachers, but they expected Elizabeth, Charlotte and Emma to be their brightest young ladies.

Snobbery or social science? Whatever's behind it, there's at least a decent case for names having a lifelong impact on us all.

Then there's the phenomenon of nominative determinism – the notion that people tend to gravitate towards areas of work that fit their names. I'd always thought this a load of rubbish until my father-in-law told me he once knew a fireman called Bernie Deadman and now I think it must be true. So choose wisely.

Words from your fellow man:

Enzo, 36, father of one: We both agreed from the outset that we wanted a name that worked both in English and Italian, that being where both of my parents were born. Luckily my wife did not want him named after her father – there is no equivalent of Ken in Italian.

Levi, 36, father of two: We had agreed on a shortlist for boys and girls. When the baby was born, I kind of gazumped my wife a bit by telling everyone we'd had a girl and that we thought her name was Rebecca. My wife wanted a good look at her to make sure she suited her name, but by then I'd told everyone anyway. I was right, as it happens.

Chris, 34, father of one: We hadn't chosen as we couldn't agree, me liking all those left field, I-agree-with-Madonna/Gwyneth-and-isn't-apple-zuton-mega-faust-sunray-a-great-name, my wife firm on the idea of something that they wouldn't get picked on at school for. We eventually went with Anouk Jasmine – so I won hands down.

BEING DAD – YOU, YOUR FATHER AND WHAT IT MEANS TO BE A DAD

There is one aspect of a man's pre-baby processing that tends to get very little airtime, almost certainly because it involves us talking about how we feel and looking into our past.

You see, there's nothing like looming paternity to bring back memories of what it was like to be fathered as a child yourself – from snapshots of playing outside, in what seem now like unfeasibly long and sunny summers, to car journeys that whizzed by at the start of the holiday, but made a young and flighty mind almost melt with boredom on the way home. There's a good chance you'll find yourself inexplicably conjuring up all sorts of images as your conscious and subconscious tries to get a handle on the fact that you're next up in Daddy Bear's chair.

Of course very few of us grow up guzzling lashings of lemonade in an Enid Blyton world. For many, memories of their father's role in childhood are far from positive. Dread, loneliness, longing, even pain, can be the predominant feelings that this sudden focus on what being a dad really means can dredge up. For those who experienced a childhood without a father, or lived through male figures coming and going in their life, the prospect of being cast in that role themselves can cause real anxiety and self-doubt. Will they be able to break the pattern, or will what they have always resented about their fathers be passed on again?

That notion – that as men we are pre-programmed to bring up our children in the same way as our fathers interacted with us, that nature and nurture have already combined to set out our parenting stall for us – obviously has a modicum of genetic truth to it. The clichés about you coming out with a lot of the hackneyed lines your parents fired at you, for instance, can become horribly accurate all too soon. I'd already said, 'Don't make me come over there,' to my son before he had reached his second birthday, which is a shameful thing to have to commit to paper.

The big truth, though, according to research, is that no matter how difficult it may be, examining your own childhood and your relationship with your parents means that you are not only much more likely to create your own personal parenting style rather than merely aping the way you were treated, but crucially that you are also much more likely to produce happier and more emotionally adjusted children. Dr Howard Steele of University College London interviewed 100 fathers-to-be, whose partners were expecting the couple's first child, to discover how they viewed their own relationship with their parents as they were growing up. Over the course of the next decade many of the men's children were interviewed and psychologically assessed at various stages of their early life. What became strongly evident was that the initial interviews with the fathers-to-be were powerful predictors of the children's emotional and mental state.

It wasn't, though, as you might imagine, a straightforward case of those dads who had a dire relationship with their own father seeing their children suffer the same fate too. What the study found was that the children whose expectant fathers had really thought about the way their parents had related to them were happier. Those whose fathers had responded to the original interview question with ambivalence, or stated that they hadn't really thought about their own childhood in relation to how they were going to approach fatherhood themselves, ended up with offspring who had more difficultly with relationships of all kinds and were generally less happy and more anxious. What also became clear was that although the amount of thought the fathers put into their own childhoods did indeed have a direct link to their own children's mental health, this didn't become apparent until the children hit puberty. Until that point the children's relationships with their mothers seem far more influential. Or to put it in another way, as men we have to put in some serious, considered effort early on, with relatively little sign of it having any effect whatsoever.

That aside, it seems that it's not a case of whether your dad preferred to stuff you 7–0 at footy in the garden rather than actually play with you; it's more a question of whether you have spent the time reflecting on what you might want to do differently – or as Dr Steele himself put it in a rather more scholarly way, 'Fathers should be encouraged to reflect on their own childhood while their child is still in the womb.'

So if you find yourself drifting back to your early years over the coming weeks, let yourself go, chances are your own kids will thank you for it.

Words from your fellow man:

Tom, 34, father of two: Expecting my own child made me consider the way I was fathered. I remembered all the good times, but I also hoped to be far better in other areas. If the first few years have taught me anything, it's that its bloody hard trying to live up to everything you'd want to be as a father.

Peter, 33, father of one: I made an extra effort with my dad while we were expecting, but it also highlighted the fact we are not that close – something I don't want to happen with my children.

Donald, 34, father of two: You find yourself examining parenthood present and childhood past as the months roll on. You tend to draw similarities and perhaps have a better understanding of what your folks have been through. Did they really deal with all this...? Was it the same for them...? Were they more natural...? Were we just easier kids... (probably not)... or have they just forgotten? You even start dredging up some old sayings from your mum or dad, which is scary to hear yourself come out with.

Enzo, 36, father of one: When I think of my father I try to picture how happy it would have made him to spend time with his grandson. The fact that Max won't experience that will leave a gap in his life, sadly.

Levi, 36, father of two: My dad died two years before I became a father for the first time and it made me miss him more without a doubt.

Oli, 35, father of one: I've never had a dad around and the constant worry was if we had a boy, would I be good enough, would I know what to do, because I had absolutely nothing to base it on. The worry was less if we had a girl, but still there.

Move along please

There's another much more intrinsically self-interested and not overly cheery thought which can pop into your head once or twice as you near becoming a father for the first time. You are going to die.

I told you it wasn't cheery. But when you think about it, getting a sense of your own mortality at the point when you are just about to introduce a new life to the planet isn't all that surprising.

For starters, on a very practical level all of a sudden your death would have a serious impact on the survival of other people – hence your thoughts can turn to wills and life insurance for potentially the first time ever. You might even find yourself driving a bit more carefully, although that's highly unlikely. Then there's the dawning realisation that the start of your son or daughter's childhood will mark the end of your own, in a very real, very, 'I'm too knackered to even think about going out and besides where would we get a babysitter at this short notice and besides we can't afford it anyway,' kind of a way. While it's not quite one in one out, your offspring's arrival does nudge you along a place towards the end of this earthly plank – or at least it can seem like that in the more contemplative moments that you may well find yourself having as the birth nears.

Don't worry, though, folklore has it that nature craftily gives the selfish gene that is the cause of all these 'What about me?' thoughts a quick call and flatters the arse off it by first making the baby look like you for the initial few weeks of his life, then a few months later as that little trick is about to wear off, making your child not only smile at you, but also start to act like you as well. Later on they even laugh at your jokes, too, and all of us love that, don't we? It's brilliant, and more than makes up for the fact that you are no longer even the second most important person in your own house and have already entered the, albeit gently paced, downhill phase of your very existence.

For now, though, you are just going to have to trust me as you enter what can be the most inward-looking phase of the pregnancy. Rest assured it doesn't last for long. In a matter of months you won't be giving yourself a second thought as you neglect to shower, shave or eat for three whole days, as you and your partner desperately try to work out why your new baby is screaming like he is being disembowelled with a soup spoon as soon as his beautiful little head comes into contact with where he is meant to be sleeping.

But don't be too hard on yourself; if you can't be introspective on the cusp of the most momentous and important event of your entire life, when can you be? The importance of the role of the dad in shaping the lives of children has been eroded and underplayed as generations of fathers were forced to spend most of their time at work.

In recent years, however, study after study has shown that how we perform as fathers profoundly affects how our boys and girls turn into men and women.

- Pre-school children who spend more time playing with their dads are often more sociable when they enter nursery school.
- Involvement of dads with children aged 7–11 predicts success in exams at 16.
- Where dads are involved before the age of 11, children are less likely to have a criminal record by the age of 21.

It's even been found that babies who miss out on regular baths by their father are more likely to grow up with social problems. No pressure then.

PROGRESS REPORT, MONTH 6

Your baby (23–26 weeks)

Your baby measures about 23cm (9 inches) from crown to rump and weighs almost 1kg (2lb) – his body is now growing faster than his head and his proportions are roughly the same as those of a newborn.

Conscious thought is now possible and your baby can learn and remember – although whether he can hold a grudge at this point remains unclear.

Your baby's ears are going from strength to strength, too, and he can move his body in rhythm with his mother's voice – like one of those dancing flowers that were all the rage one Christmas a few decades ago.

It's said that a baby whose father talks to him while he's in the womb can pick out his voice in a roomful of people from birth.

More usefully than mere recognition, though, there's a chance he will respond to it, too; that is, stop crying when he hears your voice in months to come – now there's an incentive to get talking to that bump if ever there was one.

His nostrils have opened up too, not because he's perfecting a brilliant Kenneth Williams impression to wow you both with on arrival, but because he has begun to make inhalation movements with his muscles. That's right, your baby is practising how to breathe.

Won't be long now!

Your partner

The baby's movements and hiccups are now becoming a big part of your partner's existence.

As the baby grows and the womb expands, the whole package begins to press on her stomach, exacerbating bouts of heartburn and indigestion as well as rib pain. As her muscles start to stretch and lengthen she may well also get a sharp stitch-like pain down the side of her stomach.

If stretch marks are going to appear, they will make themselves known around now, usually on your partner's stomach or breasts. See this month's must-dos for some advice on handling what, as you can imagine, is a very delicate topic.

Now is also the time that pelvic floor muscles start to become stretched. The oft-talked-about pelvic floor helps to hold your partner's bladder, womb and bowel in place – so, you know, it's worth having. The muscles also act as the valve mechanism that allows her to empty her bladder and bowels. Trouble is, being pregnant can make these muscles become very weak or overstretched and can result in a little bit of wee leaking out when she coughs, exercises, laughs, moves or remains completely still. Tips on how to help her strengthen these muscles follow shortly, but for now just remember that every gag you tell her from this point onwards has the potential to be literally piss-funny so go easy.

MUST-DOS OF MONTH 6

Give her a wedgie

Stick 'pregnancy wedge pillow' into Google and buy one. These simple little things give your partner support for her growing bump, and while

– until recently – this was just seen as a nice thing to have, there is recent evidence that there could be a link between pregnant women sleeping on their back and stillbirth.

In late 2017, the charity Tommy's launched the 'SleepOnSide' campaign, which aimed to make women aware of the research that sleeping on their side in late pregnancy could reduce their risk of stillbirth.

At a stretch

Stretch marks affect between 75% and 90% of pregnant women. The combination of more weight and higher levels of hormones making the skin thinner than usual is a pain, and can cause some serious anguish and anxiety for many women both during and after pregnancy.

There's a good chance, though, that despite your loving and magic fingers your partner may well develop a permanent stretch mark or two. Your role then is simple: tell her you love her and that she is beautiful, every single day.

Floor it

In motivational terms, the reasons for your partner doing pelvic floor exercises are about as compelling as they come. These exercises help:

- protect her from incontinence during and after the pregnancy
- support the extra weight of pregnancy and may even help shorten the second stage of labour
- heal the perineum after birth
- achieve orgasm during sex.

Makes you wonder why we aren't all doing them en masse in the work car park every morning.

If you are still enjoying some mid to late pregnancy how's your father then you can be of even more help. If your partner does the lift and squeeze movement while you are inside her, your penis can act as a detector rod and you can cheerfully inform her if you can feel her efforts.

Romance? Dead? Get outta here.

MONTH 7

BRACE YOURSELVES

(27–31 weeks)

You are well and truly in the third trimester, which means the final preparations are about to begin and you are going back to school.

That's right, it's time for you to experience the antenatal class in all its glory: the breathing exercises, the vaginal discharge conversations, the pressure to meet lifelong friends in a handful of hours. I'm excited for you, I really am.

Then there's a very different form of preparation to tackle, trying to get your head round how having a baby will change your relationship.

In many ways it's one of the most important yet neglected areas of the pre-birth period. We all focus heavily on the moment of the birth and how to deal with the baby that pops out as a result of it (although it doesn't actually pop), but often people don't give a second thought to how this new little being will change the bond they have with the person they made it with.

THE ANTENATAL EXPERIENCE – BACK TO SCHOOL

Antenatal classes often draw differing and extreme responses from fathers-to-be. Some can't imagine attempting to tackle the trials and technicalities of birth without the crash course they receive while sitting cross-legged on the floor of a local church hall. Others would do anything to get out of them, praying that extreme weather will force the primary school-style cancellation of their torment.

Although there are many types of antenatal class around these days, they tend to come in two distinct flavours: the antiseptic hand gel NHS version and the pumpkin soup with a hint of saffron private variety of which the National Childbirth Trust (NCT) classes are by far the most predominant.

Typical classes, whether NHS or NCT, often follow a course over six to eight weeks, with the majority of women in attendance due to give birth at roughly the same time.

NHS antenatal classes

It's usual, but by no means certain, that if you choose to go down the NHS route you'll have your classes at the hospital you are booked in to deliver the baby. These are usually free of charge and taught by midwives, who not only tell you about every detail of labour and birth but also about that particular hospital's policies and procedures.

Information will include what labour is like, what pain relief can and can't do, sessions on the prospect of interventions, explanation of the clinical name for when someone comes at your wife wielding a pair of forceps or a plunger-like device (a ventouse, of which there is much, much more in the Month 9 chapter) and caesarean (C-section) births. You might also be taught a few parenting skills; for example, how to bath a baby, change a nappy and, crucially, where you'll find CBeebies on Freeview and Sky.

They may also give you the opportunity to have a tour of the maternity unit, which is worth doing for sure, but is a bit like being given a detailed look at your dentist's tray of shiny instruments before he sorts out your root canal. NHS classes are often large and a bit more impersonal than their privately organised cousins, but then this is the NHS, God bless her creaking bones, so a comfy chair, coconut macaroon and foot massage were never really on the cards were they? But you know the advice is rock-solid.

Just to give you a taste of things to come in labour, you may not be taught by the same midwife for each class, as their day (and night) job can be a tad unpredictable, meaning they have to hand over to whoever is free.

NCT antenatal classes

NCT classes are the undisputed king of private antenatal tuition. Other organisations hold them and plenty of former midwives have set up their own sessions, too, but with more than 1,000 qualified teachers and an army of 10,000 volunteers, the NCT is the alpha female of the antenatal world.

Founded in 1956, the NCT looked to challenge the childbirth orthodoxy of the time, which was essentially that women kept quiet and did what their (almost certainly male) doctor told them. One of the organisation's original published aims gives us a pretty good indication of what having a baby was like back then: 'Women should be humanely treated during pregnancy and in labour, never hurried, bullied or ridiculed.'

Ridiculed! Bloody hell!

Another founding principle states that analgesia should not be forced on women in childbirth – or, please stop rendering women unconscious with chloroform the first time they so much as ask for a glass of water.

With these kind of values at its beating heart, it's no surprise that the NCT has evolved into the champion of natural childbirth and is unashamedly women-centred. Equally unsurprising is the fact that its antenatal classes reflect that ethos, which has led to them gaining a knit-your-own-lentils, earth-mother reputation from some quarters. It's highly debatable how accurate that reputation is, and it seems everyone in the pregnancy realm has a take on it.

What is for certain is that the NCT antenatal classes remain incredibly popular. Instructors are not usually midwives but women who have had at least one baby. They aren't just grabbed off the streets, though, you'll be glad to hear; they have all been trained in what they do and most deliver the classes within an informal setting, which can quite often be their own home. Small class sizes add to the friendly feel as does the often hands-on teaching style, which can see your partner, and often you too, practising relaxation skills and different positions for labour, as well as receiving information on the ins and hopefully outs of the birth itself and all the scenarios that surround it.

Costs start at around £120 per course and can rise to £300 depending on where you live, but being the good eggs they are, the NCT has a raft of payment plans and discounts to try to make it possible for almost everyone to take part in one of its classes if they want to.

With their more intimate air and informal approach, NCT classes and their ilk have taken on an interesting subtext in recent years, too, one far away from the mere imparting of knowledge and information. As you arrive at your first class, looking round the room at the glowing women and sweaty men, there's a fair chance you'll think two things. Firstly, I hope I don't have to take my shoes off because I think my left sock has a hole in the big toe, and, secondly, at least two couples in this room need to become our new best friends. It's the unspoken law of the antenatal class that because the two main stars of modern adult friendship are aligned, namely:

• Do we have something, anything, in common – er yes, something quite large and round?
• Do we live near each other? Probably.

And don't forget, this isn't just about forging friendship for friendship's sake, this is about developing an incredibly useful support network who are going through what you are, when you are.

So no pressure.

Words from your fellow man:

Peter, 33, father of one: I would recommend NCT classes to everyone – best £120 I've ever spent. You pick up a few things but the main thing was my wife picked up seven like-minded women, who in the run-up to the birth and the first year of having the little one have been invaluable. Of course the two of you together are the most important people to make sure you get through, but never underestimate the relief you get from speaking to people facing the same daunting baby mountain as you.

Tom, 34, father of two: Antenatal classes are worth doing for so few reasons. Sure we met a couple of nice people, but keeping up with your

own bestest friends is hard enough, especially when you are on permanent baby duty. Usual mix at ours I guess, with a couple of annoying
ones for good measure. The one thing I recall is that if a dog licks your
baby's face it won't really affect it. Everything else was a battle to stay
awake, let alone be interested in. But it was a key milestone, it meant
we were in the final run in, and this is the best bit about NCT. It gets
you in the zone, and it's nice to have others to share it with.

Jim, 34, father of one: For some reason I got severe indigestion
whenever we went to an antenatal class (thank God for the herbal tea).
I also always forgot all the names, all of the time, but they were good
fun when I was awake. And the teacher was supportive after the birth,
bless her.

BIRTH CHOICES – WHO DOES THE BEST DELIVERY?

If you do decide to take part in antenatal classes of any description
they are certain to throw up as many questions as they provide
answers, especially when it comes to the type of environment your
partner should deliver her baby in.

Home births

In 1955, there were 683,640 births in England and Wales, of which
33.4% took place at home. Today the figure for home births is just
under 2.5%, which actually represents an increase from a low of less
than 1% in the mid-'80s, with the vast majority of babies being
born in hospitals and other medical institutions.

Eminent zoologist Desmond Morris, in his brilliant little book
Babywatching, suggests that this shift towards medical institutions

constitutes a major difference between the labour human females endure and the relatively relaxed way in which our close cousins in the animal kingdom deliver their young. Morris proposes that because modern mothers-to-be are rushed off to a strange and daunting place with strong associations with illness and pain and then put in the hands of relative strangers, they become, understandably, anxious.

Just as nine out of 10 pregnant horses give birth in the dead of night – the mare instinctively waiting until the least stressful part of the day – Morris suggests that women subconsciously and hormonally struggle with the same intuition too, which results in labours many times longer than normal for our species compared to other mammals.

He goes on to say that while home births are, of course, possible, so out of the norm have they become that they themselves now carry bucketfuls of anxiety, too – with mothers worried that they are too far away from the expert help that hospitals have.

It's a very interesting theory and one which makes much sense. But the fact remains that while moves have been made to promote home births, they still represent a tiny minority, especially of first babies. If you would like to explore a home birth, talk to your midwife if you haven't already.

Birthing units

So the statistics say that you will almost certainly go for, or end up having, a hospital delivery. Luckily there's now some choice in this area, too, with the advent of the midwife-led birthing centre. These units often feel cosier, more relaxed and less clinical than a regular hospital and some say they even bridge the gap between giving birth at home and on a hospital maternity ward.

The obvious drawback – if indeed you see it as a drawback – is that with a somewhat low-tech approach centred on birthing pools, balls and stools, comes fewer choices on the pain relief front. For instance, your partner will have to be transferred to a hospital if an epidural is needed (although often this is essentially an internal transfer as the birthing centre may be attached to the hospital itself).

Going private

Can you buy a better birth? Some people with anything up to 20 grand burning a hole in their pockets seem to think you can.

There's a range of private birth units across the UK, offering private rooms, state-of-the-art facilities, one-to-one care during labour and beyond, top-notch meals and what is marketed as the most peaceful, relaxed and personal way to have a baby. It's worth bearing in mind that, depending on the unit, there's a good chance that in the event of a medical emergency your partner would need to be transferred to an NHS hospital.

Costs vary, but when you start to add in the consultant's fees and extra nights after the birth you are talking about many thousands of pounds for the privilege.

A cheaper alternative is to book a private room in an NHS hospital for use after the birth. Often called amenity rooms, these are private rooms situated on or close to the postnatal wards. Midwives tend to allocate them on the basis of clinical need, but it is possible to book one depending on availability. If the birth is uncomplicated your partner may well just be allowed to go back home the next day, but after something like a caesarean section these can represent a viable option. Costs vary widely from hospital to hospital, with some coming in at under £100 a night, and others many hundreds of pounds.

Howdy partner

Another area that your antenatal classes may bring into focus is who will be your partner's birthing partner. If at this point you are shouting at the book, 'Birthing partner? I'm the bloody birthing partner!' then you are probably clear that you will indeed fill that role and good on you.

But, increasingly, there are other options that are coming into the mix. Your partner may want some girl power in the room and her mum, sister or best friend may be who she wants there as well as, or even instead of, you. Tough luck. As we will see in the Month 9 chapter, there's plenty for the birth partner to do, including taking some critical decisions when acting as the mother-to-be's advocate. It's this scenario that has largely given rise to the paid-for birth partner, or doula.

Doulas almost always have experience in the delivery environment and offer continuous support and guidance throughout labour. They can either be an additional birth partner or the sole companion. It's obviously imperative that you choose one who both your partner and you get on with and can see yourself working well with under one of the most pressurised situations you will ever face.

With an estimated 5,000 births using a doula each year in the UK it's a growing trend, despite charges ranging from £250 to more than £1,000, depending on the doula's experience. The fee often includes antenatal and postnatal visits as well.

YOUR RELATIONSHIP – ALL CHANGE PLEASE

It's often said that women have an unwritten rule when it comes to telling their thus-far-childless female friends about the reality of labour. They lie.

Whether it's a Darwinian instinct to protect the future of the species by seeing someone else go through the same agony as they have, or just good manners, no woman ever tells it like it really is in the delivery room.

There is, however, a male version of this phenomenon, and I'm about to reveal it. There's no easy way of putting this so I'll just come right out and say it: there's a very good chance that your relationship as you know it will very shortly end for good. That's not to say you and your partner won't be together, or that you won't be happy. It's just that what you've had in the past and are currently enjoying the Indian summer of, will never be quite the same again. Ever. It may well be better, it could be deeper, but it'll never be as it was.

For many couples, the months and sometimes years after they first become parents usher in a period of such upheaval that it can feel as if at the moment their child arrived the person they thought they knew back to front disappeared and was replaced with some-one who looked remarkably similar, but acted very differently indeed. At the heart of this conundrum is one key question: can a truly equal partnership, the kind that most women and indeed men expect nowadays, exist with the arrival of a baby who hasn't a clue about fluid gender roles and equality movements.

When studies of British parents find that far from bringing happiness and joy, an increasing number of modern mums and dads feel that the arrival of their offspring has left them feeling 'angry and resentful' and even 'miserable, sad, distracted and depressed', it's hard to avoid the conclusion that something is going on here. Then there's the earlier work, undertaken in the USA, which followed more than 300 couples having their first child over a period of six years. The studies, which documented in greater depth than ever before the amazingly stressful social and emotional consequences of parenthood, revealed that for about half of the couples who participated, marital satisfaction declined after the birth of a first child.

Of course, having children has always been a challenge, always upset the apple cart, even in the days when the apple cart was the very height of commercial transportation tech. For your average newborn things are pretty much as they were: babies have always cried; always been a bit lax on the toilet front; always had an idiosyncratic (some might even say downright quirky) sense of day and night; and have always, always, been the centre of attention in their household.

But we – that's you, me and everyone who is having children today – are right in the middle of a seismic shift in the very way the family unit works. The foundations of the partnership men and women enter into when they start a family are moving under our feet, leaving both partners on shaky ground. Before we look into exactly how and why the modern-day relationship all too often suffers a temporary cardiac arrest when children arrive – and crucially how you can avoid it flat-lining altogether – it's worth taking a look at how being a father has evolved into what it is today.

A horrible history of Dad

Fathers haven't got a great reputation historically. The hands-on dad or 'new man' phenomenon is widely seen as just that, new; with the father figure of yesteryear almost universally viewed as a pretty uncaring beast within the stereotypical sweet of history:

- **Prehistoric Dad:** An idyllic existence for the loin-clothed old man, hunting and gathering during the day, sharing a cave with scantily clad wife (or wives) by night. Little interest taken in Bam-Bam-like infant. Occasional sabre-toothed tiger attacks don't help.

- **Medieval Dad:** Saxon fathers had a tendency to pelt offspring with parsnips when displeased with them. Aside from this occasional vegetable abuse, the father was a peripheral, pox-addled figure.

- **Elizabethan Dad:** Good practice for a father consisted of throwing their young into a woven sack, transporting them to the docks and selling them to barnacle-covered explorers as tobacco tasters and potato smokers.

- **Victorian Dad:** Children spent the majority of their time strapped into metal frames and forced to permanently pose for 10-hour box brownie photo shoots, leaving father plenty of time to cultivate his already impressive opium habit.

- **1950s Dad:** Children beaten by fathers for questioning authority figures.

- **1960s Dad:** Children beaten by fathers for not questioning authority figures.

- **2000s Dad:** Dads finally begin to get it and start to take interest in their young. The emergence of man-bags signals that the shift has gone too far, but a crisis is averted.

The reality, though, is very different. Adrienne Burgess, author of *Fatherhood Reclaimed* (Vermilion, 1998), paints a picture of historical fatherhood that bears very little resemblance to the way most of us imagine it to have been. Our view of the hunter-gatherer in primitive societies spending most of the time slaying wild boar far away from home is a dodgy one for starters. In most tribes, fathers were present for the majority of the time and in many there developed a pride among men that they were close to their children.

Jump forward an epoch or two and rural Dad wasn't too shabby on the childcare front either. With life regulated by daylight, fathers were only away from a lighted house or cottage for a handful of hours, while in summer the whole family often worked together in the fields. Even in more wealthy families, children often slept in the same room as their parents; the nursery room tucked away in the attic didn't start to appear until much later.

Then there are the stats – after formal/informal divorce, fathers often won custody of their children and when you take into account that around 8% of mothers died in childbirth, many more men than women were lone parents. In fact it's estimated that between 1599 and 1811, 24.1% of children lived in lone father households, compared with just 1.3% today. So what the hell happened to catapult us to the world where waiting until your father got home became something to be feared rather than looked forward to? You guessed it, global warming fans: the sooty paw prints of the industrial revolution are all over it.

The main way in which both physical and emotional distance has been put between fathers and their children is through the idea of the father as sole provider for the entire family. The man-as-breadwinner model might seem as old as the family unit itself to us now, but it wasn't until the steam-driven late 19th century that bringing home the bacon began to be seen as the male's raison d'être.

But rejoice, my brother, because fathers are making a comeback. After more than 200 years of being set apart from our own families, cast as the provider but never carer, we're trying our best to become a true part of it all again, which is great, obviously, but far from straightforward. While we've been trying to change, wrestling ourselves away from our desks, diggers and dustcarts, and moving heaven and earth to make it home for bathtime, things have changed at home too – in a big way. Being a 'husband' in Britain is in many ways unrecognisable from how it was just 50 years ago for one woman-sized reason – being a 'wife' has been utterly transformed too.

Woman, wife/partner, mother

When I was five years old, my dad walked into our house one summer's evening and proudly told us all that the family had a new car. By new he meant a very old Austin Princess but that's a minor point – what's interesting now that I look back to that day in the late 1970s is that this revelation was news to my mother too. My father had sold our old car and bought a new one without consulting with my mum and it didn't so much as raise a matrimonial eyebrow.

Do you know a man under 40 who has done anything even remotely like that?

The car was Dad's domain, together with providing for the entire family, filling out the pools coupon and getting the fire going. Bringing up the children on a day-to-day basis, running the house and keeping everyone fed, washed and watered was, by and large, what Mum did. For all seven of us. Thank you and goodnight.

You don't need to be a social historian, or indeed a woman, to see that the clearly defined gender roles which many of our parents and all of our grandparents operated within have changed profoundly and forever. It's only a handful of decades, for instance, since the stipulation for a woman being granted a mortgage was that she must get either her husband's or her father's signature. A woman was her father's daughter before becoming her husband's wife.

No longer, of course, at least not in many parts of the world. The women's movement turned all the old assumptions about the roles of the genders on their head, a shift which also coincided with a fundamental change in the very nature of work itself. As the old heavy industries were replaced with knowledge-based jobs, the need for brawn and physical strength was replaced with the need for people who were at ease with human interaction and emotion, as well as being able to carry out more than one task at a time. Now let me think, which gender would that suit best?

Professional satisfaction as well as personal and sexual freedom is rightly on the menu for today's women, and ambitions for many don't just centre on being wives or mothers. This in turn has also had a subtle effect on the laws of attraction and partner selection. Whether your potential wife is a good cook, keeps the house nice and tidy or has child-bearing hips are questions that have been consigned to the dustbin of male chauvinist history. Now we look for partners not cleaners; it's a soulmate we want, someone who we can share our lives with; a companion.

When we've found that special person, often nowadays someone who earns as much or more than we do, life can feel pretty sweet for both parties. Every couple is different, of course, but in the main, the number of relationships in which the man could change the family car without a by your leave from his partner is falling rapidly. A more typical scene now would be hours of joint research, followed by much debate and list-drawing before they finally reach a compromise or go with one choice over another, leaving the loser to persistently pick holes in the wretched automobile for the next five years. A palaver for sure. But a relatively fair and equal one.

It's no surprise then that faced with the opportunity to establish a career, achieve some level of financial security, be part of a true partnership with someone and just have a bloody good time, the average age of the first-time mother has jumped to 29 and counting. Foreign holidays, cool careers, good food – oh yes, this is what dreams are made of, this is what relationships have evolved into, this is what real equality between the genders can bring.

And then you have a baby.

A nappy-wearing cluster bomb lands right in the middle of your serene and blissful partnership, and not having read much Germaine Greer or indeed giving a toss about the hard-fought gains of the feminist crusade, his prime concern is to be fed, winded and changed. Now.

The ideology of equality that many of us now live by within our relationships has come on leaps and bounds for sure, but babies – tiny, innocent little mites with not much on their minds but milk – have the power to shake your new and happy world to the core in those first few months especially.

Now, it's down to us to work out how to stop the baby bomb from causing some serious collateral damage in our households, and what follows is some of the fallout to watch out for. Thinking about it ahead of time may not provide you with all the answers, but looking after your first baby is tough enough without being blown away by the sheer shock of how much the rest of your life seems to have changed, too.

Turn and face the strange

So, things are going to change, but how?

Here's a whistle-stop tour of the two main areas in which your bundle of joy will indirectly alter how you and your partner get along. If, in the early weeks and months of being a father you spot one of this troublesome pair, and chances are you will, you might just stand a chance of summoning up the time, forethought and energy to adjust what you are about to say or do and avoid a flashpoint that everyone could do without, especially the smallest one of your trio.

Bond, maternal bond

Everyone knows that mothers and babies bond. It's one of nature's staples, like needles playing hide and seek in haystacks and bears preferring to do their business outside. There's no two ways about it, early on babies only have eyes, ears and nostrils for Mum and often the same is true in reverse.

For some new fathers this can hit home more than they ever imagined it would. Feelings of jealousy towards this unfeasibly cute little intruder who has so besotted their loved one are well chronicled and while for some men this can be a real problem, what is much more common is the feeling of total and utter uselessness that washes over fresh-faced, keen and achingly well-informed new dads. You've done the antenatal course, you've watched the DVD, you've even bought a bloody book with sperm on the front for crying out loud, but the 50/50 spilt you employed before the arrival of the little one is often nowhere to be seen.

This one-sided scenario, as we will see in a short while, can cause problems aplenty for your partner, too, but in the first few weeks it's the dads who run the risk of feeling like they've put a lot of thought into what to wear to a party, only to be asked to wash up when they get there. That's a pretty stark picture, of course, and you may not feel as edged out early on – your partner may even have had a caesarean, in which case you'll be a very busy boy indeed, but no matter what your personal circumstances are, there's a strong chance that you'll feel a little sidelined as the overwhelmingly powerful surge of love between baby and mother kicks in.

When you stop for a second to compute the fact that just the sight, smell and sound of her baby can make a woman flood the place with the milk she needs to support him, you can see that mums make decisions at this extraordinary point in their lives based on hormonally driven instinct, an instinct that just days before didn't exist. There are no brochures to consult, no Googling the answer, she often just knows, feels, what is right for the baby at this crucial early stage and you as the father just plain don't.

There will be conversations, of course, even the odd compromise, but when push comes to shove, your partner will almost always back her intuition to tell her the right thing to do by the new arrival. It's the way it is and always has been. That's not to say all women know what to do from the off, and harnessing this intuition, this feeling, can be an overwhelming and daunting task in itself.

When you consider that it was only around 100 years or so ago that infant mortality rates in the fantastically prosperous UK were at levels that would turn even the most relaxed of women into fiercely protective sabre-toothed tigresses, it's a wonder we are allowed to stay under the same roof, let alone be tolerated when it's suggested that it might be good to give the week-old tot his first bath.

In the mid-1950s, eminent paediatrician, psychiatrist and psychoanalyst Donald Winnicott identified and highlighted this early state of intense mother–baby bonding, naming the phenomenon 'primary maternal preoccupation'. Winnicott observed a special mental state of the mother that involved a greatly increased sensitivity to, and focus on, the needs of her baby, starting near the very end of pregnancy and continuing for a few weeks after the birth.

It's also been noted that not only does a mother need support and protection while she is in this phase, but that the benefits of the secure attachment it creates can have positive effects on the child right through childhood and into adult life. Which is a polite way of saying, 'Butt out numb-nuts.' But what's key to remember is that the early days and weeks of your new family's existence are like no other. No matter what plans you had made, no matter how interwoven you and your partner were before the arrival, nature is calling the shots; and although you play a very important role in those early days, you are very much the best supporting actor rather than the joint lead.

Fear not, though, the time when you will be expected to step up to the plate is just around the corner, bringing with it another set of challenges to negotiate.

Jobs and doing them

After the first few weeks of a baby's arrival things start to get back to normal. Well, not normal, just a different kind of different.

What stops are the visits from friends and relatives and the arrival of presents. Even the nice old woman from over the road comes round to collect the dish she brought the shepherd's pie in during the baby's first week at home.

What starts is the graft. It's hard to overestimate the wonder/panic you'll feel at how such a small and defenceless little thing can generate so much work for two adults. This outrageously increased workload also sits against a backdrop of complete and utter knackeredness.

It's hard to put into words just how exhausted you'll both be: FUUUUUUUUUUUUUUUUUUUUUUUUCCCCCCC CCCCCCCCCCCKKKKKKKKKKKKKKKKKKKKKKKK KKED was the best I could come up with.

Sleep deprivation has been used as a means of interrogation, most famously by the KGB. Menachem Begin, the prime minister of Israel from 1977 to 1983, who was unfortunate enough to have experienced the technique while a prisoner in Russia, described it as follows: 'In the head of the interrogated prisoner, a haze begins to form. His spirit is wearied to death, his legs are unsteady, and he has one sole desire: to sleep . . . Anyone who has experienced this desire knows that not even hunger and thirst are comparable with it.'

Yep, that sounds about right.

Then there's the fact that you will almost certainly be back at work, too. Deep joy.

So, with all those ingredients in the pot we have a potentially explosive situation on our Sudocrem-covered hands. Here's how it may pan out.

After a pitiful amount of sleep you make your way to work like a mole with a bad headache. Your even more shattered partner spends the entire day with a life form that is only capable of doing the following things: eating, pooing, vomiting and crying. Not surprisingly, pretty soon the charm of this four-pronged approach wears a little thin and your partner, now permanently smelling of regurgitated milk and drowning under a sea of off-white cotton clothing, asks you to help out more – to not only do your fair share but above and beyond that, too. Slightly stung, you swallow hard and try to do what you think is being asked of you, be more proactive and take some of the pressure off your partner. Now's not the time, you are proud of yourself for thinking, to point out that between the hours of 8am and 6pm you are actually working rather than – as she seems to be implying – being massaged for 10 hours while watching the cricket. So you get involved more, but this can lead to . . .

Scorekeeping

This is a game invented by the devil. To start off with, both you and your partner keep a secret tally in your heads of the chores you've performed over the course of, let's say, a week. On the unspoken scoreboard you are getting murdered of course, absolutely hammered out of sight. In nappy changing alone you are down by more than 40 points and if she's breastfeeding as well, my word, you might as well pack up and go home. Except you can't because that's where the game is being played.

Then one day, after you have yet again put one of the few nappies you have changed on the bin rather than in it, she explodes and proceeds to douse you in a torrent of pent-up point-scoring. You attempt to come back, of course: you de-iced the car the other day, and so often are you spotted late at night in the super-market that the security staff are beginning to become suspicious. But it's a feeble defence, because she's at home with the baby and therefore does the lion's share of the baby stuff. Stands to reason, doesn't it?

Under no circumstances point that out. None whatsoever.

You see, this isn't really about who does what, it's about your partner's expectation and reality of motherhood smashing into each other like they have been sent round the Large Hadron Collider. It's a snapshot of the schism we are in as a generation when it comes to the roles of men and women. After years of progress to gain sexual equality, this tiny throwback lands in the household and not only is the woman forced to put the career she's worked so hard to achieve on hold, she also now finds herself spending her days wondering what would best remove faeces from sheepskin. It's an enormous shift and what compounds it is how things look from the other side of the fence. After doing your best to be useful at the labour you have a fortnight off work to glory in the gifts and the visits that a beautiful new baby attracts before slotting, albeit wearily, back into your old life.

With this kind of hellish dance going on, there's little wonder surveys are finding that relationships are struggling to survive with this kind of deep dissatisfaction and resentment knocking about.

Or you might be fine. None of this may happen to you and yours. You may crack the code and nail it at the first time of asking. If you do, would you mind writing a book about how you did it please?

Seize the day

If you don't want to just hope it's going to be alright on and indeed through the night what can you do to prepare? Well, the answer to that question is simpler than you'd imagine: talk, and start talking now.

There's a chance, of course, that you might have the most angelic baby ever conceived, or you might be independently wealthy or incredibly stealthy and get out of any baby duties by either employing an army of staff or pretending to have a hernia and taking to your bed for six months.

But more likely than not, new and fiendishly testing situations will arise within your relationship at a frequent rate and trying to calmly pause, identify and discuss what is at the heart of them will be your undoubted objective. The only trouble is it will be 3.47am, one of you will be singing 'Hush little baby don't say a word' for the thousandth time while a burning pain starts to spread through shoulders and back, and the other will be hunting frantically for the gripe water.

But for the next month or two before your baby arrives you've got the opportunity to spend an hour or two, at the very least, trying to set a few ground rules, to promise each other that no matter what happens love is indeed all around and tolerance will be your watchword. It mightn't make all that much difference in the frantic first few months, but when tiredness seeps through every pore, even one flash point averted will make your pre-birth efforts more than worth it.

Once you both find your parental feet, the utter joy of the little person you created will flood your lives, but as you both adjust – and especially as the enormity of becoming a mother begins to dawn on your partner – you need to be as kind to each other as you've ever been. And the groundwork for that can start right now.

Words from your fellow man:

Kevin, 50, had two children in his early twenties, followed by two more in his forties: I honestly can't remember changing a single nappy when my first two were small. And I'm not some sort of 'Where's my dinner, woman?' brute by any means – you just didn't get involved back then. My wife gave up work as a matter of course and I expected to and was expected to provide for them all. I worked hard and when I got home from work the kids were bathed and tucked up in bed.

Second time around it's been totally and utterly different. I've changed nappies, had them screaming on my shoulder at 4am and made bathtime my own – I've been totally involved and it's been absolutely fantastic.

I think people forget just how much attitudes have changed in such a short space of time. You got funny looks and even the odd comment pushing your child in a pram as a bloke just 30 years ago. Now I wander down the street with my nipper in the sling and no one bats an eyelid. It's great but it's a mind-blowing change.

Nick, 35, father of two: The change to our relationship was huge. I expected it to be much easier. The penny really dropped when I was having to read the instructions of the breast pumping machine (which were in German) at 2 in the morning. That was indicative of what our relationship now revolved around.

At the beginning my opinion on what to do with our son didn't carry equal weight at all.

My wife was great and I felt like a weekend dad at times – mostly because I was. In fact that was probably the cause of quite a lot of issues – I came home from work after she'd had a really heavy day with Lucas and I'd throw my tuppence worth in without thinking.

You are very much in the thick of it together and while it was easy to blame each other for lack of sleep we were also focused on the new baby. It's not really your relationship that changes, it's your lives.

Jim, 34, father of one: We are a partnership, a team. We talk about everything and always did before the baby arrived, too. I think we are doing all right; it's a tough job. In some ways we are closer yet further apart, perhaps because there is someone else in the middle.

Suki, 34, father of one: You have to get used to doing things differently and obviously you have to plan your lives a lot more than you did before, a lot more. You also have to accept that you are no longer the most important person around; in fact, you're not even the second most important person around.

David, 34, father of one: I got home from work one day and my wife handed me a leaflet from our local opticians: 'I'm worried', she said 'about your eyes, I think you might be short sighted.' 'Really?' 'Yes, I don't think you can see anything that is below your knees – it's the only explanation I can come up with as to why you constantly walk up the stairs and straight past 20 fucking things that need taking up there.'

PREMATURE BIRTHS – KEEPING THE FAITH

In 2019 more than 61,000 babies were born prematurely in the UK, which equates to around 8% of all births. That's a staggeringly high figure when you give it some thought and it is very much on the increase.

Pre-term is defined as being born before 37 weeks' gestation and in truth the condition is still not well understood, with most early births still happening without any clear reason. It's hard to say who will have a premature birth, but it seems you're more likely to if your partner:

- has given birth early before
- has had a miscarriage late in pregnancy
- has had an infection in her birth canal or womb
- has a weak cervix and tends to open early (our old friend cervical incompetence)
- has a bleeding placenta
- is carrying more than one baby (half of all sets of twins and most sets of triplets are born early)
- is a smoker

It pays to be on the lookout for the very early signs of labour, which include: any type of contraction-like sensation; low, dull backache; pelvic pressure or pain; diarrhoea; vaginal spotting; bleeding; and watery vaginal discharge. As ever, if your partner has so much as a scintilla of doubt, get in touch with your doctor or midwife ASAP.

Born survivors

Survival rates for premature babies in developed countries have been creeping up and up in the past 20 years as technology and expertise have moved on. As a rough guide, around 80% born at 26 weeks survive nowadays and about 90% of those born at 27 weeks do – stats that would have been all but unimaginable a generation or two ago.

By the 34th week, it's reckoned that a prematurely born baby has almost the same chance of survival as a full-term baby. Even extremely premature babies are now enjoying astonishing survival rates: for those born at 23 weeks it is 19% and at 24 weeks 40%.

Long-term effects

Despite the improved survival rates of premature babies, it's clear that many still face a number of challenges, both immediately after birth and in later life. In the immediate aftermath of their birth the tiny tots are susceptible to breathing problems due to underdeveloped lungs. They are also at greater risk of cerebral palsy and a number of life-threatening infections. Later on in life there seems to be some evidence that they are more likely to have learning and developmental disabilities.

An academic study analysed the IQ and academic ability of 219 children born extremely premature – before 26 weeks. The children's performance was compared with that of 153 classmates who had all been born after a normal length pregnancy. One in three of the prematurely born children found reading a real effort, while 44% struggled with maths. These children also scored slightly lower on IQ than their contemporaries.

Keeping the faith

Despite all the worries and anguish that inevitably come with a premature birth there are plenty of stories to give hope to everyone who goes through one.

Perhaps the most astonishing is that of Amillia Taylor, who was born on 24 October 2006 in Miami at just 21 weeks and six days' gestation. At birth, she was 23cm (9 inches) long and weighed 283g (10oz – so about as long as a pen and no heavier than a can of Coke). Given that the American Academy of Pediatrics states that babies born at less than 23 weeks are not 'viable', she not only cheated nature, but she also cheated the law as well, thanks to the fact that, in desperation, her mother Sonja didn't let on to doctors just how early she was.

Nine days after Sonja showed signs of labour at just 19 weeks, her doctors realised that they couldn't delay the birth any longer and performed a caesarean. Unbelievably Amillia came out breathing without assistance and even made some tiny, tiny attempts to cry. At this, medical staff assumed that she might be 23 weeks old and understandably Sonja didn't put them right, fearing what the consequences could be.

Despite suffering digestive and respiratory problems, as well as a brain haemorrhage, Amillia was discharged from hospital four months later and is now a healthy little girl.

If you go through a premature birth, keep the faith and take heart, not just from Amillia, but also from the fact that Isaac Newton and Winston Churchill were both believed to have been born early, and they made a half decent fist of life. Having had one of our children arrive seven weeks early, a mere trifle for modern medicine these days but enough to put several shades of fear into us, I can honestly say the care he received was breath-taking. Sitting in the premature baby ward and realising that there isn't a single moment, day and night when it isn't staffed by a highly qualified nurse will stay with me forever. Truly the NHS at its very best.

PROGRESS REPORT, MONTH 7

Your baby (27–31 weeks)

Bad news tumble fans, this is the last month that your baby can turn a somersault in the womb. He can still kick, though, and will do so increasingly – probably because he's raging that he hasn't got room to do acrobatics anymore. That's it, no more fooling around now little one, it's time to get ready for the serious stuff.

By the end of this month your baby will measure around 28cm (11 inches) from crown to rump and weigh in at about 1.5kg (3lb 8oz), which is starting to sound a bit more like a baby's weight, isn't it?

As well as fattening up, your baby is continuing to mature and become more independent, ready for going it alone in a few weeks' time. He can now control his own body temperature and his bone marrow has now taken complete responsibility for the making of his red blood cells. I've got this, Mum.

He has also developed a mature breathing pattern by now and the air sacs in his lungs are beginning to get ready for his first breath. Chances are that he would still need initial help in breathing if he arrived now, though.

He is now passing urine into the amniotic fluid at the rate of about a pint every day, which seems like a lot for someone so wee, as it were.

Mind you, now they have fully functioning taste buds on their tongue and inside their cheeks they must surely be starting to realise that the amniotic marketing board may have been over-stating its product's appeal ever so slightly.

Your baby's brain is also starting a growth spurt this month and to squeeze inside its skull it starts to fold over on itself, which is why brains take on that weird walnut look.

At about this time your baby's eyelids begin to open, too, and studies have shown that when a torch is shone against the stomach, the baby may move towards or away from the beam, which when you think about it doesn't prove much really, does it? But there you go, I thought I'd pass it on.

In all probability though your baby is becoming more sensitive to light, sound, taste and smell.

The colour of your baby's eyes begins to appear around now, but the real colour won't show until six to nine months after birth, because eye pigmentation needs light exposure to complete its formation – or you could just shine that torch at the bump a lot more to speed things up a bit. I'm joking of course, but you knew that.

Your partner

It's a big welcome back to utter tiredness for your better half as the third trimester kicks in. It's a state that in truth she, and indeed soon you, will remain in for the next two or three years. Fatigue will become like an old, crotchety, short-tempered companion that will never really leave your side for very long. Enjoy.

Apart from that, there are all sorts of exciting anatomical and physiological things going on as your partner prepares for the most complex, overwhelming and at the same time breath-taking thing she will ever do.

She may well be already producing colostrum, the sweet, watery fluid which is less rich than breast milk proper and easier for a baby, so far used to a diet consisting exclusively of amniotic matter, to digest. This is the stuff that will, all being well, provide your baby with his first few meals and it is so packed full of antibodies and nutrients that I'd be here for the rest of my life if I attempted to list them.

It's also 'hello old friend' to needing to go to the loo 250 times a day. As the baby grows and grows it begins to press on your partner's bladder in a big way.

This is also the stage in which lower back pain forces pregnant women to stand hand on hip like a little teapot. A combination of the alteration of her centre of gravity and the slight loosening of the pelvic joints to allow for a baby to pop out are the culprits.

Bump-wise things are getting quite prominent now and it's only a matter of days before someone plucks up the courage to offer her a seat on the bus.

There's a fair chance your partner will be offered an antenatal check at least every two or three weeks from now until around the 36th week and she can ask about anything that's worrying her. Things such as varicose veins can cause real anxiety at this stage, as can breathlessness, which can occur as her lungs absorb about 20% more oxygen and expel more carbon dioxide with each intake, as she essentially breathes for two.

Finally, you may notice your partner's tummy button starting to become stretched and elongated, or even protrude. No matter how it looks, the baby will not – repeat, will not – be coming out through the navel, and all will be back to normal after the birth. Just wanted to put your mind at rest on that one.

All in all though that's quite a list, isn't it? It might happen everywhere all of the time but the fact remains that what your partner is going through right now is mind-blowing.

MUST-DOS OF MONTH 7

Belt up

If you've not done so already, a pregnancy seat belt extension is a very good idea. It essentially means that in the event of an accident, the belt doesn't put pressure on the bump.

Treat her

A pregnancy massage, a pedicure, a manicure, a face mask – booking a little treatment treat for her at this stage, when the chances of her reaching her toes to paint them is receding by the second, will go down a storm.

Stroll on

Walking is your friend. It's not only a great way to spend some time together and talk about how you are both feeling, it also means your partner is getting some gentle but invaluable exercise and fresh air.

Give some back-up

Back pain is a nightmare at the best of times. Suffering from it when you're pregnant, though, is as annoying as it is inevitable. That doesn't mean you can't do something to keep your partner's discomfort to a minimum.

Buying her a pair of low-heeled or flat shoes that don't look they have been stolen from a bowling alley is a good start. Gently encouraging her to sit with a straight back on a hard chair or the floor is smart, too, although be prepared to be told occasionally to stop acting like her mother. There are also bump support belts available, which take some of the strain off the back. If you get one of these, under no circumstances refer to it as her Liz Truss.

LAST ORDERS PLEASE

(32–35 weeks)

Everyone knows that pregnancy is nine months long. As soon as you enter the first day of that final month the baby could arrive any day, any second, or at least that's the perceived wisdom.

So what does that make the eighth month, then? Busy, that's what it makes it, very busy.

The reality of the ninth month being a quick hop, skip and a jump to the delivery can be very different, of course. For a start you've often got four weeks of the bloody thing to negotiate before full term is reached and even then around one in every five women goes over term and needs to be induced.

But none of that matters, especially when you're having your first baby: nine months is when it's due, so eight months is your last chance to get things sorted before your little family increases in size.

As if to bolster this chronological logic, our old pals the pregnancy hormones bring the nesting instinct to the party, with all its quirks, idiosyncrasies and Hoover-mania. And I'm not just talking about your partner here, as we've seen on the phantom pregnancy front there is increasing evidence that men's hormones lead them a merry dance in the lead up to pregnancy, too. So then, eyes down for a frantic four weeks.

GETTING READY – YOU'VE GOTTA LOVE A LIST

If lists weren't invented by men, it was certainly something we would have got round to doing. Lists are a man's best friend; put something down on one and you've as good as done it, or at least as good as stopped having to think about doing it.

There's an awful lot to do this month and even if there wasn't, it seems we are programmed to feel like there is, both socially and hormonally – the eighth month is the pregnancy equivalent of the pre-Christmas rush.

So let's throw ourselves into it and look at what needs to be done, what's the best way to do it and how, among all the hullaballoo, everyone involved can find the time for a good sit down, too.

The birth plan

Viewed by some as the chocolate fireguard of the pregnancy process, the birth plan is a way of rationally and calmly telling the people who are caring for your partner what she would like to happen and what she would most certainly not like to happen.

Your partner will, of course, communicate in no uncertain terms with the health professionals when she is in labour, but the calm and rational bits will go out of the window, along with the doctor's stethoscope if she can get near enough to grab it. So this written plan essentially acts as a letter written by your partner when she was pain and push free. It's surely only a matter of time before boring old paper is replaced by a short video projected on the wall of the delivery suite for all staff to watch.

'Hello, the fact that you're watching this means I'm lying on a bed with my legs in the air screaming some fearful obscenities.'

No matter what format it's in, though, one thing is for absolute certain about your birth plan: it will always be a work of fiction to a less or greater degree – and so it should be.

Sitting on your couch a month out and writing with a great deal of sincerity and conviction that 'under no circumstances do we want any pain relief outside of gas and air to be administered' is fine. Were your midwife to wave that very piece of paper in your partner's face seven hours into labour as she's screaming for every drug known to modern medicine, you'd wish you'd kept your pen in its holster.

But luckily that's not how it works at all. Most smart birth plans are written very carefully like a communiqué at a G8 summit, with certain avenues favoured, but leaving none blocked off.

Given the unpredictable nature of childbirth and the differing ways in which people cope with what it throws at them, there's every chance that the midwife or doctor may well need to recommend a course of action that is not what either of you had in mind, but one which is in the best interests of your baby and your partner.

Writing it

There are no hard-and-fast rules about how to write a birth plan. As you can imagine, the web is awash with print out and fill in templates, but as this is such a personal document you may find that you use these as just a guide and essentially go it alone.

Some people structure them chronologically: early stages, transition, delivery, etc; others write theirs issue by issue: pain relief, favoured positions, feeding the baby. Whichever way your partner prefers to tackle it, it's an idea to bear these three points in mind:

• Make sure it's no more than one page in length. It has been scientifically proven that no one has read anything longer than one side of A4 since 1981.
• Do your research beforehand – don't mix up an episiotomy with a cup of sweet tea.
• Be direct, but be nice.

Is it worth it?

Good question.

Some say that the best thing you can do with your birth plan when you arrive at hospital is to keep it in the bag. Walking into such a fluid and unpredictable situation with a semi-rigid set of demands doesn't help anyone, they say. If you brandish it too lustily there's also the fear that it could even mark you out as a patient from hell, although that theory does the medical staff who will be on hand a massive disservice in my opinion. Even worse, though, it could act as a stick to beat yourselves with, a record of the control you'd like to have in one of the most uncontrollable environments you'll ever find yourselves in.

On the other hand, there's no doubt that the very act of think-ing about and writing the birth plan together as a couple means that you both focus on the potential issues that may arise at a time when you can think clearly and at least go some way to addressing them mentally. For that reason alone it's got to be a list worth making.

> **Words from your fellow man:**
>
> **Stuart, 37, father of two:** Our birth plan said gas and air and epidural as a very last resort. Within half an hour with gas and air my partner was begging for the epidural. The birth plan for your first baby isn't based on any kind of reality. It's like trying to imagine how you'd feel taking a penalty in the World Cup final while sitting in your armchair with a beer in your hand.
>
> **Peter, 33, father of one:** We had planned for a water birth but as things went really quickly we didn't have time to run the bath. Ironically I have been plagued with shit baths all my life that only ever dribble out water from the taps, but I did expect the NHS to have got round this problem. We took lots of CDs and candles as well but they are still in a plastic bag in the boot of the car.
>
> **Levi, 36, father of two:** We did pretty much stick to our birth plan, although our baby did get stuck upside down for five hours in my wife's nether regions. Otherwise it went like clockwork.

The hospital bag

There's nothing like the sight of a fully packed bag sitting quietly, expectantly, in the corner of the bedroom, to remind you that at some point soon everything you've been reading about, talking about and thinking about for months will begin to happen.

In many ways, though, the hospital bag has also become a sign of the times: a pregnancy icon, a window into our world of gadgetry and deep-seated fear of missing a trick – if only, if only, we'd brought the colander.

But really it's just a bag of stuff you might need but probably won't use and more often than not your departure for the hospital isn't anywhere near as Hollywood as you are led to believe it will be. The process of labour itself is also often such a long, drawn-out business that you'll be able to knit your partner a new cardigan should you have left the blue one at home. But, as ever with pregnancy, you never know.

So what do you really need to take? The potential list is endless, although I'd leave the dog at home if you can. I've tried to cut out as many of the pointless suggestions that get made; there are lists that recommend taking a pack of cards, for instance, in case things get a bit dull. The chances of your partner wanting to play a few hands of knockout whist while in labour are staggeringly remote, unlike the chances of you being served up a volley of abuse for suggesting it.

If you don't understand fully what a few of these things are yet, don't worry, the Month 9 chapter is about to give you a run-down on all the runners and riders in the delivery room stakes.

For your partner

- The birth plan – seeing as you've spent all that time on it, it would be a shame to leave it on the kitchen table. You could even make multiple copies and start handing them out from the car park onwards to make sure you don't miss anybody out. Or not.
- Medical notes of your partner's health and pregnancy to date.
- Nightdress or pyjamas, dressing gown, slippers, socks – fair enough.
- An old nightdress or T-shirt to wear in labour – things could get a bit messy, you see.

- Lip balm – sounds ludicrous, but dry and chapped lips after hours of labour is all she'll need.
- Books and magazines – in case of an elongated early labour.
- TENS (transcutaneous electrical nerve stimulation) pain relief machine, if you are planning to use one (more about this very soon).
- Toiletries – complete range of.
- Music – smartphone and speakers or CDs if the hospital has its own system (some hospitals don't let you plug in your own equipment, on the off-chance that it shorts the whole place and causes the death of hundreds of people; which for the sake of a Celine Dion album would be a very high price to pay indeed).
- Breastfeeding kit – bras, pads, nipple cream, etc, if you plan to give it a go.
- Maternity pads – as I said earlier, things can get a bit messy.
- Old, cheap or disposable knickers – ditto.
- Going home clothes – not quite time for the skinny jeans yet mind you, as immediately after the birth she will feel like she did at about the six-month mark.
- Snacks and drinks – more snacks and drinks – low-fat, high-carb fare is what's usually on the menu. In truth, many women try to load up in the early stages and then can't face a thing until the job is done, when they will attempt to eat the midwife's arm. Plenty of fluid is essential.

For yourself

- Water spray – this enables you to carry out one of your traditional and almost useful labour tasks – trying to keep your partner cool and (relatively) refreshed while she's in labour. Practise your nozzle skills before the big day but don't pick up the Windolene by mistake.

- Digital camera or camcorder – some hospital staff can be funny about you taking pictures, but this is the biggest day of your lives so distract them by pretending to spot a foot-long MRSA bacterium under the bed and snap away at your beautiful new arrival and the wonder woman who brought him into the world. Resist Instagram Live at all costs.
- Snacks and drinks – you need to keep your strength up too, tiger. Don't go mad, though; the sight of you tucking into a three-course meal with coffee and mints to finish will not go down well with a certain person in the room. Also take real care not to take stuff that's too stinky – I'm not sure if anyone has ever tried to eat a Peperami in front of a labouring woman, but if they have I'm hoping it's somewhere on YouTube.
- Bribes – a lot of people send flowers to the midwives after the birth, but a bag of Revels 'to keep the team's strength up' before it all kicks off could pay big dividends.

For the baby

- Baby blanket – to wrap the little mite up in as you take him into the big wide world for the very first time.
- Nappies – the hospital might provide a few, but best to have your own, too.
- Socks or booties – bless. Socks on his hands will also prevent him scratching himself with the sharp little nails he may be born with.
- Hat – for his exposed little bonce obvs.
- Babygrows in newborn, up to 1 month and 0–3 months – who knows how big he's going to be.

- Muslins – let the sick fest begin.
- Infant car seat – not going to fit in the bag this one, obviously, but learning how to fit this tricky beast in the car takes a fair bit of time and patience and is best done at home ahead of time, well out of earshot of the midwife. She may not want to entrust a newborn baby to a man who is repeatedly calling a seatbelt a fiddly little bastard.

Even with some of the sillier suggestions not making it through the net, it's still a shedload of stuff. Let's just all take a moment to be grateful that Ryanair haven't yet taken to running hospitals, shall we? The excess baggage costs would be enormous.

Getting to the hospital

Not technically a list but the chances are you will become strangely obsessed with the various routes you can take to a hospital you know well and have been past many times before. Don't be alarmed – it's perfectly normal. You may even go a stage further and do the journey at eight or nine different times of the day or night and plot a chart of the best route for each hour. That's not so normal.

But hey, this is a big deal and driving your pregnant partner to the hospital is one of the traditional, cast-iron father-to-be jobs of all time, so why not get serious on its ass? Besides, it's worth doing a bit of preparation to avoid being stuck at a set of temporary traffic lights for 20 minutes with a passenger who would happily wring your neck should she be able to get off the back seat to reach.

If you've not been to a hospital for a few years, allow me to also tell you about a major change you may not be familiar with – the revenue generated by hospital car parks now makes up just under

75% of the entire gross national product of the UK. Or at least that's what it feels like. Take change, take cash, take cards, take gold. If you're in for a long labour you'll need all of them in vast quantities.

One other tiny thing to bear in mind while we are on the transport front, is that as your booze-free partner has probably chauffeured you around half-cut for the past eight months, it wouldn't look great if you suddenly realise you're over the limit when the big moment arrives.

Persona non driva

So what if you don't drive, what are your options?

Calling an ambulance is frowned upon because labour is not classed as an emergency, even though with your first baby it will feel like the most emergencified of all the emergencies you have ever found yourself in. If you do call one out, the chances are that it will take you to the nearest maternity ward rather than the one you are booked in at. If in doubt, always ring the delivery suite at your hospital first and speak to the midwife who will tell you the best course of action to take.

So for most people, calling a taxi or Uber is the main option open to them. Stories abound of taxi firms refusing to take labouring women in case their car seats take a hammering, so a bit of research beforehand to check who is OK to do the job is a smart move.

NESTING – NOT JUST NEARLY CLEAN, BUT REALLY CLEAN

Your partner is going to start getting very tired this month, very tired indeed. As the baby gets heavier, her energy levels will drain away as the day wears on and the chances of her making it to the end of the evening news will start to dwindle dramatically.

Unless there is decorating to be done, of course; or cleaning; or washing all the baby clothes for the second time to get that new smell out of them; or hoovering. Tiredness won't affect any of those things, it seems.

Welcome to the world of the nesting instinct, where Mother Nature turns pregnant women into frenzied cleaning machines ahead of the new arrival.

Or so the story goes. Is it real or just another pregnancy myth?

Well, it's real and as well as often being amusing and sometimes bizarre (some women, rendered so immobile by the sheer size of their bump, have been known to sit in the middle of the floor with the longest vacuum extension they can muster sucking up dust from as wide a radius as they can stretch to), there is something incredibly humbling about being around a nesting woman.

Nesting essentially brings us down from our self-constructed plinth as a super species and acts as yet another reminder, should we need one, that we are really just monkeys with hats on. I say we, because the urge to nest towards the end of pregnancy doesn't just affect women, you can get caught up in the hormonal house cleaning too – you clucky old thing you.

What's the cause?

Prolactin (which is responsible for, among other things, lactation and orgasms, and increases in both men and women during pregnancy) is reckoned to be the biggest culprit. Tests on animals show that as nesting and nurturing behaviours in both males and females increase the more prolactin is present.

In fact, so potent is prolactin, on occasion it's not only been nesting and nurturing that it has brought on in males. A Scottish billy goat named Claymore, who was reported to have had an extraordinarily high prolactin level, actually started to produce milk. Indeed, so taken was he by the taste of his own milk, that he would often 'nurse himself' – which is one of the most disturbing phrases I've ever had the misfortune to write.

As filthy old Claymore demonstrates, prolactin is one powerful substance and if it can get a billy goat to breastfeed, turning you and your partner into cleaning machines is no sweat.

How bad can it get?

Pretty bad. Here's a smattering of what could happen:

- throwing away almost anything, because if it's not new, it's a potential death trap
- taking apart door knobs and cupboard handles to not only clean inside, but also disinfect the very screws which hold them together
- adopting the toothbrush as the primary cleaning implement of the household
- organising kitchen cupboards into package size or alphabetical order depending on what day it is

- folding and refolding the baby's clothes until they no longer look brand new; which can then invoke the first point on this list.

Despite bringing on some pretty irrational behaviour, the only real area to keep your eye on in terms of your partner's nesting instinct is decorating. Climbing ladders and painting aren't the smartest things for a pregnant woman to do, given what a fall could mean and the potential damage that paint fumes can do. By far the safest option is for her to place herself in a comfy chair and creatively direct the whole project as you do the donkey work.

STOPPING WORK – KNOWING WHEN TO SAY GOODBYE

Choosing when to stop work towards the end of the pregnancy can be a very tricky decision for your partner. Some women, imagining that they will want to work until the very last second, find themselves dragging their weary bones on public transport and up office stairs wishing that they hadn't been quite so gung-ho early on, while for many others finances dictate they have to keep earning for as long as they can. For some, who have given themselves plenty of time off ahead of the big day, finding themselves bored and marooned at home with hour after hour to think about what awaits them on the big day can be a real drag.

It's a hard one to judge and everyone is different, but what's for certain is that whether or not your partner continues to work through to the final knockings, taking it easy as things literally come to a head is a must.

The whole working during pregnancy debate is a thorny one and some studies have claimed that pregnant women who work past the recommended time are up to five times more likely to have conditions associated with increased blood pressure during pregnancy (including pre-eclampsia) – the inference being that high stress at work causes high blood pressure, which in pregnant women can be deadly.

Whatever the medical facts might be, flexibility is king if your partner is lucky enough to work somewhere that will play ball. Missing the morning rush hour, working from home or trying to avoid the jobs that wind everyone up are all well worth doing at this stage of the game.

If none of them are possible no one, but no one, is going to question an almost full-term woman having a sickie or two – although if anyone asks, remember it wasn't me who suggested that.

PROGRESS REPORT, MONTH 8

Your baby (32–35 weeks)

Your baby's main preoccupation at the moment is trying to get himself settled into a head-down position and adjust to the increasing lack of space in the hitherto roomy womb. Once they have found the slot, some babies do decide to turn back round again, although attempted escape at this stage is futile.

By the end of this month the average baby weighs in at around 2.4kg (5lb 4oz) and is a touch over 32cm (12.5 inches) long, crown to rump.

Because of the nice deposits of fat he is building up, his skin is now a pleasing pink colour rather than a worrying red.

The baby's eyes are now fully functioning and he can focus and blink. And as for his ears, it's safe to say that his hearing is better than yours now. Finger and toenails are also fully formed and some babies will even have a full head of hair at this stage, while others might just have a few wisps.

The lungs are still developing, however, but even they will be the real deal very soon indeed.

If your baby is a boy his testicles should have dropped from his abdomen into his scrotum. In some cases, though, one or both testicles won't move into position until after birth and in two-thirds of these babies, the condition corrects itself by the time of their first birthday. Which seems a long time to wait, doesn't it?

The baby's skull is still pliable, to help him ease out of the narrow birth canal, but all his other bones are hardening, a fact your partner may become well aware of as elbows, feet or even the head itself can start to protrude from her stomach at this point – making you think of, but never mention, the scene from *Alien* where John Hurt has a very bad case of tummy trouble.

Your partner

Antenatal checks will almost certainly be more regular now as blood pressure, urine and the baby's position are kept under a close eye. The level of all-round discomfort felt by your partner also increases this month on a lot of fronts.

Thanks to a pregnancy hormone fantastically called relaxin, your partner's pelvic joints expand and therefore, unsurprisingly, ache in preparation for birth. There's also more discomfort to be had as the ever-expanding baby forces the womb against your partner's lower ribs, as well as the abdomen, often becoming so stretched that her navel sticks outwards instead of inwards.

She may also notice that her feet and ankles are pretty swollen by the end of the day, thanks to water retention.

Drinking lots of water actually reduces water retention. Your partner's body – and indeed the baby – need plenty of fluids at this point so rather than doing what seems logical and reducing the amount of water she takes in, she needs to increase her intake.

However, if she suddenly feels swollen or puffy in her hands or face, you should contact your doctor as this may be an indication of pre-eclampsia, a condition covered in the glossary at the back of this book.

To top things off nicely, her nipples will also be starting to enlarge and her breasts become heavier; and oh yes, those pesky Braxton Hicks contractions from earlier can be full on at this stage, too, making all concerned very jumpy for the 30 seconds or so they tend to last.

As far as rays of sunshine go, they are few and far between. If the baby has already moved into the head down position, your partner's breathing may become a little easier and indigestion should start to improve, which is something, isn't it?

Your partner may also have some fantastically vivid dreams at the moment, too. Although, given that they are primarily driven by the thoughts that an almost fully formed baby is moving around inside her and she is about to experience childbirth, painting them as light relief may be stretching things a little.

Carpal tunnel syndrome

This annoying late pregnancy complaint deserves to be looked at in a little more detail. Carpal tunnel syndrome (CTS) is a medical condition in which a nerve in the wrist is compressed, leading to numbness, muscle weakness and pain in the hand.

Symptoms are often worse at night and guess what? Pregnant women are highly susceptible to it as weight gain and swelling are also contributory factors. Although not all pregnant women suffer from it, it's estimated that between 20% and 60% do, which is a hell of a lot considering the relatively low profile the condition still has.

For most women who do experience it, CTS is generally mild and temporary, disappearing soon after the baby is born, but for others it can be a debilitating and severe problem which can last well into the baby's first year.

A weakened grip, numbness, pain and a burning sensation around the thumb and fingers can combine to make CTS a nightmare for some mothers-to-be and if it does last post pregnancy, it can seriously hamper their ability to lift and carry their newborn.

Flexing wrists and fingers regularly throughout the day is said to help by some and make matters worse by others, so wrist splints worn at night are often the only treatment of any worth. These keep your wrists in a position that provides space in the offending area and eases the problem.

Month 8 isn't much fun for your poor partner, is it? Not long now, though (although again that's something to be thought but rarely said).

MUST-DOS OF MONTH 8

Ring the changes

Haemorrhoids, an ugly-looking word for an ugly complaint. If your partner is suffering on the pile front, buy in a job-lot of witchhazel – a good natural remedy – and offer to apply it regularly. It's the least you can do.

Clocking off

Whether your partner is ecstatic to be finishing work or nervous about putting her hard-fought-for career temporarily on hold, psychologically it's a big moment and one that does signal the end of one era and the beginning of another.

Make a fuss of her and although you'll be hoarding any spare holiday you have for when the baby is born, taking a day off to spend at home with her after she's jacked in the job is a nice gesture that will almost certainly be appreciated.

Footloose

You've not got long until you are parents. If your partner can handle it, make the most of your last few weeks of no-babysitter-required freedom. Eat out, go to the cinema, see friends, and lie in. Then lie in again.

Blowing raspberries

The raspberry leaf contains something called a uterine tonic and, taken daily in the final weeks of pregnancy, it could well help to prepare the uterine muscles for labour and maybe even make the process ever so slightly less painful. In an Australian study 192 first-time mums were given either a 1.2g raspberry leaf tablet or a placebo twice a day from 32 weeks onwards. The lucky ones who were given the real deal were found to have a shorter second stage of labour – which as you are about to read about is the pushing phase – and a significantly lower rate of forceps delivery – 19.3% versus 30.4% in those given placebo. It's fair to say that this was a pretty small study and hardly what you could class as conclusive proof – but it's got to be worth a shot hasn't it?

It's best to start with one cup of raspberry leaf tea a day or one tablet and build up gradually as the due date nears to a maximum of four cups of tea or tablets daily. Your partner can take the tea during labour as well if she's up to it. To the health food shop with you. As ever its best to check with your midwife or GP before you do.

IT'S SHOW TIME

(36–40(+) weeks)

WAITING FOR CURTAIN UP – ANYTIME SOON

So here we are, you and your magnificent partner have made it to the ninth month and all you need to do now is take your seats and the performance will start shortly. Trouble is, as with all the months you tend to come across these days, this bugger is four weeks long, with each day of each week needing to be negotiated individually.

As for the due date you've been given, it's best not to get fixated on it, as only a miserly 5% of babies arrive bang on the money. Out of the remaining 95%, three in every 10 arrive early and seven in 10 late. So the odds are that your partner has still got a fair bit of incubating to do yet – even as much as six weeks more from the start of this month, in fact, which is pretty much the longest the medical profession in the UK will let you wait before they deem the placenta too old and inefficient to properly nourish the baby any longer.

All that of course presupposes that the due date itself is based on sound medical and mathematical principles. Which it isn't.

Most estimated due dates are calculated using a formula devised by a German obstetrician named Franz Naegele in the 1850s. The rule estimates the date from the first day of the woman's last menstrual period by adding a year, subtracting three months and adding seven days to that date. This equation, that has a straight-from-a-Christmas-cracker aspect to it, roughly works out that the average normal human pregnancy lasts around 280 days, or 40 weeks, from the date of fertilisation.

Among the many inconsistencies of this outdated method is that it relies on the notion that in 19th-century Deutschland women evidently ovulated on the 14th day of a 28-day cycle without fail or they would be locked in the woodshed to think about what they had done.

Another of its drawbacks is that it relies on each month having 30.4 days in it exactly – so get pregnant in May, or God forbid in a leap year, and your due date stands a very good chance of being well out.

Basically, it's a bloody rubbish system that almost always gives us due dates that are too early. But we just haven't got round to replacing it yet, what with climate change to sort out and whatnot.

All of which means that before you get to the main event, there's a good chance you'll have to get through another month to six weeks of being pregnant – which is a pain in the arse for you and a pain absolutely everywhere for your poor partner. So let's quickly zip through what's what in month 9 before it all kicks off.

PROGRESS REPORT, MONTH 9

Your baby (36–40 weeks)

Your baby is considered full term at 37 weeks, meaning that he can be born any day. If labour starts now no effort will be made to delay it; it's happening.

On average your baby will measure about 37–38cm (14.5–15 inches) from crown to rump, with a total length of about 48cm (19 inches), but of course as we already know, all of the little bubbas are different.

The final pieces of the baby's anatomical jigsaw are put into place this month: the central nervous system is all but fully wired; the digestive system is complete; and his lungs mature to full capacity, leaving him ready to breathe his first ever breath.

His skin is smooth and soft as a baby's bottom, especially his bottom, and there is still the odd dollop of the cream cheese substitute vernix around, mostly on his back to help his passage down the birth canal.

His fingernails are probably long, too, due to him not being able to remember for the life of him where those tiny nail clippers have got to – something you will come to empathise with very shortly – and he may well have already scratched his face, bless him.

Most of your baby's lanugo – the fine downy hair that's covered him for a good portion of the pregnancy so far – has now been shed. Delightfully, he will now swallow the lot along with other secretions, and store them in his bowels ready to form his first poo – a tacky, post-Guinness-drinking-session-like stool called meconium.

All in all, after nine remarkable months of growth the goose is cooked – transformed from a bag of cells to a stunning little person – who's heading your way.

Your partner

The poor, poor woman – even though there's only weeks, even days left to go, time may well feel like it's standing still as she wrestles with her sheer size. Posture-wise she could well find herself making up for the extra weight out front by leaning backwards, hands on the back of her hips in classic double teapot style.

Such is the change in her centre of gravity she could also find herself bumping into things or losing balance, so one of your many jobs this month is to be a helping hand where needed.

In most first-time mothers, the baby's head drops down or engages into the pelvis at about 36 weeks – although in subsequent pregnancies it's normal for your baby to get cocky and not to engage until the last minute.

The most important thing for your partner to do at this stage is to sleep and rest. The most difficult thing for your partner to do at this stage is sleep and rest.

Those jolly japers, the Braxton Hicks contractions, will still be knocking around, too, scaring the bejesus out of her, although she's probably an expert at spotting their phoney baloney twinges by now. If they become painful, though, then it's time to take notice. Excitement, nervousness and even fear can be swirling around in pretty significant measure as the countdown begins. Some women even experience depression in late pregnancy, because of lack of sleep and a deep, deep desire for the baby to be outside rather than in. Combine with trepidation to produce an overwhelming cocktail. It's pretty rare, but keep an eye out for it and keep talking. Another uncommon thing to keep a little watch out for is the onset of severe itchiness in your partner. This can be a sign of a serious liver problem called obstetric cholestasis. If this is the case, the itchiness will be very widespread and often includes itching of the hands and feet. It may also be accompanied by nausea, vomiting, loss of appetite, fatigue, pale colour, red stools and jaundice.

Make an appointment with your doctor or midwife if you are worried.

Something not to be too concerned about is if your partner's weight plateaus now – a few women even lose weight in the last week or so before the birth. This barely needs saying, but the main issue in month 9 is that your partner's stomach is being crushed by a great big baby – she is going to be one uncomfortable soon-to-be momma and it's down to you to keep her, if not happy, then at least on the right side of volcanic.

MUST-DOS OF MONTH 9

You'll be the first to know

Get into the habit early of politely telling friends and family that you'll let them know as soon as something happens, rather than them needing to ask.

It's a long enough month without having to field daily requests asking for 'any news', and although reading this you may think me a miserable so and so and that you will never react to people's interest with anything other than unbridled gratitude – I promise eventually it will annoy you to the very core of your being.

Cook up a storm

When your baby arrives home you'll be all over the place for a few weeks as the normalities of everyday life, such as eating and sleeping, get hijacked by the new person in the nappy.

While you can't really prepare for the sleep deprivation, you can make moves to ensure you and your partner (who will be recovering from a major trauma and even major surgery if she's had a caesarean section, and may also be breastfeeding and needing to keep her food intake up) aren't reduced to consoling yourselves that the corn on the cob in the KFC bucket you've just bought at least constitutes one of your five a day.

Fill the freezer with frozen shepherds' pies, lasagnes, (mild) chillies – whatever nutritious comfort foods you fancy in fact, and you'll be glad to call on this scrumptious stockpile when times get tough.

Chill

Sounds obvious, but the pair of you should do your best to relax as much as possible this month.

Walking remains a great option if your partner's up for it and the movement is even thought to bring on labour. Or if something less strenuous is in order go to the pictures or, you know, just Netflix and chill. But really chill.

As far as you're concerned, you could squeeze a last round of golf in if that's your thing – not last game forever, but last for five years or so, or go to a football match. My personal recommendation is stay in bed as much as you can and savour the knowledge that you could get up if you wanted to – but crucially you don't have to.

Coiled spring

Just in case you've forgotten, your partner could go into labour at any second so keep your mobile on, the car full of petrol and your bloodstream free of too much alcohol so you can drive the thing.

And relax.

THE BIRTH PLOT – WHAT'S MEANT TO HAPPEN

You are about to play a part in one of the biggest and most dramatic scenes of your entire life. It'll have the lot: tension, agony, despair and elation. And although you'll be familiar with the general thrust of the story, this is no re-run; this will be unique to you and your partner, and guaranteed never to be forgotten.

Before we get on to who the main players are and how the action might unfold, it's worth taking a quick look at the mechanics of how a birth works, at what the script says should actually happen. According to the textbooks, labour moves forward in three clear stages:

The first stage of labour

During the first stage, contractions will gradually open up the neck of the cervix. This stage is itself split into three sections: early labour, active labour and the transitional phase.

Early labour: Sometimes referred to as the latent phase, early labour sees the cervix soften, open and widen thanks to various chemicals acting on it. This process is to allow the baby to pass through it and down into the birth canal before it sees the light at the end of the tunnel and makes a break for freedom. The cervix will go from being tightly closed to about 3cm or 4cm open or dilated – once this happens active labour has started.

Active labour: At this point contractions usually become longer, more frequent and often more painful – the cervix is now opening from 3cm or 4cm to the magic 10cm needed. The contractions themselves could come as often as every three to four minutes and last 60–90 seconds at this stage, or they can even be as frequent as five in a 10-minute period.

Transition: The transitional phase is when your partner moves from the first to the second, pushing, stage. It's often talked about as the period when the cervix moves from 8cm dilated to the full 10cm – the hard yards.

While contractions may be less frequent during this phase, they can be much stronger and longer and can even come in a double wave, with the fading away of one being overtaken by the rise of the next.

It's quite common for your partner's waters to break just before or during transition. During pregnancy the baby is protected and cushioned inside the uterus in a bag full of amniotic fluid. When the bag tears and fluid leaks out, it is the waters breaking. Most women's waters break towards the end of the first stage of labour, but for about 10% of women the waters break before labour starts (in this situation a doctor or midwife should always be seen to reduce the risk of infection) and for the remaining 2%, the waters break before they are 37 weeks' pregnant. The amount of fluid that comes out will vary from a discreet trickle to a take-cover tidal wave.

After such an intense phase, you, your baby and – especially – your partner will need a rest, and nature often provides this through a short lull in the contractions before the big push begins. As rests go, your partner will have had more enjoyable leg waxes, but it's at least a tiny breather.

In terms of the length of this first phase for women carrying their first baby, the average rate of cervical dilation is 1cm per hour in active labour (i.e. from around 3cm dilated onwards). There are huge variations in labour length but the average length of time for the cervix to dilate completely is 9.7 hours. Durations longer than 24.7 hours are considered prolonged – which you'd bloody hope they would be.

The second stage of labour

Once your partner has reached this point she is ready to push your baby out through the birth canal – a distance of around 23cm (9 inches) – and into the world. She'll feel the pressure of the baby's head between her legs and with each contraction will come a strong urge to push or 'bear down'. (*Very* strong, like stronger than you or I have ever felt the like of before.)

With every push, the baby will move gradually through the pelvis a little until the almost-mother starts to feel a stinging sensation – which is caused by the opening of the vagina starting to stretch around the head. Once the midwife can see the baby's head she may ask your partner to stop pushing and take short breaths for the next couple of contractions to help ensure that the baby is born slowly to reduce the likelihood of tearing occurring or the need for a cut called an episiotomy to be made to allow the baby through.

A few more pushes, and the baby is born. The average length of the second phase for first-time mums is between one and two hours.

It's like nothing you've ever witnessed. Shocking, awe-inspiring and ultimately utterly uplifting. And all you're really doing is watching it – but we're getting ahead of ourselves.

The third stage

Once the baby is born, the third stage begins. A new batch of contractions, thankfully weaker this time, will start up again and gradually force the placenta away from the wall of the uterus.

With the aid of the odd push, the placenta, with the membranes of the empty bag of waters attached, will drop out through the vagina. In many hospitals, new mothers are routinely given an injection that makes the placenta come out without the need for any pushing.

The midwife will then examine the placenta and membranes to make sure that nothing has been left behind and check your partner's abdomen to ensure that her uterus is contracting to stop the bleeding caused by the placenta coming away.

The cast list – who will be in the room

Guess what? It hardly ever goes like that. Very few births run anywhere nearly as smoothly as a quick one, two, three and out you pop – especially when the baby is the woman's first.

One of the many reasons why childbirth is so unpredictable is that the process of giving birth that we have adopted tends to involve an awful lot more people than you'd imagine. So before we look at what's likely to happen rather than what should happen, let's just find out who's who on the delivery cast list for the average hospital birth.

The mother-to-be: If you're not recognising her at this stage you really are in deep trouble – or possibly the wrong delivery room. The absolute star of the show – until she gets upstaged in the final scene by a devastatingly endearing child actor. Although prone to foul-mouthed outbursts, she is a truly committed and focused performer – grappling with the job in hand with such gusto and courage that no one can take their eyes off her.

Midwife: One of life's natural super supporting actors – attentive, caring and knowledgeable, although not beyond delivering a forceful word or two should the situation require it. Increasingly, though, there are tragic occasions where time and shift patterns get the better of these devoted helpers and they have to exit stage right before the dramatic final scene.

Second midwife: A notoriously tricky role. Entering the fray part-way through, she often has to gain trust and respect in double quick time and can find herself on the receiving end of one of the leading lady's legendary tirades. Despite these initial tensions, most understudy midwives turn out to be good eggs in the end, but some are condemned to remain peripheral figures, never overcoming the lateness at which they joined the performance.

Doctor: Often cast as the portent of doom, this white-coated will-o'-the-wisp makes rare and fleeting visits to check on progress – until something is amiss, when they swing into action and take charge of proceedings, often putting noses out of joint in the process.

Student doctor: Green behind the gills but eager to learn, these pasty-faced trainees often pop up nowadays. Hovering over the midwife's shoulder, it takes all their might to keep the air of doctorly superiority that is being ingrained in them under wraps. Can occasionally be heard to mutter, 'That's that done, geriatrics next,' once the show is over.

Doula/birthing partner: A relative newcomer on the hospital scene, these guardian angels exist for one reason only: to act as the experienced eyes and ears for the mother as she throws herself headlong into her role. Not for the faint-hearted, this is a part often played by those with a natural propensity to speak up rather than keep their own counsel. Can be a generator of flying sparks.

Baby: A scene stealer is born. Despite only making the briefest of appearances towards the very end of the script, this tiny totem manages to make his presence very much felt.

And finally . . .

The father-to-be: A well-intentioned but peripheral figure present throughout but never managing to establish a clear role. Often gives off a self-conscious air of being neither useful nor an ornament.

Or so popular culture would lead us to believe. The panicking and ineffectual father flapping around the delivery room, water spray in one hand, roast beef sandwich in the other, has almost become a comedy staple. Yet figures put the percentage of men attending the birth of their children in the UK at somewhere between 90% and 98% – which is a staggering number when you consider that 50 years ago the practice was all but unheard of.

The debate rages about the positive and negative effects, on both the mother and the father, that being there brings; the main negative cited being that labour can be longer, more painful and more complicated because she senses his anxiety and becomes nervous herself. It's an interesting argument and one that very quickly arrives at the point that says exclusively female birth environments (including no male doctors etc.) are the least likely to add to the labouring woman's troubles.

Chances are, though, you are going to be there, so assuming you can stop yourself screaming, 'Blood, blood, I can see blood!', let's look at the crucial role you can play in supporting your partner.

First things first, no one in that room – not the doctor, the midwife or the doula – knows your partner better than you do. If you've been to antenatal classes together and talked about what her fears and expectations are, you are perfectly placed to be her advocate, the person who can speak up when you feel the need.

That's easier said than done, for sure. A delivery room full of medical professionals can be a very intimidating place, a factor which is behind the rise in popularity of professional birth partners and doulas, who have experience of intervening in those pressure-cooker situations.

But you're not just there to be a thorn in the side of the midwives. One study showed that fathers are five times more likely to touch their partner during labour and delivery than other support figures; and the women rated the fathers' presence more helpful than that of the nurses.

Providing you keep your emotions in check, you can bring calm and comfort to your partner in a way that no one else can. Just being there can often be enough. It's a tough job, of course, and you'll get cursed and worse, but let's face it, you'd take sitting next to the bed over being the one on it any day of the week, wouldn't you?

But let's not get ahead of ourselves; we're about to find out what having a baby is really like – from the initial faint twinge to first family cuddle.

ACTION! – WHAT ACTUALLY HAPPENS

So far we know what's meant to happen and we know who's meant to be there – but how do things tend to pan out? What's having a baby really like?

Are we nearly there yet?

For many years, it was believed that the mother's body was responsible for starting labour, but research now points to the baby itself as the one to kick the whole thing off by pressing the hormonal eject button and sending a message to his mum to get a move on.

One theory is that the baby's lungs secrete an enzyme when they are fully developed which triggers contractions, while another is that glands near the baby's kidneys do the deed and expel a hormone that starts things moving.

Whatever starts it, one of the most curious things about childbirth is that for something so profound, so dramatically life-changing, it almost always starts with more of a whimper than a bang.

In fact, it's next to impossible to be absolutely sure in the very early stages whether this is the start of it all, or just a bit of backache. To add to the frustration, when you ask someone in the know how you'll know, they just say with a smile, 'Don't worry, you'll know!' Just writing that has brought all the annoyance that phrase conjures up flooding back.

The only other time in my life I remember being given such wet advice was when learning to drive.

Me: 'When do you change gear?'

Instructor: 'You'll know.'

Me: 'No, I don't know, how will I know when to change gear?'

Instructor: 'Don't worry, you'll just know.'

Me: 'I won't, I'm telling you, I don't know.'

Instructor: 'You'll know, the car will tell you, you'll just know.'

CRASH.

What's even more annoying was that my driving instructor was right of course – drunk but right – and so it is with the onset of labour. You, or rather your partner, will just know when labour has started because she will have some or all of the symptoms listed below.

- Your partner could experience lower back or abdominal pain that persists and is often accompanied by a crampy premenstrual-type feeling.
- Some women get diarrhoea-like symptoms in early labour as the body has a good old clear out ready to give birth.
- A brownish or blood-tinged mucus discharge called 'the bloody show' comes away (please avoid using the line about making a bloody show of yourself, no matter how tempting − now really isn't the time). This is the mucus plug that blocks the cervix, helps to keep the baby in and infection out − and it's not there anymore! Get the bag, we're off to the hospital! Not so fast, mucus man − this could be a sign that labour is imminent, or it could be several days away. Bugger. Either way, though, it is a sign that things are moving along nicely.
- Painful contractions that occur at regular but shortening intervals and become longer and stronger − bit of a giveaway that one.

Some or all of the above may happen in the early stages, but don't expect fireworks to go off when labour actually starts, as the whole thing is much more of a fluid process than the stage 1, 2 and 3 model would suggest.

It's official

Once your partner's body is telling her unequivocally that she is in labour, when the pains she's feeling are becoming longer, stronger and more frequent, you are on your way. It's a very strange time in many ways, this event that you have been waiting for every day for nine months has finally started to happen and your natural reaction is to call in international rescue, but instead you'll probably just put the kettle on.

Many women describe this early stage as feeling like a bad period pain cramp that reaches a peak, eases off and returns at regular intervals. The contractions may only last about 20 seconds and be 15–20 minutes apart when they first start, or they could start off much stronger and closer together. Because first labours are usually at least 12 hours long it's probably best not to go to hospital too soon. Your partner will be infinitely more relaxed at home than she will in hospital, no matter how swanky and covered in soft plastic furnishings it is.

And so begins a game of contraction chicken/guess the width of the uterus – which sees many a couple trying to hold off for as long as they can, but secretly scared witless that they will leave it too late and be left alone with the hot towels and the marigolds.

It's a very good idea at this stage to try to time the contractions, from when they first come on to when they begin to ease off, and then also the space between them. That's two stopwatches' worth. This will at least give you a rough guide as to how labour is progressing and as a rule of thumb, you don't need to go to hospital until your partner's contractions last at least 45 seconds and come five to 10 minutes apart.

But if you're in any doubt whatsoever, don't be all British about it and think it best not to bother the midwife; it's absolutely what she's there for and she'll be able to tell an awful lot just by hearing how your partner sounds on the phone. If this is your first baby you'll have no real idea what's coming next, so leave the informed guesswork to your seventh, eighth and ninth labours when you will be probably running a sweepstake on when you'll reach the 10cm mark.

Also, if your partner has any semblance of a symptom she is worried about, from the colour of her show, to a headache or worries about the baby's movements – get on the phone and get it checked out. If the midwife is at all concerned about how you're coping, or even if she just wants to check your partner in person, she will call you in for an assessment. There's a strong chance that you will then be sent home again to wait for things to move along a bit further before going back in. It's frustrating, but unavoidable.

While you are both at home, try to encourage your partner to stay as relaxed and rested as she possibly can, given that every few minutes she is laid low with an ever-increasing pain. She could watch a favourite film, take a warm (but not hot) bath or just try her best to put her feet up in between the contractions. If she feels hungry, eating and drinking something she fancies is a brilliant move to gain some fuel for the heavy, heavy going ahead.

When she's having a contraction, help her to get in whatever position gives her the most relief. Now's also the time to start using any breathing or relaxation techniques you've learnt at your ante-natal classes.

This early stage is also when a TENS (transcutaneous electrical nerve stimulation) machine can be of some use. This little box of tricks sends electrical pulses through your partner's back via pads placed at bra-strap and lower-back level.

No one really knows how TENS works, but it seems to. It may stimulate your partner's body to produce endorphins, it may prevent pain signals reaching her brain or it may just be that it's such a bloody palaver to use that it acts as a distraction to what's actually happening.

Endless fiddling with the TENS machine is high on the list of things to keep the expectant father occupied and some men become so attached to them that the machine has to be prised from their hands long after the birth is over. Or at least that's what happened to me.

Time to make a move

As the contractions really start to kick in, you'll decide that it's time to hit the road. Every woman copes with labour pain differently and when it's her time to go in, it's her time to go in.

When you arrive at hospital, it would be lovely to say that you will be greeted at the door by the midwife who has coached, cared and caressed your partner for the past nine months, but especially if you live in a city, the chances are that you won't.

Whoever it is, though, will almost certainly go through the same procedure – she will ask what's happened so far, take a look at your partner's maternity notes and carry out a series of checks on blood pressure, temperature and urine, if there's any of the latter to be had. She will also measure and feel the bump to ascertain which way round your baby is and whether the head is fully engaged in the pelvis. Once that's all done, your partner may be asked if she would like an internal examination to find out how dilated she is.

This can be a crushing moment. If your partner has been really suffering contraction-wise and feels like she must be a fair way down the road, only to find out that she is only 1cm–2cm gone, the wind can be knocked out of her. So be prepared to be there for her and tell her how fantastically she is doing.

Now's potentially a good time to get the birth plan out if you like – double-checking with your partner, of course, that she doesn't want you to put a big red pen through the painkiller-free bit first.

Pain relief – what's on the drugs trolley today

As the contractions become ever more powerful and painful, and your partner moves towards being fully dilated, the pain relief options available to her come into play.

Here's a quick guided tour through what's on offer on the drugs trolley.

Gas and air

Otherwise known as Entonox, this colourless and odourless gas comprises half oxygen and half nitrous oxide – or laughing gas. The gas enters your partner's bloodstream via a two-way mouthpiece or mask just as a contraction is starting. It has the effect of dampening the pain, relaxing the muscles and making her feel a little light-headed, sometimes, just sometimes, even making her laugh. If you fancy sneaking a quick slug of it yourself at a discreet and opportune moment, just make sure you don't have too much, for Christ's sake.

Gas and air is most often used at the end of the first stage of labour as contractions intensify in frequency and strength. Some women swear by the stuff, but for others it just isn't strong enough, or the light-headedness or even nausea that it can cause puts them off.

In terms of any effects on the baby, the gas is quickly flushed from the system and there is even evidence to suggest that the high oxygen content is good for the little mite.

Pethidine

Pethidine is a proper painkiller, part of the opiate family and very similar to morphine. In fact it is morphine, just a synthetic version.

It's mainly administered via injection and is only given during the first stage of labour. There's no doubt pethidine will help your partner relax; it essentially makes the person as high as a kite and gets to work in no time at all. It means business, does pethidine.

It doesn't slow down labour either, just dulls the pain significantly, although not totally. Sounds great, I'll have some right away please.

Whoa there: pethidine has its issues. For starters, one in three people find opiate drugs such as pethidine unpleasant and the drowsiness, nausea or even bouts of sickness it can bring on are not nice.

But pethidine's main drawback is that it crosses the placenta; in other words, the baby takes it as well as the mother. The effects this can have range from affecting your baby's breathing and making him drowsy for several days afterwards, to potentially stifling the baby's rooting and sucking reflexes in the days after birth – making breastfeeding more difficult.

These types of problem seem to be particularly present if your partner's birth progresses more quickly than expected and the baby is born within two hours of the drug being administered.

Meptid and diamorphine – or heroin to you and me – is also sometimes available for labouring women. Both are opiates and have similar advantages and disadvantages to pethidine.

Your partner will not become a heroin fiend as a result of choosing to use diamorphine. I thought that was worth clarifying.

Epidural

The Johnny Big Bananas of all labour pain relief, an epidural sees painkilling drugs passed into the small of the back via a fine tube.

An anaesthetist administers a local anaesthetic in the lower back and then inserts a hollow needle between the small bones in the spine. The needle then slides into the space between the layers of tissue in your partner's spinal column, handily called the epidural space, and a fine tube is then passed through the needle. Wincing yet? The needle is then removed and the tube taped up your partner's back and over her shoulder. The drug is then injected around the nerves that carry signals from the part of her body that feels the labour pain.

And, my word, it's become a wildly popular procedure, too – official figures show that the number of mothers-to-be who have had an epidural has risen in recent years to a whopping 36.5% of all births in the UK.

An epidural can be given at any point in labour, but the majority of women go for this option when their contractions are getting pretty fierce as the cervix moves towards its full dilation.

There's one big, shining benefit of the epidural route – it more often than not provides excellent pain relief during labour. The mind remains perfectly clear, unlike with the pethidine route, and while your partner will be aware of the contractions she's having, if the epidural is working correctly, she will feel no pain. That's quite a draw.

It's not without its problems and risks though – and there are quite a few to consider.

- Firstly, the buttock-clenching procedure takes about 20 minutes itself and another 20 minutes for the anaesthetic to kick in – which may not happen first time of asking – and there's a relatively short window in which to have it administered.
- Your baby's heartbeat and your partner's blood pressure will be monitored continuously for at least 30 minutes when she's first given an epidural, and after each top-up of the anaesthetic if it's needed. There's also a higher risk of the labour needing to be speeded up using a hormone drip once an epidural has been given.
- Not being in full control of the nether regions can also mean that the pushing stage of the delivery may last longer with an epidural.
- Itching, fever or the shivers can occur and your partner may also need a catheter to empty her bladder.
- There's a higher chance of your baby needing to be born with the aid of ventouse or forceps, which may be because epidurals make it difficult for your baby to move into the best position to be born.
- There's also a very small risk of the procedure leading to nerve damage. Although this rarely happens, the risk is about one in 1,000 for temporary damage and one in 13,000 for permanent problems.

The wider debate about the benefits of drug-free births is a thorny and complex one, with one of the UK's most prominent midwives suggesting that the increase in pain relief during labour undermines the mother's bond with her child.

All I'll say is that if men delivered the babies, we would be asking for all of the above in giant pill form.

Transition – not as easy as it sounds

Maybe it's because it sounds a bit like intermission, but whenever anyone mentioned the transition phase of pregnancy I used to conjure up images of a small oasis of calm in which people come into the room handing out choc-ices while making you a G&T, and you are invited to nip to the loo if you like, or go and put some more change in the parking meter.

I got that very wrong.

The transition phase is, for many women, the most difficult part of the entire labour; it's the point where even the steeliest of resolves to avoid pain relief are tested to the maximum. This is the point when the cervix moves from around 8cm to the full 10cm dilation, and the second, pushing stage of the pregnancy can begin.

It's often said that contractions become less frequent at this point, but that's only really because they become so long and strong that they seem to merge into one. It's also common for your partner's waters to break as this stage begins and she may also get an urge to do a poo, as this is the time when the baby's head touches the rectum. That urge may well turn into a reality, too, although your partner may or may not be aware of the comings and goings down there. If it does happen, do your best to play the whole thing down – it's obviously as natural as having the baby itself and your partner shouldn't feel embarrassed for a single second.

Getting her through it

Transition is a tough, tough time and it can often be arrived at after many hours of energy and spirit-sapping early labour. Helping your partner through this often-dark period is one of the most important jobs you'll ever do. That help can come in many ways:

physically helping her to find the best position, comforting her if she feels shaky or shivery, encouraging her to release the guttural noises she's making, or ensuring her pain relief choices happen – no matter how much they might differ from the birth plan.

It might just be, though, that you need to bear the brunt of some pretty fruity and forceful outbursts from the love of your life. Don't be surprised if you are showered with more than the odd volley of obscenities as each contraction takes hold – there's even scientific evidence that swearing does actually alleviate pain.

Whatever it takes, getting to the next stage is the name of the game, because at the end of that, you are both going to see your baby for the very first time.

Almost there – the final push

The cervix is fully open and your partner is ready – or as ready as she'll ever be – to push her baby out into the world.

If she's lucky she may well have experienced a spell without any contractions in between transition and this, the second stage of pregnancy, called in some quarters, mainly by people who dress up as Victorians at weekends, as the rest-and-be-thankful phase. If that little spell of calm didn't exist you'd imagine the childbirth marketing board would invent it to give labouring mothers the tiniest of life rafts to cling to.

Although there are different approaches to pushing, the one that is overwhelmingly favoured by UK midwives is that women push when they get the strong urge to do so and rest when they don't – the other largely discredited method being that they push throughout once they have reached full dilation.

With every push and contraction – which at this stage are around

60–90 seconds long and come at two- to four-minute intervals – the baby will move through the pelvis a little, but as the urge dies away he'll probably slip back a bit again too. Fear not though, progress will be made – albeit slowly.

Gone are the days when women dutifully and utterly inexplicably lay flat on the bed, legs up so the doctor didn't have to strain his neck to see what was going on and attempted to essentially push against gravity. Out-of-bed positions are becoming more and more popular and it's not hard to see why – squatting, for instance, opens the pelvic area by an additional 10%. Birth stools and balls as well as water pools are all options to be considered and if it's where your partner wants to go, it's your job to help make it happen.

Whichever position does it for your partner, the art of pushing effectively these days is characterised by her not holding her breath and turning purple, but rather going with the contractions and the urge, burying her chin into her chest, letting out a deep growl and pushing through her bottom as if she were having a nice poo – which again, she may well do.

Once the baby's head is way down the pelvis and your partner can feel the burning sensation that characterises crowning – when the baby's head starts to stretch the opening to the vagina – she really is getting close.

Assisted deliveries

But things don't always go smoothly and while around 12% of UK births are assisted using instruments that figure increases to 55% for first-time mums. There are several reasons why an assisted birth might be recommended. Your baby might be getting distressed as he is being pushed down the birth canal, or he may not be budging much at all, or your partner simply might have zero energy left to push with. So what high-tech tools has modern medicine developed to help in this delicate procedure then?

A plunger and some giant medieval tongs.

The plunger is, of course, the ventouse: a cup with a pulling handle attached to it, which is linked to a small vacuum pump. Sophisticated, it's not.

The cup fits on top, and the back of your baby's head is held firm(ishly) by the vacuum and the cup is then pulled on during the next contraction. This will be tried around three times to see if the little one can be convinced to make an appearance.

Be warned: babies born using the ventouse sometimes come out with cone-shaped heads or looking like they are wearing some sort of Olympic cycling helmet. This effect of the suction almost always wears off after a few days.

Despite being a pretty basic way of helping a delicate little baby along its way, the ventouse is positively feather-like compared with the other instrument available – forceps. These satanic salad servers come in two interlocked parts, and have curved ends to cradle your baby's head.

Your doctor will need to make a cut to the back of your partner's vagina, called an episiotomy, so the forceps can be inserted to put round the sides of your baby's head. Once they are in place, the doctor will gently pull during a contraction to try to lever the baby out of his hidey hole.

Although forceps have a higher success rate than ventouse, your partner is also more likely to sustain some damage with their use. As it is much more painful, there is also a higher chance of her needing an anaesthetic to be able to cope with the use of forceps.

Most forceps births are straightforward, although your partner may experience some soreness and bruising afterwards. Your baby may be slightly bruised too and conditions such as torticollis (wry neck), which results from damage to the neck muscles during the procedure, should be looked out for in the weeks after birth.

If after three attempts with the forceps your baby is still refusing to move it's almost certainly time to stop tugging and think about a caesarean section.

A caesarean section (C-section) involves making an incision into the woman's abdomen and uterus to manually remove the baby. Most C-sections are performed under epidural rather than general anaesthesia, and if this is decided on, you will be able to stay with your partner throughout. You'll be transferred to a nearby theatre and a screen is usually put up while it takes place so you and your partner don't have to witness what's going on – many men can't resist a peek, though, and some regret it, given what they then see.

While a C-section is a serious medical procedure, it can be over remarkably quickly, and before you know where you are, after hours and hours of labour you can suddenly be holding your new baby.

Delivering the placenta and the stitch-up job can take half an hour, so you become the caregiver for the baby there and then. As you'd expect after having major surgery, your partner will be pretty immobile and in considerable pain for a good while afterwards, meaning your role once you get home becomes even more crucial.

The number of caesareans is on the increase; in 2018 around 29% of all births happened that way, some through choice and some through necessity. Many bodies, including the Royal College of Obstetricians and Gynaecologists, have expressed concerns over the trend.

The birth – it's a baby!

If your partner is fortunate enough to avoid having an assisted birth in any of its forms, the midwife will tell her that she can see the baby's head and that he is no longer slipping back between each contraction. After a pause from pushing on the next contraction or two, to help ensure that the baby is born nice and gently, and to help avoid any tears or the need for a last-minute episiotomy, the final pushes will begin.

The majority of babies emerge with their chin down on their chest. Once the head is fully out, one shoulder is delivered, swiftly followed by the other one and the rest of the body slides out at quite a pace.

However your baby is delivered, and whatever your partner has to go through to help your little one make the final few inches towards life on the outside, there will come a moment when you both get to see your baby boy or girl for the very first time in the flesh. After hours or even days of unprecedented effort your truly amazing partner has achieved something so extraordinary that you'll never see her in quite the same way ever again – she's moved from woman to superwoman.

Then, covered in blood, cream cheese or amniotic fluid, your baby will be handed to your partner and neither of you will have seen anything so amazingly beautiful in your entire lives.

You, my friend, are a father. Congratulations.

Tying up loose ends

Immediately after your baby is born, if all is well with both mother and child, skin-to-skin contact will be established between the two without delay to start the bonding process. There's also plenty of evidence to suggest that you should get your shirt off and get close to your little one too at some point, as well as fixing his gaze with yours – both of which are thought to help form a lasting bond between you and your new child.

One job that needs to be done before you do that is, of course, the cutting of the umbilical cord. The midwife will clamp it in two places and, if you wish, you can do the honours in what has become a well-practised symbolic gesture of the establishing of true independence. In reality it's like cutting a very tough and gristly German sausage.

Before you can start to really get to know the new arrival and your partner can begin the process of establishing breastfeeding, if that's the way you intend to go, there are a few quick tests and measurements that need to be taken.

The baby's airways will be cleared of any mucus, and after the weight is recorded, the APGAR score will be taken. This is a simple method to quickly assess the health of newborn children immediately after childbirth by measuring Appearance, Pulse, Grimace, Activity and Respiration. This test is done twice, at approximately one and five minutes after birth.

Afterbirth afterthought

While all the loveliness of meeting, bonding and even feeding the newborn little bundle is going on, the third stage of birth, the process of delivering the placenta, is already underway. Contractions begin again, although thankfully weaker this time, with the aim of making the placenta gradually come away from the wall of the womb. A lot of hospitals give new mums an injection to speed up this process.

It's hard not to feel that this is a pain in the arse – the job has been done and all your partner wants to do is cuddle her new baby. Luckily, on most occasions this is a relatively straightforward procedure with the strange bagpipe-like sack of membranes which has kept your child alive just dropping out without much fuss.

In Mali, it's thought that the placenta can affect the baby's mood and it's washed, dried and placed in a basket to be buried by the father. In Cambodia, it's carefully wrapped in a banana leaf, placed beside the newborn for three days and then buried. In South America and Korea, it's ceremonially burned after birth to neutralise it. We tend to put it straight in the bin, providing we've not been persuaded to turn it into a pâté by Hugh Fearnley-Whittingstall.

Occasionally, getting the placenta out can be much more complicated, and leaving even tiny fragments of it inside the uterus can lead to heavy bleeding. When all other avenues have been explored and it hasn't come out, an operation will be required to remove it – meaning that even if a woman has avoided having an epidural to deliver her baby, she may be forced to have one to allow her doctor to remove the placenta manually. As well as being painful and stressful for your partner, this means that you are Charles-in-charge when it comes to your baby's first hour or so on the planet.

And breathe

Your first experience of witnessing childbirth will never leave you. Shocking or sentimental, traumatic or transformational – the memories of the moment you became a father and what your partner went through to make that happen will live as long as you do.

No matter what friends who've been there tell you ahead of the event, no matter what you see on the television or at the movies and no matter what you read, yes even in books like this one, nothing even gets close to how you will feel.

As you leave the hospital and begin to call or text friends and relatives with the big news, you will be physically drained, emotionally spent and probably not smelling too great either, but chances are you'll be as happy, as genuinely, undoubtedly happy as you ever have been.

Cherish every moment of this day and the days that follow it as you burst with pride for your new family – it really is life at its very best.

STORIES FROM THE FRONTLINE

The birth story is, quite rightly, the preserve of the mother.

In the weeks and months after your child is born you will hear it told and retold, mainly to other women, all of whom listen intently. Those who have recently given birth themselves will wait for a suitable moment to cut in with their own story and the ones yet to experience childbirth will sit dead still, the colour draining from their cheeks, as they wonder whether they could cope.

But just this once, just because we can, let's hear what it was like for the fathers. All right, so we've not had the unspeakable pain, the needles in our spine or the stitches in our unmentionables, but we were there, we were there.

Chris, 34, father of one: *We arrived at the hospital at about 8am. Anouk was born at 8.47am. So we held on at home with those contractions a fair while!*

They did say come in at the last possible moment. My wife actually collapsed in the reception – apparently the receptionists hate women having babies in the reception area, so my wife was quickly ushered to her feet and up we went to the birthing room.

I'm an old hippie, so remember hoping that my wife would get in the bath for a water birth and, as it turned out, she actually was up for it, but couldn't get over to the bath. Anouk was on the way, born on the floor of the birthing room. I remember being fascinated at the way the head turns and the shoulders squash up to get out . . . and being slightly amused when the midwife asked my wife if she wanted a mirror (to see what was going on – she didn't – obviously).

Colin, 33, father of one: *After I got 'the call' at work to say Susanne's waters had broken, I responded in time-honoured fashion and prepared to race home there and then, only to be told to stop being a numpty and come home after work . . . This was going to take a while.*

And it did.

That evening we went for a long walk and a curry and at around midnight the contractions really started to kick in. We phoned the hospital and they told us to come in. Susanne was examined and told she was only 1cm dilated and we went home again, arriving at about 6am.

At about 5pm that evening the contractions were getting fast and quite strong and at sevenish I called the hospital back and was told they were full. Full, like an NCP car park.

The suggestion we were given was to go to another hospital nearby – one which we had heard from friends with first-hand experience was horrific. So we waited as long as we dared and I called back at about 10pm hoping against hope that it would be open – and it was.

We raced in, expecting to be near the big moment, but no, Susanne was still only 1cm. But at least we were in the bloody place now and nothing was going to shift us.

Susanne took some pethidine and we managed to get four hours much needed rest. My big fear was that when things did eventually get moving she would be completely and totally spent, having been in labour for almost two days already. So it's 4am now, the pethidine has all but worn off and it's time for another examination. 4cm.

Four hours later – 6cm. The following examination two hours after that, still 6cm.

That was when things suddenly got very clinical. We were taken to theatre where Susanne was put on a monitor and given a hormone drip to increase the contractions. Serious pain at this point – it later turned out Isabella was 'back to back' with her back against my wife's spine – so Susanne decided to have an epidural.

As the anaesthetist was attempting to find the right spot in her back for the injection, the baby's heart rate kept on plummeting and for the first time I began to contemplate something going seriously wrong.

Then Susanne let out an almighty scream and there was the head! Bin the epidural and push, push, push. More than 90 minutes later after trying stirrups and birthing chairs, the midwife called the doctor with the ventouse.

Luckily, before she could get that far, Isabella popped out aided with a few snips from the massive scissors.

A huge, huge effort from my wife and one I will never forget or stop admiring her for.

Donald, 34, father of two: *Quite near the end of the pregnancy my wife had woken up screaming in pain during the middle of the night and I* immediately thought this is it . . . but when I realised it was merely a bit of cramp I soon fell fast asleep, after performing the obligatory 'leg in the air, rub the calf' footballer's treatment, of course.

I won't call it crying wolf, but when my wife woke me again 10 minutes before my alarm was due to sound for work and said her waters had broken I'll admit it took me a while for things to register, but once the penny had dropped I sprung to life. Our first visit to the hospital – like many on their big day – was in vain and we were sent home with the advice that she should be going into the early stages of labour by the close of play that night.

When she did go into labour at about 3pm that afternoon my parents, who had been notified early, decided they would show up unannounced . . . bad idea. By this point the contractions had started and the doorbell went. We were mystified as to who it could be but a simple peek out the window alerted us to it being my parents. My Japanese wife, who never ever shouts, screamed, 'Get them out of here, they are not coming in!'

I ushered my parents away before they caught sight of my wife, but left them with the news that she may be going into labour (resulting in a machine gun-like response by way of text messages over the hours that followed).

I got back to my wife, who was clearly in pain, and (forgetting all I had been told and shown in my NCT classes) I tried to massage her back during contractions instead of between – an error of quite enormous proportions. 'Get your fucking hands off me!' Wow!

My wife, who, as well as never shouting, certainly never swears, suddenly does both – very well!

I took that as my cue to call the hospital and spoke to a midwife, who was surprisingly unhelpful. She said she could hear by the sound of my wife in the background that she is clearly not ready and we would only be sent home; now, that is talent bordering on the supernatural. She said I can't tell you not to come, but I believe you will be wasting your time. Bugger her, I thought, rush hour is on its way and my wife's newly discovered expletive vocabulary would surely expand rapidly should we get stuck in traffic, so we left at once.

At the hospital we were quickly shown to a room and then left completely on our own for about 40 minutes. My wife was in such excruciating pain that I slightly lost it and told the desk of doctors, nurses and midwives to stop chatting among themselves and get someone in to look at my wife . . . please. This seemed to do the trick and a midwife followed me back very casually. She was less casual when she took one look at the business end of my wife and shouted 'Don't push, you're 10cm dilated and I can see the head!'

From then on, we had what felt like hundreds of midwives crowded around the water birth pool. I was made chief fisherman in case unusual pieces of . . . well, anything . . . should appear in the water. At one point, when the baby's head had nearly come out and my wife's contractions stopped she promptly fell fast asleep. We all started shouting at her and she awoke startled like she'd been sleeping for hours. After an initial look of sheer bewilderment she remembered where she was and went straight back to the push and grind . . . I was so impressed and still am.

When Emily was born, I cut the cord and she was passed to me. She opened her eyes and two blue marbles looked up at me . . . It was amazing . . . the world stopped.

It wasn't quite over for my wife though. The senior midwife asked if a student doctor could deliver the placenta, which she did, only for it to fire out and explode in the student's face. Her hair was covered, her glasses were red, and her chin was dripping. We never did find out whether this young fresh-faced girl did pursue a medical career or finish her course or even make it to the shower.

Going home to an empty house that night was very strange. I was so excited I wanted to celebrate and wake the world.

Unfortunately it was now about 1am on a school night and I had to make do with a couple of cold beers on my own, while mulling over the events of the day. This was not out of the ordinary, kids are born all over the world all the time but nevertheless 'new life' was amazing!

Jim, 34, father of one: We had a 26-hour labour all in. For the first 20 hours I was pretty relaxed, and thought we were all doing well. I was in control and going to boss the situation.

The next three hours were really long, draining and increasingly worrying. It began to get a little messy. The dried apricots failed to re-energise anyone and I had forgotten the sandwiches in the car. I could not do the mantra anywhere near as good as the midwife. Gooood, Gooood, Very Gooooooooooood: my timing was not up to scratch and I had no idea she was coordinating her 'Goods' with breathing and pushing. I took some stick for that!

The next two hours were increasingly alarming and I began to think these people did not know what they were doing. We could see Paul's little head, but they couldn't get him out. My partner's face was red and full of burst blood vessels.

The last hour consisted of an emotional schizophrenia, the like of which I've never experienced before – horrified/serene/angry/grateful/scared/proud and back to the beginning again. I had no idea, no control, so I just held my Anne all the time, taking the squeezes, the pinches but thankfully no punches.

She was incredible. The most amazing woman – incredible to think all mums have been through this. I look at mothers in a different light now.

On arrival, Paul looked like a shrunken scraggy old man, and a lot like my nan.

Levi, 36, father of two: It's not quick like on the telly, with rushing and hot towels and then birth. Labour was long and boring, and watching your wife in regular, gut-wrenching pain is not fun at all.

You're also excited, but you want this bit over. Like when you have to finish something truly horrible on your plate before getting a big bowl of crème caramel. I only felt useful at the end, when my wife was being urged to really push, and I held her hand and counted to 10 with her and urged her on. A bit like a boxing coach in the corner but without pouring cold water on her genitals.

Our child was forceps-delivered. I thought the doctor was pulling my wife off the bed at one point. Horrendous, and the baby was born with red marks on her jaw where the clamps were fitted.

We had agreed that I only had one job and that was to tell my wife if we'd had a boy or a girl. The moment was so shocking that I could only splutter in wonder, 'It's a baby,' much to the midwives' mirth.

I cut the cord, but only because I was asked if I wanted to and not because I felt like I was giving life to this bundle – I didn't, my wife did that bit. People who think cutting the cord is really meaningful and symbolic are dreaming.

You wait all day in an unpleasant, hot, pretty sterile, not particularly chilled-out environment. You're worried and everything takes ages. You've waited nine months for this day. Nine months is an unexpectedly long time. You know it's coming, that's why we're all here, isn't it? Yet, I was STILL gobsmacked when a baby came into the room. An extra person was magicked in there. An awesome feeling.

I drove home at great speed, exhilarated and listening to Mozart at full blast in the middle of the night. I thought about my dad, too, and felt very happy.

Nick, 35, father of two: We had a planned C-section. It was incredibly weird going out for dinner the night before knowing that we were going to have a baby the next morning. Sleep was at a premium that night, too.

The taxi driver knew and wished us luck! The theatre was strange – a place of work for the staff in there, something inevitable and predictable for everyone except us.

Then he came out – he looked exactly like my dad – my wife had given birth to my dad . . . It was . . . surreal and amazing.

Peter, 33, father of one: Many things stand out from the birth for me, *but there were a few key moments. First of all it was the only day of the year it snowed and a 20-minute journey took about an hour and a quarter – including a bit of skidding on icy roundabouts and 10mph on the dual carriageway in blizzard conditions. Despite really close and hard contractions my darling wife still felt compos mentis enough to criticise my driving – but at least it took her mind off the impending pushing.*

When we finally got to the hospital, as always, I was told I'd parked in the wrong spot and was made to find another despite the contractions coming long and hard. Once we were inside, my wife was off her face on the gas and air. So much so, she actually couldn't remember how to push when the moment came. However, the mild threat that a doctor may have to be brought in to examine her when there was a 15-minute lull got things moving very sharpish. I remember that, just like in the sitcoms, you can actually hear the occasional primal scream from elsewhere in the unit. It's odd to admit, but even when you get near to the very end it always takes 10 times as long as you think. A minute seems like an hour.

The only scary moment was when Sam came into the world and the midwife pressed the emergency button, but that was just to get another midwife to help her cut the umbilical cord. For a split second I thought there were massive problems, but everything was OK.

In contrast, the most emotional moment of the lot was telling my wife that we'd had a boy. Actually seeing him brought tears to my eyes and my voice went all wobbly. I didn't feel instant love – I was in awe of the little fella; how he had all these toes and fingers and how he knew he should breathe. Just incredible.

And the most surreal experience was about 30 minutes after Sam was born. The midwife told us Alex had a tear that needed stitches. A couple of minutes later a small doctor came in and asked her to open her legs before he put them in stirrups. 'Pretend I'm not here,' he said, before strapping a kind of pot-holing light to his forehead, turning it on and proceeding to insert the stitches.

As we attempted to talk softly and gaze lovingly at each other and our new son, the thread was lifted high into the air time and again as this tiny little doctor with a miner's lamp on stitched my wife's nether regions.

Stuart, 37, father of two: *After an unsuccessful induction attempt at the doctor's we were told to ring the hospital a few days later. And as we were almost two weeks overdue at this point we were up bright and early, ready to go.*

After initially being told there were no beds, we called back again and got the go-ahead to come in, so picked up our bags and travelled in style to the hospital on the bus. After being induced a second time we were told that it could take a while and, despite going for a walk to get things moving, so it proved.

It wasn't until 8 or 9 at night that the contractions started to kick in, by which time my partner was on the antenatal ward, meaning I had to leave, which was a nightmare knowing that she had a night of pain ahead of her, but they insisted and kicked me out.

After a restless night's sleep at home with the phone on my pillow I made my way back to the hospital as soon as I was allowed in to find my partner in even more pain and having had no sleep at all. The fact that she had to go through that night on her own was a scandal.

By 3 o'clock that afternoon we were in full flow, with the birthing plan thrown out of the window and the epidural administered. By 10 that night our daughter still refused to enter the world and there was talk of an emergency caesarean which would have suited me fine because by this point my better half looked totally shattered after 24 hours of labour.

Luckily, though, she is made of stern stuff and had a bit more fight to push, and with a little help from a scalpel Lily was born at 1.13am.

A few hours of getting to know my new little girl were magical before I was kicked out again to do the ring round, float home and then float back again first thing.

Suki, 34, father of two: *The first time around we went into hospital two or three days on the trot after minor contractions had started, only to be told baby wasn't ready each time. Once the waters had partly broken, we went back and then had to start on what turned out to be a 20-plus hour process of induction, which ended, as a lot of them do I believe, in a forceps delivery.*

I was totally exhausted so I can't even begin to imagine how my wife felt. The arrival of the baby was simply the best feeling ever; the mum carries it for nine long months and to be able to finally hold this tiny little being your-self is fantastic.

Tom, 34, father of two: *I remember my back killing me during the labour and as my wife had had an epidural by then I popped on a redundant TENS machine – queue funny looks from midwives, of course.*

I mainly juggled monitoring the monitor with keeping the music fresh. And once we got down to crunch time, I even managed to use the rose petal spray, which was both ineffective and camp all at once.

We were far more casual the second time around. Arrived nicely dilated thanks to my magnificent wife, worked through the following hours superbly and because Jane seemed so in control I could really focus on the music.

Both arrived to Norah Jones, God bless that woman.

Oli, 35, father of one: *The birth was horrible, to be honest.*

Firstly, if you like to be in control, then this is the one moment when you're not. You mostly hang around, generally on the fringes of what is going on.

I hate hospitals anyway and don't like needles, so when they did the epidural, I went out of the room. I was very emotional, particularly as we had an emergency caesarean.

Both A and J were in a lot of distress, so after about four hours they rushed us in to do the caesarean.

Seeing someone you love in immense pain and distress, particularly when you can't do anything is horrible. When people say it's a wonderful experience, I think that's bollocks; in my mind, get it over and done with ASAP.

David, 34, father of one: *After 10 days of curries, pineapple and anatomically awkward but surprisingly sexy sex we had to face the truth – we were going to be induced.*

Arriving at hospital I was utterly amazed just how calm my wife was. To me this was like a horror film – voluntarily checking yourself into somewhere in the absolute knowledge that unbearable pain was the unavoidable conclusion.

But she was cool. She's been happier, obviously, but so strong was the desire to finally see the baby that had been inside her for what seemed like three and a half years, that she was virtually guiding the midwife in like an air traffic controller when the time came to apply the gel.

Despite what we had read, contractions didn't begin there and then with a fearful and thunderous crash.

In fact, nothing happened, so we went for a walk and even decided to go for some pasta at a place near the hospital to boost our energy levels for the night ahead.

About three hours later my wife started to feel back aches and mild stomach cramps which got worse pretty quickly – and we knew things were starting.

By the time Sarah got into bed on the pre-maternity ward she was in a fair bit of pain but still pretty calm. When the nurse came round and we told her we thought labour was starting she came out with the classic line that it couldn't be labour because my wife looked too happy and if it was labour she'd know about it.

Wrong.

The time was gone 11pm and it was kicking-out time on the ward for men, including me, and I was ushered out – leaving Sarah in increasing pain. After half an hour pacing outside the hospital I knew I had to go back in and tailgated someone through the doors. When I got to Sarah's bed she was out like a light and the midwife, surprised to see me back, told me that she had been given pethidine after asking for painkilling help.

Even more worried that things would soon be kicking off I pleaded to stay but was told to leave the ward, go home and get some sleep – as soon as anything was looking like happening I'd be called, but they didn't think anything would be happening for hours.

Wrong again.

Just as I walked in the front door of our house after a half-hour drive my mobile rang and I was told my wife was about to start pushing and that I needed to rush back.

I raced back and was just in time for the start of the pushing phase – she had gone through full dilation on her own.

The pushing stage was thankfully very quick and almost straightfor-ward and an hour and a half after it had started we had a beautiful baby boy.

And we thought that was that. But it wasn't. The bloody placenta refused to come out, despite the midwife pawing at it like James Herriot. A full two litres of blood later and the doctor was finally called. She took one look and whisked my poor wife off to theatre to have an epidural so they could get the placenta out with impunity. Resisting an epidural for the baby but being *forced to have one for the placenta felt like a real kick in the teeth for my wife, but soon enough the trauma began to fade for her.*

It goes without saying, though, that we will be giving that hospital a miss should we be lucky enough to have a next time.

BEING OVERDUE

As we've seen, the due date of your baby is a rough estimate at best and a load of old cobblers at worst. But even with that knowledge lodged in your partner's brain, the very second the given date comes and goes you are officially overdue. It's a blunt word for a pretty blunt time and one which unites womankind in frustration, uncomfortableness and not a little irritation.

Once your partner reaches her 41st week she will be checked out by an obstetrician to see if the aforementioned dodgy due date really is dodgy. The position of the baby will be checked as well as its size and there may even be an internal examination carried out to see whether the cervix feels soft and ready for labour or hard and ready for a fight.

You may also be offered a sweep – a word which will take on a whole new meaning to you in the coming days. It refers to the procedure of sweeping the membranes, which while sounding like a grunge band from Devon, is actually a medical procedure and a pretty unsophisticated one at that. It involves the midwife or doctor sweeping a finger around the cervix during an internal examination to try to separate the membranes around the baby from the cervix itself. This in turn releases hormones which could kickstart labour. It won't come as a shock to anyone to discover that having a sweep can be somewhat uncomfortable or even downright painful – but it does increase the likelihood that labour will start within 48 hours and poses no risk of infection whatsoever.

As a manual introduction to induction it's worth a go, because the medical alternatives that come into view as time ticks on don't take many prisoners.

A helping hand?

Nobody wants to be induced.

Apocryphal stories abound of going from nought to 10cm dilation in 90 seconds and contractions so strong that they cause structural damage to the hospital.

So why don't we all just wait until the little 'un is good and ready?

The reason overdue mothers-to-be make obstetricians very nervous indeed is because the risk of the placenta beginning to fail in its task of keeping the baby alive increases ever so slightly as the pregnancy goes past full term. The risk of stillbirth in the UK is around one per 3,000 pregnancies at 39 weeks, four per 3,000 at 42 weeks and eight per 3,000 at 43 weeks. It's those figures that are the driving force behind the fact that in England something like one in every five women is induced.

Once the membrane sweep has been tried and is unsuccessful, a range of induction options will be offered to your partner. She, by this time, will not only be climbing the walls wanting to get her enormous child out of her body but also swearing on all that is holy – the next person to ask if there's any news will be attacked with a fully charged TENS machine.

The midwife or doctor may also arrive at something called the Bishop's score, which is a scoring system to predict if an induction is required and/or would be successful. Based on five elements assessed during an internal examination, a grade from 0 to 13 is given. A score above 9 means labour will still most likely start spontaneously, anything beneath 6 and an induction is probably needed.

Five and the bonus ball and you could pay your mortgage off.

THE 'NATURAL' WAY – MYTHS WHICH ALMOST CERTAINLY DON'T WORK

It's a measure of just how royally pissed off overdue women get at not being able to get shot of their stowaway that over the years they have been prepared to try so many bizarre and, more often than not, utterly ineffective ways of starting off labour. Here is just the merest handful.

Sex

Now, let me see, I wonder who could have come up with this? So determined was the man who cooked up this one that he even took the time to invent three separate ways in which it works.

Firstly, orgasm helps to stimulate the womb into action (a little presumptuous given how logistically difficult the act of sex is at this stage, never mind good sex). Secondly, semen helps to ripen or soften the neck of the womb (the guidance is unclear whether this should be applied directly or taken orally). And thirdly, the jiggy-jiggy nature of sex itself can kick things off.

You've got to admire him for his thoroughness, but it's almost certainly a load of old twaddle.

Castor oil

Taking castor oil to bring on labour is an ancient trick that is thought to get the uterus going by serving up a bad case of diarrhoea, with a side order of nausea.

While a few small studies have shown this to be somewhat effective, the dehydration that can be caused at such a critical time marks this method of induction down as only slightly less undesirable than your partner hanging upside down until things get a move on.

Eating pineapple

The enzyme bromelain that is found in fresh pineapples (it's lost in canned or juiced varieties) is thought in some quarters to help soften the cervix.

Given the tiny amount of the enzyme in each pineapple, your partner will need to eat a lorry load, by which time she will have such a case of the runs that she will no longer be aware she is still alive, never mind still pregnant.

Eating curry

Almost certainly another poo-related method and as such pretty meh.

Homeopathy

Who knows whether the root of the shoot of the lesser nettle buckweed shrub, or whatever is the recommended potion, actually does anything, but one thing is for sure: when a homeopathist puts a bottle of tiny, tiny tablets into an overdue woman's hand and says that under absolutely no circumstances should she take any more than one of those tablets, you can be assured of a couple of things.

- The woman will believe that these tablets hold the answer to her prayers.
- She will take five of them.

What doesn't help is when her husband then tells her that they taste like Tic Tacs and are almost certainly a placebo. Take it from me, not a good move.

The last resort

The final and almost foolproof way of bringing on labour is for the expectant father to drink two bottles of red wine very quickly. He is almost guaranteed to be required to drive to the hospital within the hour, but will end up being forced to drunkenly beg taxi firms to ignore their 'no amniotic fluid on the leather policy' and take them in.

THE MEDICAL WAY – DRUGS THAT DO

If your partner has made love to a pineapple while munching on a castor oil-drenched onion bhaji and there's still no movement as she approaches the 42nd week mark, the medical induction options come into play.

Prostaglandin

Prostaglandin is a hormone-like substance which helps stimulate uterine contractions and can be administered via a gel, pessary or tablet into the vagina. The drug tends to kick in over the course of a few hours, although a second dose can sometimes be needed.

There's a very small risk that, as with Syntocinon below, the uterus may become over-stimulated or hyper-stimulated, which can reduce the amount of oxygen getting to your baby – if this happens yet more drugs are given to slow things down.

Syntocinon

Syntocinon, a synthetic form of the hormone oxytocin, is only given if prostaglandin has failed to do its thing. Your partner would be given this via an intravenous drip, meaning it goes straight into the bloodstream.

Syntocinon is a powerful drug and can cause strong contractions that could put the baby under stress, meaning continuous monitoring is necessary. Women who are given Syntocinon often choose to have an epidural as contractions brought on via this route can be more painful than natural ones. You may also be offered a caesarean before choosing to try Syntocinon.

Artificially rupturing the membranes

This is a scary sounding method of breaking the waters that is fast becoming a thing of the past or a last resort if for some reason prostaglandin can't be given.

A midwife or doctor makes a small tear in the membranes around the baby using either a probe with a hook on the end, or a glove with a needle-like prick at the end of one of the fingers.

The words Jesus and wept spring to mind.

COPING

With the prospect of induction looming larger every day that baby chooses to stay put, it's no wonder that the post-40-week phase of a pregnancy can be among the most trying of the whole thing for your partner. Your job is to keep her as calm and as occupied as possible. Sitting in the house and thinking about nothing else is a recipe for a serious case of cabin fever.

Despite the dubious scientific evidence for all the old wives' tales remedies, what they all have going for them is that they give you both something relatively positive and proactive to talk, try and obsess about – although if you are seriously considering the castor oil route it's time to go and see the midwife again!

Remember, 80% of all births don't require induction and if you fall in the remaining 20%, you'll both find a way to get through it, because you are very nearly parents and that's what parents do.

FAMILY MAN – YOU, YOUR BABY AND SUPERWOMAN

Once the sheer drama of childbirth has passed and you have called and texted almost every human being you've ever met, you'll regretfully say goodbye to your new little family and almost certainly drive home, shattered but as happy as you've ever been.

There's something incredibly special about travelling to hospital to visit the two most important people in your life – full of pride, full of love and in awe of what your partner went through. This short little spell before they come home is one of those intensely personal and joyful times in your life that you'll never forget.

Of course for your partner the next few weeks or even months is a period of recovery. In the immediate aftermath there could be tears to be shed, stitches to heal, heavy postnatal bleeding to stem and stretch marks to come to terms with. She could feel elated, delighted, overwhelmed or depressed; childbirth is a huge event and everyone deals with the fall-out in different ways. If she had a caesarean, walking, standing or even just sitting up could be real problems, and your help and support will be vital.

On the plus side, their job done, the hormonal hordes quickly start to slink away, meaning the unholy trinity of heartburn, piles and constipation are relieved pretty quickly.

Going home – the rest of your life starts here

Postnatal care in the nation's hospitals varies wildly. Some women receive attention, advice and support that genuinely help them in the testing days and weeks to come. For others the post-delivery ward is a place to escape from as soon as possible. A noisy, impersonal hell hole that stuffs in new mums and their babies like brooding battery hens.

Either way, after anything from 24 hours to a handful of days (or a week or more in complicated cases) the time to take your baby and its mum home will come.

After the tentative drive back, there will come a moment when you both sit down in the familiar surroundings of the place where you live and the penny will drop – you are parents, you have an utterly dependent little baby and it's down to the pair of you to provide for him and protect him. Bloody hell.

Having your first baby is like nothing else and I truly envy what you've got to come.

Talking of which . . .

THE NEXT STAGE –
BABIES AND TODDLERS

WHAT HAPPENS IN THE HOSPITAL?

Entire books could be taken up by your first month of fatherhood.

In fact, entire books could be taken up by your first few *days* of fatherhood, so powerful can the post-traumatic tidal wave be for all concerned.

You have your partner who, even if she has just performed the most straightforward birth ever recorded in human history, has still undergone physical and emotional upheaval on a quite massive scale.

Having come out the other side of the labour ward she isn't, as feels wholly appropriate, prescribed two weeks of recuperation on a beach, but rather handed a helpless and utterly dependent newborn baby to fathom out and keep alive.

Then there's the little one herself. Imagine for a moment, if you would, what that poor mite has just been through. She's just spent nine months lounging in the amniotic pool, her heavenly life occasionally punctuated by the odd somersault or thumb suck. Then she has, and there's no nice way of saying this, just been forced out of an unfeasibly small hole, or grabbed from above in the most undignified of fashions.

As if the method of her arrival into the world wasn't distressing enough, she's then faced with more bright lights, noise and prodding than her little mind could ever have dreamed existed.

And what about you?

You've tried to do your bit to make life easier through the pregnancy. You've desperately attempted to keep yourself together and be strong through the labour. Now the task in hand is to get to grips with fatherhood and help your new family settle in at home before you are yanked back to work after a few measly weeks.

So all in all, the three of you have had quite a time – and there's a lot you as the proud, excited, but perhaps somewhat daunted father will need to get involved with to make sure these first crucial few weeks and months are navigated as well as possible for your new family.

Before you can get started with family life at home, there will almost certainly be a little (or longer) spell in hospital for your partner and baby to negotiate.

YOUR PART IN THE RECOVERY

Around 97% of mothers in the UK give birth in hospital. This section focuses on what you can expect to happen in the hours, days, or even in the thankfully rare cases where the baby needs special care, weeks before your new son or daughter can come home.

If your partner has given birth vaginally without complications, she could be back home together with your new baby within hours, at most a couple of days or so.

Given the dire call for beds in most NHS hospitals, the notion that your partner can get some rest and TLC before she is discharged to embark on motherhood is sadly often overridden by the pragmatic need for space.

Having said that, even if there were beds aplenty, your average postnatal ward isn't what you'd call relaxing. The combination of crying newborns, other new mums in turmoil and visiting relatives can combine to make a pretty hectic and unsettling environment and many new mothers can't wait to get home as soon as possible.

In many non-Western cultures, once women are at home there often exists a 30- or 40-day 'confinement' – which sounds beastly and lockdownish until you realise that during that time most household activities are carried out by others so the mother and baby can recuperate.

It's also interesting that many cultures overtly and deliberately celebrate childbirth rather than the birth of a baby. The mother's role, efforts and well-being are seen on a par with the joy of a new arrival.

While there's tea and sympathy for new mums in our culture, there's no doubting that the star of the show is the bundle of joy in the corner. In many ways, such is the medicalisation of labour it's easy to see how that subtle but important shift happened.

Being there as much as you can for this short but sometimes stressful stay in hospital is a must. Your partner is grappling with a whole world of immediate challenges, including establishing breast-feeding; trying to figure out just when she is meant to rest; wondering what the hell to do with the alien-like umbilical cord stump; or, in many cases, just coming to terms with the reality of being a mother.

Night-time can be especially tough and often lonely for your partner after you've been turfed out on your ear at 10pm or so. It's a good idea to keep your mobile on overnight in case she needs to talk. Arriving, cavalry-like, as soon as you're allowed back in the morning will go down well after a tough evening. If you also come armed with something you know she'd love to eat for breakfast you will be a very popular chap indeed. While the NHS can and often does excel on the maternity care front, it's not in any danger of winning a raft of Michelin stars any time soon.

Your partner's postnatal check involves pulse, temperature and blood pressure readings. Her midwife will check that her womb is beginning to contract to its normal size and position. After that, your partner will be able to go home. As long as she has had her first post-birth wee, that is, just to check that all is well with the piping.

If your baby was born by caesarean section, your partner will often stay in hospital for between three and five days, all being well. As we will see later, once you get home, you will play a vital role in aiding her recovery from the major surgery she has just endured.

The midwife will want to be sure your partner can walk, albeit gingerly, to the toilet and once there urinate without the need for a catheter, as well as keep food and drink down without vomiting.

Told you it was major surgery.

The baby needs checking out, too, and a paediatrician or a specially trained midwife will carry out a set of remarkably thorough newborn checks before you can take your new family home.

BABY'S FIRST CHECK-UP

Your baby will be given its first test at just one minute and then again at five minutes after the birth – and you thought setting SATs for seven-year-olds was tough.

The APGAR test, devised by the eponymous Dr Virginia Apgar, has been standard practice since the 1950s. The midwife will watch your baby's colour, breathing, behaviour, activity and posture, and then score each of these five factors between zero and two.

A perfect 10 out of 10 is what every new parent wants to hear, but an eight or a nine is still great news. A score between five and seven means your baby is in fair condition but may require some help with breathing. Your midwife may vigorously rub your baby's skin or give her some oxygen if this is the case.

Newborns who score under five are considered to be in poor condition and are often placed on a special unit, which looks, it has to be said, a bit like a doner kebab grill, where heat, light and oxygen are on tap to help warm them up and aid breathing. A paediatrician will also be called to help with initial treatment and decide on the best course of action.

The APGAR score is then repeated for babies with low scores, until your baby is in a good and stable condition, or as we will see later, it's decided that treatment in a neonatal ward is a good idea.

Most babies score well, though, and the next job for the midwife is to weigh your baby and measure the circumference of her head. Seven and a half pounds (3.4kg) is seen as the average weight for a newborn these days, although all sorts of factors mean you could have either a petite little thing or a big bouncing bundle of joy that tips the scales above or below that.

This average birth weight has been creeping up for the past 30 years in the UK so that now your average baby boy comes in at 7lb 8oz and girls at 7lb 4oz. The number of babies born weighing more than 9lb 15oz has increased by 20% recently – so be prepared!

Head circumference is a key measurement medically speaking, but it isn't anywhere near as celebrated a birth dimension as weight, is it? If you fancy redressing that balance and sending a text to friends and family reading:

> We are delighted to announce the arrival of a baby girl. Mother and daughter doing very well after a tough birth. Olivia Jane is perfect, beautiful and has a head circumference of 34cm.

Do let me know how it goes down.

Then there's the heel-prick blood test, usually carried out sometime before your baby is one week old. Although only a tiny amount of blood is taken from the heel, it's a tough one to watch. It goes against every instinct you've got to let someone stick a pin into this delicate and vulnerable little vision of loveliness, but it's for the best, especially when you look at the conditions it is screening for:

- sickle cell disorders
- cystic fibrosis
- medium chain acyl dehydrogenase deficiency (MCADD), a rare condition that affects the way the body converts fat into energy
- phenylketonuria, an enzyme deficiency
- thyroid deficiencies

The main event, though, is the full newborn examination, a head-to-toe look at your baby that will normally take place between four and 48 hours after birth.

A paediatrician, or midwife with extended training, will check for any health problems or conditions. Ideally you should be there so you can ask questions as it happens, and answer any questions the health professional has about your family's medical history.

Here's a rundown of the main things the examination looks at.

Head

Fear not, some babies often have a strange, almost moulded shape to their head after a vaginal birth caused, as you can imagine, by being squeezed through the birth canal.

Most of these cases will resolve themselves within 48 hours or so. The fontanelles, or soft spots, on your baby's head, which make the whole journey possible for your little one's skull, will also be checked.

If the birth required intervention with either ventouse or forceps, there's also a small risk of your baby's head being bruised or even their neck muscles being damaged, and this will also be looked at.

Mouth

The doctor or midwife will check that the roof of your baby's mouth is complete. If a cleft palate is detected, it will need surgery and could well make feeding difficult.

Eyes

The doctor or midwife will shine a light from an ophthalmoscope into your baby's eyes to look for a red reflex, the same red reflex that ruins many a photo. In this case, red eye is a very good thing indeed as it means cataracts or other rare conditions can be ruled out.

Heart

Your baby's heart will be listened to for heart murmurs or any other sounds that shouldn't be there. Murmurs are not uncommon in these early days – your baby's circulation goes through some pretty major changes as it adjusts to life without the umbilical cord. Heart murmurs often require a second opinion and further investigation, but they often disappear on their own.

Genitals

Your baby's genitals can often give you a bit of a fright when you first see them after birth. Sometimes swollen or a dark angry colour, or even both, this is down to the maternal hormones your baby was exposed to before the big arrival.

These are the same hormones which could also cause your baby to have engorged breasts, regardless of gender and for girls to have a clear or even slightly bloody vaginal discharge for the first few weeks.

In boys, the scrotum is checked for undescended testes and his penis will be checked to ensure the opening is at the tip and not on the underside, which would cause all sorts of problems, as you can imagine.

Lungs

Your baby's breathing pattern will be observed and her lungs will be listened to with a stethoscope to ensure there is a clear equal entry of air into them both.

Skin

Your baby's skin will be checked for all manner of exotic sounding birthmarks, including stork marks, strawberry marks and Mongolian spots.

Hands and feet

As you'd expect, fingers and toes are counted and the feet are checked for webbing (around one baby in every 2,000 is born with two or more toes fused together).

The resting position of your baby's feet and ankles will also be checked for club foot, which is where the front half of the foot turns in and down.

Hips

Your baby's hips will be given a good old to and fro to check the stability of the joints. Most NHS trusts routinely scan hips these days, too. If any instability or clicks are picked up, further tests will be carried out.

Reflexes

Your baby's reflexes are truly a thing of wonder. The innate ability to suck that most babies possess at birth is impressive in itself, but the rooting reflex, nature's way of helping the most helpless of tots find their food, is nothing short of amazing. Gently brush one of your newborn baby's cheeks and chances are she will instinctively turn her head to that side on the hunt for milk.

Then there's the grasp reflex. So strong is it that many newborns can cling on to your fingers and support their own weight – not that it's advisable to try this out!

Why a seemingly frail and needy little newborn should be able to perform this extraordinary gymnastic feat is even more astonishing than the act itself. Anthropologist Desmond Morris explains that the ability to cling on with such intensity is a reminder of our close evolutionary ties to the monkeys and apes, whose young grasp their mother's fur for all their worth from the get-go, as they are transported through the tree canopy.

Most modern mums give the Tarzan routine a miss nowadays, so this initial reflex soon fades, but when your finger is grasped by a tiny hand you'll be witnessing many thousands of years of evolutionary history.

The examiner will test that all of these reflexes are functioning properly and will also carry out the Moro test. This entails holding your baby face up with one hand under its bottom and one holding its head. The hand holding the head is allowed to drop by a few centimetres. The Moro reflex should then kick in and your baby will fling out both her legs and arms with fingers spread. The examiner is looking for symmetry here.

Your baby will probably cry for a little while after this, which is perfectly understandable.

Ears

Many hospitals now give babies a hearing test before you are discharged. This is often carried out by a specialist nurse or midwife who brings two very special bits of kit to your partner's bedside.

The first test is called otoacoustic emissions (OAEs). A miniature earphone and microphone are placed in the ear, sounds are played and if the baby hears normally, an echo is reflected back into the ear canal and is measured by the microphone.

The second test is the auditory brainstem response or ABR, in which electrodes are placed on the baby's head (it's nowhere near as bad as it sounds) to detect brain responses from sounds played via earphones.

So as you can see, your newborn will be given a pretty rigorous check-up in her first few days. If, as most babies do, she passes her first ever set of exams with flying colours, you'll be relieved and proud in equal measure.

But things don't always go to plan where delicate new lives are concerned. Between 6%–10% of babies spend some time in a neonatal or special care unit through ill health, premature birth or because they need special monitoring (for example, if the mother was diabetic).

SPECIAL CARE IN A SPECIAL PLACE

There are many reasons why your baby could be admitted to the neonatal ward – including being born prematurely, underweight or because of a range of illnesses or conditions, including any maternal conditions that may have affected the baby.

Although the circumstances may vary, what's true in every case is the utter shock that you as parents feel watching your son or daughter struggle.

When our youngest son was born unexpectedly six weeks early, we spent almost a month helplessly watching as he fought off severe jaundice. He was fed via a tube into his tiny stomach while he slowly learnt the sucking reflex he'd not had time to perfect in the womb.

Compared with many of the other children in the unit he was a big healthy boy at four pounds odd and he had no conditions that required surgery. But to us it was the most intense and initially bewildering period of our entire lives.

We sat for hour after hour peering into the incubator, listening to the beeps of the monitors plugged into our boy. The sight of another couple on the ward getting ready to take their baby home filled us with hope and a desperate longing to be able to do the same.

As the days passed, and we got to know and talk to the staff as they expertly went about their business, we began to realise how lucky we were. Neonatal nurses and doctors are the crème de la crème. While in the labour ward, it's sometimes the case that dads are treated, or at least can be made to feel, like a spare part, I never felt this once in the neonatal unit. Every dad I spoke to during my time there said the same.

There are usually three different levels of care on neonatal units depending on your baby's needs.

1. Intensive care (neonatal intensive care, or NICU), for the most gravely ill or premature babies.
2. High dependency (HD) care, for babies who are not on the critical list but who still need complex care.
3. Special care (SC), for otherwise well babies who are catching up on growth and development after a premature birth, or those who are getting better after more complex treatment.

Some babies move through these levels as they improve, or heart-breakingly back again if they regress.

Most neonatal units are open 24 hours a day for parents to visit. When you can't be at the hospital – or when you wake up in the morning at home after a fitful night's sleep and the memory of what is happening floods back – you can call the nursery and talk directly to the nurse who is caring for your baby.

Remember that just because there's a high level of medical care being delivered, you and your partner still know your baby best and your instincts are to be trusted. In my experience, the staff recognise and encourage this and treat you as part of the team.

There are many ways you can help your baby, such as getting involved in the feeding, even if this is via tube. Most wards have breast pumps and cold storage space so that new mums can express milk so that even if the baby can't suckle yet, they are still getting their mother's milk and all the benefits that brings.

You can also do all of the usual baby-care duties such as washing and changing them if your baby is strong enough. If your baby is small, this will take some getting used to, especially for first-time parents, but the staff generally have infinite patience and expertise and will guide you through.

'Kangaroo care' is also something that not just benefits your baby, but also does you the power of good. It's nothing complex, but the results have been proved to be remarkable. You simply hold your nappy-only baby inside your shirt upright against your bare skin with her head turned so her ear is above your heart. The technique, pioneered in the mid-80s in Bogotá, Colombia, was devised because of the lack of reliable power and equipment available – almost immediately the mortality rate fell from 70% to 30%.

The most important thing you can do is to look after yourself and – crucially – your partner during this tough time. Leaving a baby in hospital after she has been discharged is perhaps one of the most painful and unnatural of experiences a mother can have. You need to be there to help her come through it, despite the worry and angst you are feeling yourself.

What's for certain is that if your newborn has to spend time in neonatal, they could not be in better hands.

In a strange way we left the ward feeling that in an ideal, budget-no-issue world, this is the kind of post-birth care everyone would receive. Not the incubators and the feeding tubes, but the one-to-one care; the staff with the time and expertise to reassure and educate; and the sense that when you depart, you do so with real confidence that you and your child have been looked after to an exceptionally high standard.

Words from your fellow fathers:

Ben, father of two: The care my wife and baby received was amazing on both occasions.

We had our first at a hospital with a doctor on call as we were worried about complications. However, after the baby was born we then transferred to a midwife-led unit at our nearest hospital. It was like a baby hotel and the staff were incredible. It was very relaxed and there was plenty of time for the midwives to help my wife learn how to bath the baby, feed, etc. They even took him for a couple of hours to make sure she got some sleep.

We had our second at the midwife-led unit and they all remembered my wife and this made her feel at ease during the birth. Five-star service.

Nick, father of two: Evenings were quite lonely for my wife and a more brutal nurse type tends to be on duty.

My wife spent the days complaining that her new first born was ginger – my fault due to an unrevealed gene that had crept in a few generations back. She was quite vocal about it until the curtain around the bed next door was pulled back and revealed a young family together with close relations, all of whom were about as ginger as it gets.

In the end I upgraded her to a private room. Money well spent – comfortable, quiet and relaxed. Only disturbed once or twice by the delivery of Bounty baby bags made up of baby brands such as Pampers, nappy rash creams and – scarily – Red Bull (someone knew what I was in for).

A man came in and asked if we would like a family photo for £10. I then realised what a baby factory I was in, complete with cross-sell and up-sell opportunities.

Stuart, father of two: Our hospital experience was pretty good all round except being turfed out at four in the morning after my partner had been in labour for over 27 hours.

Leaving her alone to fend for this new little person that we'd made together made me feel sad looking back, but at the time I was still shell-shocked that it was all for real.

I was allowed back at about 8ish, so for the sake of a few hours you'd think they would have let me stay?

PROGRESS REPORT, EARLY DAYS

Your baby

Life outside the womb must be pretty bewildering in these first few days for the newborn baby. Understandably, they spend much of their time becoming accustomed to the light, noise and amount of space they have to unfurl their scrunched-up limbs.

Your newborn's vision is pretty blurry at this stage. She can only see well up to about 45cm/18in away – which, as it cleverly happens, is about the distance from the breast to the mother's face – so keep close to her whenever she's alert.

Her specialist subject is the face for this early spell and you'll catch her staring you down at any given opportunity. This intent study is her way of memorising your features so she can recognise the people who are legally responsible for her welfare should any litigation be required at a later date.

While it's a strict diet of milk at this stage, your baby's taste buds can already distinguish between sweet and sour flavours, so she can tell the difference between fresh and gone-off versions of the white stuff.

Other than perfecting face recognition technology and establishing a burgeoning career as a milk tester, she will also be weeing up to 18 times a day and pooing anything between four and seven times daily. As long as she is having at least one bowel movement a day, things are probably OK in that department. A single 24-hour span without a poo isn't cause for panic as long as the nappies continue to be wet, but any longer than that and it's time to seek medical advice. Your baby should poo within 24 hours of birth.

In terms of colour and consistency, in the early days, a newborn's poo tends to be thick and dark green in colour. This first proto-poop is called meconium – which is so sticky and seemingly indestructible that it could be the answer to the pothole problems that blight our roads.

As your baby starts to feed properly you will be confronted, on opening the nappy, by yellowish matter which has more than a passing resemblance to chicken korma. It is usual for your baby's poo to vary in colour each day depending – if she is breastfeeding – on what your partner has been eating.

Your partner

If all has gone well, your partner will be beyond relieved that your baby is healthy and that she herself has managed to get through the labour, which has hung over her like the sword of Damocles for nine months.

As we will see in the next chapter, there's an awful lot of physical recovering to be done. But for now the sense of post-birth achievement, pride and love mixes in nicely with exhaustion and a healthy shot of anxiety and apprehension at how she will perform as a mum. As far as I can tell, this cocktail is ever present throughout parenthood to a greater or lesser degree.

Being in hospital is rarely a joy, no matter what the circumstances, so being there to make life even a modicum better for her is a must. Speaking to the staff, taking charge of your baby so she can go for a tentative wander, bringing in her favourite food, whatever it takes, she'll really appreciate it.

As if she needed any added pain, it's normal for your partner to be constipated for at least a couple of days after having the baby. She's had high levels of the hormone progesterone in her body during pregnancy, and her digestive system has almost shut down completely during labour as all available resources were mustered for the main job in hand. It may well be a while before normal service is resumed.

If she's anxious about the first time she does do a 'number two', try and reassure her about it and suggest she tries to take her mind off it by reading a magazine. She doesn't need to make life harder than it already is by being tense in the vital area. If she's had a C-section, she might have been given a mild laxative to make things a bit easier.

Welcome to your new world!

You

There's something magical about the few days between when your first baby is born and when mother and child finally arrive home.

I remember prancing around about like Norman Wisdom after my eldest was born. I floated into the florist to get my wife some flowers and told the kindly woman who ran the place just how beautiful my son was and how in awe of his mother I felt, like I was the very first new father to have happened across her shop. (I didn't know that the flowers would end up on the nurses' desk because they were banned from the ward for hygiene reasons.)

That's how you feel – yes you know that during the time it's taken you to choose between fuchsias and roses another 20 infants have been born elsewhere on the planet, but it matters not – you feel elated and proud and special and why not?

You are.

Milk it and enjoy every minute. If you have a second it will still be amazing but because you'll have another youngster in need of some care and attention back home you won't be able to give it the Mr Grimsdale impression in quite the same way.

THE FIRST DAY OF THE REST OF YOUR LIFE

The time has come to take your new family home and begin your life as a father.

From the moment you check for the ninth time that the car seat is secured properly before you drive away from the hospital, you will feel the weight of responsibility and nervousness wrestling with the giddiness of excitement and pride inside your overcrowded head.

It may be a cliché, but when your front door closes behind you, the chances are you and your partner will glance at each other in time-honoured fashion and wonder – what now?

The answer will soon become very apparent.

This first intense three-month spell is about one thing: getting to know the little person who has just moved into your home. Getting to know how she feeds, how she reacts, how she sleeps (good luck with that one) – getting to know who and how she is.

You should have at least two weeks' paternity leave (the generosity of it) so you can explore and enjoy the new arrival with your partner as you both begin the ever-evolving process of finding out how you will parent your child.

Perhaps the most fundamental of all the areas you'll be tackling as a couple will be how to keep your milk-obsessed baby well fed. As we will see in detail, fundamental it may be, straightforward it most certainly isn't.

A very close cousin of the M word is the T word – thrive. Your baby's growth, general health and toilet habits will become your household's new fixation. Forget the football, forget the holidays, forget the extension to the kitchen you've always talked about; centile lines, Sudocrem and mastitis will be the new idiom at your place.

Like the earliest people on the planet, you now live in a world of firsts; the first bath, the first cry you can't calm, the first smile – they just keep on coming. Each one represents a challenge or a moment of joy (often at the same time) that will grab your undivided attention in a way you would not believe.

Your partner, as well as facing the biggest challenge of her life, is also recovering from the kind of physical and hormonal kicking that only women have the fortitude to withstand once, let alone a number of times.

'Baby blues', a term so weak and patronising that it should be booted from the baby lexicon for good, can and often does strike. The more you know about it ahead of time, the more you'll be able to help. Its bigger and altogether more serious brother, postnatal depression, is also something you need to be clued up on.

And don't think you're immune, either.

These first three months may sound daunting, and I won't lie to you, it is, but you'll get through it. What's more, I hope that amid all the nappies and the night feeds you'll be able to find moments when you can breathe in the magnitude and magnificence of what you are doing.

And you can help your partner take time away from the coalface to do the same.

I promise you'll be through this stage before you know where you are and you'll probably even begin to miss it.

It just doesn't feel like it's ever going to end at the time, that's all.

FEEDING YOUR BABY

I remember thinking as I skipped into hospital swinging an empty car seat to and fro that in half an hour's time or so everything would be different.

There's no other moment in your life when you will be entrusted with something so delicate, fragile and precious as when you collect your baby and head for home.

Once you've had the obligatory GULP! moment when reality dawns that the pair of you need to immediately transform from looking after yourselves pretty badly, to taking care of someone else fantastically well, stuff begins to happen.

For your baby this isn't a particularly momentous occasion. This is just the next moment on her unstoppable march towards growth and development. In the first few weeks a huge driver of those twin objectives is eating.

There's very little that's as fundamental or as emotive for you and your partner in the first few months of parenthood as the process of feeding your baby.

You'd think it would be a doddle – what could be more straight-forward? The hungry little one can either take sustenance from the two ready-made milk dispensers that your partner has cleverly developed, or if for whatever reason that doesn't appeal, formula milk is a tried and tested alternative that works perfectly well for millions.

Job done, let's move on, time to start worrying about university tuition fees.

Not quite.

For many, many mothers breastfeeding is incredibly hard. It can be excruciatingly painful. Given that the breast has yet to evolve into a translucent container with clearly defined ounce markings it can also be very hard to know, especially in the crucial first few weeks, when and if your baby has had her fill.

Then there's the stigma, guilt and even shame around the whole area of 'breastfeeding failure' which many new mothers feel when things don't go to plan.

You have a big part to play here, not just as chief bottle washer if that's the route you end up taking, but also in supporting your partner through what can be a highly emotional and devilishly difficult time.

To do that you'll need to understand some of the details at the heart of the breast vs bottle debate.

Breastfeeding

Barely a week goes by, it seems, without a new study reinforcing that breast is best on all sorts of levels.

As well as providing the most nutritious food for newborns and infants, breastmilk contains antibodies that help protect against a host of childhood illnesses and chronic diseases. It has also been claimed that breastfeeding can reduce the incidence of childhood obesity.

According to studies, infants who are breastfed also have lower risk of gastroenteritis, respiratory tract infections, childhood leukaemia, asthma, allergies, diabetes, heart disease, hypertension, cot death – the list just keeps on growing.

Even the act of breastfeeding appears to be capable of developing proper jaw and teeth alignment in your child. Some studies have also indicated that breastfed babies have slightly higher intelligence quotients (IQs) than those who are bottlefed.

A study published in May 2011 even found that children who are breastfed for four months or more develop fewer behaviour problems in later life. This is believed to be due to the make-up of the milk itself and/or the better mother/baby interaction that breastfeeding fosters.

It doesn't stop there – mothers also benefit. Breastfeeding mums burn more calories and can drop pre-pregnancy weight more quickly and according to research they even have decreased risks of postnatal depression, type 2 diabetes, breast and ovarian cancers and bone density problems.

The US Department of Health even goes as far to say that the American nation benefits when mothers breastfeed. It explains that if 90% of US newborns were breastfed exclusively for six months, the US would save $13 billion per year because medical care costs are lower for fully breastfed infants.

Just in case the message hasn't hit home hard enough, Uncle Sam also lobs in that breastfeeding contributes to a more productive national workforce because mothers miss less work to care for sick infants.

And – oh yeah – it'll also help save the planet because it produces less waste.

No pressure then.

A lot of that impressive body of evidence is common sense. Breastmilk is a dynamic fluid that changes throughout your baby's life. It's the food nature intended them to have and it's available without the need for spending money on formula and discarding the empties.

As ever, it seems that there's another argument to listen to. In 2009 Michael Kramer, a professor of paediatrics who has advised the World Health Organization and UNICEF (the United Nations Children's Fund) claimed that much of the evidence used to persuade mothers to breastfeed was either wrong or out of date.

He observed that because mothers who breastfed were often more likely to follow advice on all health issues in general, their conscientious approach was more likely to explain a lot of the benefits attributed to breastmilk, rather than the miraculous substance itself.

While he said that some of the claims were well-founded, he added that:

> The formula milk industry jumps on every piece of equivocal evidence. But the breastfeeding lobby have a way of ignoring the evidence. Both sides are not being very scientific.

Despite some doubts over the degrees involved, it does seem pretty clear and in many ways logical that breast is indeed best for the baby – but is it always an achievable or even desirable goal for every mother? The answer is no. Many new mums find the mechanics of breastfeeding impossible or that simply making a choice right from the off isn't for them.

While what's been called the 'breastmilk mafia' has a habit of sneering somewhat on those that make the latter call, it's crucial your partner feels you back her to the hilt, whatever she decides.

The elusive 'latch'

The Department of Health's recommendation for feeding infants is that exclusive breastfeeding for the first six months is the best approach.

The Department's own Infant Feeding Survey painted a picture of a reality in sharp contrast with that ideal.

While 76% of mothers said that they wanted to breastfeed at the very start of their pregnancy (this number had encouragingly risen to 80% in the preliminary findings of a 2010 study), just one week in, the number exclusively doing so was down to 45%.

By six weeks the figure had dropped to 21% and at the four-month mark just 7% of babies still had breastmilk as their sole sustenance.

By six months the figure was, in the words of the survey, 'negligible'.

When you consider the same survey found that eight in every 10 mums said they were aware of the health benefits of breastfeeding it does raise the question: What the hell's going on?

The answer seems to be that while women are encouraged to start breastfeeding by the state and the medical profession, the support that many new mums need to become comfortable and confident with breastfeeding isn't there for long enough. So they move on to bottle-feeding. One study showed that two-thirds of midwives interviewed did not even discuss formula feeding with new parents.

The trouble is that breastfeeding, despite being as natural a bodily function as sneezing, is a fiendishly delicate thing to perfect, with the latch at the heart of it all.

If your baby isn't connecting with your partner's nipple in the right way (there are a plethora of videos on YouTube showing the 'correct' latch if you want to see for yourself) it can cause the devil's own trouble with cracked, painful or even bleeding nipples rendering the whole process a nightmare.

While you can't guarantee a pain-free breastfeeding experience for your partner, you can make a tangible day-to-day difference when she is attempting to make it work. Breastfeeding seems to bring on an instantaneous killer thirst and major hunger pangs. So: is she comfortable, does she have a drink and a snack and has she got somewhere warm and quiet to focus on the task in hand?

Even with all the environmental touches in place things can still be tough and painful. Mastitis, when the breast tissue becomes inflamed and then often infected due to milk build-up, is also an all-too-common occurrence. It can lead to a thoroughly miserable time for your poor partner.

And the physical pain often isn't even the worst of it. What adds to the pressure is that while each feed seems to become more of a disaster to the increasingly fraught mum, you are both faced with a newborn baby who needs to be fed.

The logical response in this situation is to express some milk and bottle-feed while still trying to get the hang of the breast technique. Or, if expressing is too painful, use bottle-fed formula to buy some time to get things right.

Logical but very controversial – welcome to the 'nipple confusion' debate.

This hot issue centres around advice often given in recent years that if your baby so much as looks at a bottle teat they will reject the real deal out of hand.

The thinking being that the bottle offers up a reservoir of milk so easy to get at that your canny baby will simply cock a snook at Mother Nature's finest from that moment onwards. (By the way, both shaking your head for no and sticking your tongue out for displeasure are believed to be derived from ways that babies tell you they've had enough milk.)

This line of thinking is slowly being debunked and the pressure on new mums to perfect breastfeeding within the first few days, without having the safety net of the bottle to see them through, is gradually being lifted.

Clare Byam-Cook, a leading feeding specialist, is particularly vigorous in putting the boot into the nipple/teat naysayers in her book *What to Expect When You're Breastfeeding . . . And What if You Can't?* giving realistic and pragmatic advice to mums.

Technique is at the heart of many a breastfeeding problem and conflicting or mis-information abounds from midwives, health visitors, friends and even parents. So doing some research ahead of time and calling in help when things are tough will pay dividends.

The first few days after birth are crucial for breastfeeding success. The super-rich, super-powerful colostrum is up for grabs before your partner's milk is 'let down', but statistics show that, the drop-off is a very steep one after that first week.

If your partner needs help with her technique in those first few days, don't be shy in getting on the phone (with her consent) and talking to community midwives. Ideally, ask a breastfeeding special-ist, if there's one in the area, to come round and help out. Or there's the National Childbirth Trust Infant Feeding helpline on 0300 330 0700 and the NHS national breastfeeding helpline on 0300 100 0212 – both of which can hook you up with a specialist breastfeeding counsellor quickly.

If you don't ask, you won't get, and it can make all the difference.

Quantity

Another issue that can kick breastfeeding into the long grass is the fact that you never really know just how much milk your baby has had – and there's no conclusive way of finding out.

There are signs you can look out for, which – while not being as decisive as an empty bottle – at least give you both a clue how things are going.

If your baby is feeding at least six to eight times a day that's a very good sign. And so too if the act of breastfeeding itself is painless for your partner.

While the feed is taking place, your baby should be noticeably swallowing and changing her rhythm of sucking and even pausing during the feed to take a breather. Wet nappies are another key indicator – once she's past five days old or so your baby should have at least six to eight wet nappies every 24 hours, and the wee itself should also be pale and relatively odourless.

Your baby's poo should be a yellowy mustard colour if feeding is firing on all cylinders. Looking at the Dulux colour chart, you're after a deposit giving off a 'sunflower symphony'-type glow. And your partner should sense that her breasts feel emptier and softer after a good feed, too.

So you can see there's a lot going on for the new mother in your house. If things take a turn for the worse early on it really can reduce the first few weeks of motherhood to a guilt-ridden carnival of cracked nipples and crying.

Not good.

Your support, love and understanding are crucial. The social and moral pressure that some mums feel to succeed as they put themselves through hell can be overwhelming. Knowing that you support her whatever the outcome will go a long way to giving her the belief to either carry on trying or to make the switch to formula. She can feel safe in the knowledge that it is a joint decision free from shame, blame or judgement.

Bottle-feeding

If, for whatever reason, you decided to go down the formula route, rather than being the social pariahs you may consider yourselves, the figures, as we have seen, show you are in the majority. So give yourselves a break and crack on.

There are father-specific benefits to bottle-feeding. You can help share the burden and take the strain of some of the feeds, especially the night-time ones.

Yeah! (More enthusiasm needed please.)

What is unequivocally joysome is the fact that you get to share in the closeness and serenity of looking into your baby's eyes as you help them grow and thrive. It's a very lovely thing, feeding your baby, and while down the line you'll no doubt have your phone on the arm of the sofa, the TV on silent and a paper balanced on your feet, it's worth, for these first few months at least, finding a peaceful spot and lapping up every moment of your babe in arms. She will be a running, jumping, talking little person very soon indeed.

Not that bottle-feeding is a breeze. You've got to sterilise the equipment, make up the bottle in the correct way and give your baby said bottle while causing as little wind and vomit as possible. You can manage all that, though, you're a dad now.

If you notice any lingering guilt your partner may be feeling about bottle-feeding do your level best to expel it. Your lives as parents are full of decisions and choices you'll need to make that affect your child, and this is just one of them.

If your baby is content, enjoying every drop of their bottles and vitally, as we are about to see, thriving, then just count your blessings and enjoy.

THRIVING

No matter how you decide to feed your baby you will become obsessed, consumed and just a little boring to almost everyone else on the planet about how your little one is progressing on her growth chart in her first few weeks and months.

Most babies lose some weight in the first two weeks of life as they shed the extra fluid they are born with. A healthy newborn is expected to lose 7%–10% of their birth weight but should regain that weight by about two weeks after birth. During their first month, most newborns continue to gain weight at a rate of at least five ounces (141g) a week. Many newborns go through a period of rapid growth when they are 7–10 days old and again at three and six weeks.

If your baby was born significantly prematurely, your health professionals will use what's called her corrected age, taking account of her early birth date, when they mark her progress on the chart.

Many factors determine how heavy or tall your baby will be. If and when you are told that your little beauty is on the 11th centile for weight – essentially meaning that 89% of other babies her age weigh more, try and curb any competitive, 'there must be some mistake, do the calculation again, do it again I tell you!' outbursts.

It's fine.

What matters is that your baby sticks pretty much to that line as she grows. Whether she is on the 1st, 50th or 100th mark doesn't really matter. What quickly becomes important is that she doesn't consistently dip below where she should be. If she does, there's a chance you could hear the words 'failure to thrive' mentioned by a doctor or health visitor. Some babies gradually slide up or down the centiles over the first year. This is usually normal, and called 'catch up' or 'catch down' growth and is due to genetic factors kicking in.

Failure to thrive

It's hard to think of a more dread-laden phrase. It's immediately terrifying and has the potential to extract more fluid from your guilt glands than anything you've ever heard before in your entire life. All it really means is that your baby is growing more slowly than other children of the same age.

There's no real agreed definition for the term. The diagnosis usually comes about directly from the lack of the required progress over a period of time as shown on the growth chart, rather than from any specific physical signs.

If you find yourself having to deal with this situation, don't let guilt dominate your thoughts. The problem may well be easy to put right and feeling guilty isn't going to help make that happen.

What will get things back on track is working with your health visitor or doctor to find the cause. As part of that process, they may well watch your partner breastfeed or you both bottle-feed your baby, to see if there are any obvious issues with the amount of milk your baby is getting.

Sometimes the problem can be caused by an allergy or intestinal problems. In very rare cases it can indicate a more serious underlying problem – and it goes without saying that the earlier anything like that is spotted the better.

Words from your fellow fathers:

Murray, father of two: I remember a general feeling when we first got home that I/we weren't competent enough to look after such a small thing that relied on us totally.

You realise that in time that instinct is generally right – this is what you are meant to do.

Mark, father of one: My wife tried breastfeeding for the first month and she didn't really get on with it, she found it painful and we had a hungry baby on our hands!

She tried expressing which helped but we didn't last long. There was not much I could do other than be supportive of what she wanted. She was trying her best and it was all new and daunting so no point creating more stress than we needed, particularly when there seem to be so many good alternatives.

Colin, father of two: Breastfeeding was a nightmare to begin with. My wife suffered terrible cracked nipples, bleeding, infections, the lot. To her credit, though, she pushed through and ended up feeding for seven months.

I felt so helpless during the tough times – the hardest thing was not knowing how much milk baby was getting and how much is left in the boob.

If only there was a gauge to let you know how much is left. Maybe someone will design an app for that!

Steve, father of two: *I actively encouraged my wife to breastfeed for as long as possible . . . 'it's amazing for the baby, you've got to persevere.'*

Some argued that my enthusiasm was partly because it meant she always had to get up with the baby when she cried for food and I didn't have to – and in hindsight they probably had a point.

I remember thinking so clearly after a while that maybe we needed to go to bottles when my wife had reached a level of exhaustion which is difficult to articulate. She was trying to feed our daughter in bed but kept falling asleep. Olivia was inches away from the breast dripping in milk, but could not quite reach it.

This wake-up call for me meant that from then on we used the bottle and our daughter got stronger faster and as a result slept more – resulting in more sleep for ourselves.

I learnt to not be so selfish with our second child, although my wife had heard all of my lines before and would never have fallen for them the second time round anyway!

Nick, father of two: *My wife didn't enjoy the breastfeeding experience. She found it really painful.*

The other challenge was pumping. It becomes quite clear that pumping unused milk was essential. We went for a double pump (we're those kind of people – a double pump family). I was in charge of trying to get the pump to work. Reading the German instructions, at 2am, crouched on the landing in just my boxer shorts, was a low point.

THE S WORD: PART 1

Sleep is going to become your new obsession.

Your sleep, your baby's sleep, your partner's sleep – you'll come to think about them all an awful lot.

In fact, it could keep you awake at night, if you were getting any sleep to interrupt, that is.

Rather than trying to re-establish a 'normal' sleeping regime in your household it's best, for these first few weeks at least, to just accept it.

Accept that you will be tired, accept that you will be beyond tired and accept that despite it all, you'll just have to carry on. Think of it not as something to be endured but as a rite of passage, an extreme sport to be taken on and beaten.

With that in mind, let's leave the tips and techniques for later when your baby is ready to play ball.

Sleep: the facts

New-born babies sleep a lot – up to 18 hours a day for the first few weeks and 15 hours a day by three months.

Sounds great, what's all the fuss about? Thing is, she'll probably never sleep for more than three or four hours at a time, day or night.

Killer that it is, this is a crucial phase for your baby. These short sleep cycles mean she will spend more time in rapid eye movement (REM) sleep, allowing her brain to carry out the truly remarkable changes it needs to.

The phenomenal transformation you'll witness in your child over her first year, from her behaviour and understanding to her interaction is driven by a period of brain development and activity which puts us adults to shame.

Interestingly, boys' and girl's brains develop differently in a very physical sense. A boy's brain develops from the back – the doing part – towards the front – the thinking part – whereas a girl's brain develops in the opposite direction. What that means is that boys develop their physical abilities before they start to think about them.

Sounds familiar.

Whereas girls develop more of their thinking and language skills first, which helps to explain why girls seem to race ahead when the time for school comes around.

In some small way the knowledge that your disturbed sleep is helping your baby to think for herself might help you feel a bit less cranky as you walk up and down the landing for the third time that night – not that much less, mind you.

Things change quickly. At six to eight weeks, most babies begin to sleep for shorter spells during the day and longer periods at night, although most continue to wake up for at least one feed.

It is possible, apparently, for some babies to sleep through the night when they are as young as eight weeks old, but it's the exception to the rule. It won't feel like that when seemingly every other couple you know is claiming to have a 'go-through-the-nighter' from about day four. They are liars, liars I tell you! In all probability your little one will be up at night for at least the first few months or, often, for much longer than that.

Sorry.

There is a whole world of techniques, methods and philosophies for getting your baby to sleep. We shall wade into the sodden fields of the 'baby wars', as the fierce debate around them has been dubbed, in the next chapter.

For now, let's look at one area of the sleep arena that has claimed thousands of utterly tragic casualties over the years, but which finally seems to be on the retreat – cot death.

Cot death

If miscarriage is the spectre that haunts early pregnancy, then cot death is the dark cloud hanging over the new parent.

Cot death, also known as SIDS – sudden infant death syndrome – isn't an illness but a diagnosis given when an apparently healthy baby dies without warning.

There are around 135 cot deaths in the UK each year – a number which represents more than an 85% fall since the introduction of the Reduce the Risk campaign in 1991. At the heart of this campaign was the message that putting your baby to sleep on its front was a contributory factor in cot death.

Since then, 'Back to Sleep' has become a watch phrase in baby care and taking the simple measure of putting your little one to sleep on their back is proving to be a key factor in winning the battle over this truly petrifying phenomenon.

But despite the success of the past 20 years, no one knows for sure why SIDS happens. Ongoing research points to a number of potential factors at play. They include the suggestion that certain babies have a problem with the part of the brain that controls breathing and how they wake.

Whatever the true reasons, cot death can occur not just over-night in the cot, but also during a nap at any time of day. For reasons that are not fully understood, it also seems to be more common during winter. The second month is when most deaths occur and nearly 90% of cot deaths happen in babies under six months, with the risk reducing as the baby grows older. Very few cot deaths take place after one year old.

So there's a lot we don't know, but what do we know about the risk factors and how to mitigate against them? While there's no way to guarantee the prevention of cot death there are a widely accepted set of steps which can help keep your baby safe.

- Cut out smoking in pregnancy. That's both of you – and once your baby is born don't let anyone smoke in the same room as your baby.
- Place your baby on her back to sleep – and not on the front or side.
- Do not let your baby get too hot, and keep her head uncovered while she sleeps and/or while she is indoors in general.
- Place your baby with her feet to the foot of the cot, to prevent her wriggling down under the covers. You can use a baby sleep bag from three months onwards.
- Never sleep with your baby on a sofa or armchair. By far the safest place for your baby to sleep is in a crib or cot in a room with you for the first six months.
- It's particularly dangerous for your baby to sleep in your bed if you or your partner:
- are a smoker, even if you never smoke in bed or at home
- have been drinking alcohol
- take medication or drugs that make you feel drowsy
- are just very tired (which you will be), or
- if your baby was born before 37 weeks or weighed less than 2.5kg or 5½ lbs at birth.
- Using a dummy to settle your baby to sleep can reduce the risk of cot death according to some studies, potentially because the

handle of the dummy keeps air flow open if they end up on their front. The advice is if you plan to breastfeed make sure you are well established before introducing the dummy.

• Breastfeeding itself is also thought to reduce the risk.

In other areas, the debate around SIDS is an ongoing and, in some cases, confusing one. For example, how useful are baby movement monitors that sound an alarm if they cannot detect a baby's breathing movement?

Another contentious issue is around swaddling. This ancient technique of pacifying infants has made something of a comeback in recent years.

But recent research has advised parents to proceed with caution – a view echoed by the leading body in the field, the Foundation for the Study of Infant Death.

What is key to remember is that cot death is uncommon and becomes increasingly rare after the age of five months – which is about the time when babies are able to roll over and move a bit under their own steam. The measures listed above reduce the small risk of cot death even further. If you can, try not to let this nasty unsolved mystery play on your mind constantly to the point that it becomes debilitating for you, your partner and ultimately your baby.

Words from your fellow fathers:

Murray, father of two: *Lack of sleep was the worst bit of the whole thing and the major factor in nearly every argument we had. I think we both suffered really badly.*

Nick, father of two: *I found the lack of sleep the toughest, it is not the first night of no sleep – to be honest we have all been through no* *sleep in our lives pre-babies – you just deal with it. The thing that is hard is the constant lack of sleep, you can never catch up. It goes on and on day after day. You have to change your lifestyle in the first few months (I didn't). It is not the all night of not sleeping either, it is being woken in the night (even if you aren't doing anything) and the early morning and late nights due to feeding the baby. It is the broken sleep, that lack of quality sleep.*

Winston, father of two: *Even four years into being a dad, I never sleep for eight hours solid. I may well have had my last night of unbroken sleep. I didn't used to look my age but I do now.*

Ben, father of two: *The adrenalin is incredible when you have a baby and I think we both managed well for the first couple of months but it hit us both around three months when you are just worn down by it all.*

You just have to take it in turns to get a lie-in, afternoon doze, anything. Never ever turn down the opportunity of sleep, even if it is just at traffic lights, preferably when they are on red.

THE FIRST TIME FOR ABSOLUTELY EVERYTHING

Having your first child changes your entire life, everybody knows that.

On all sorts of serious, grown-up levels, becoming a dad can rearrange the furniture in your head and give your emotions a good rinsing at the same time.

But as well as the profound stuff, fatherhood also does something much more prosaic. It takes the confident, worldly, knowing man that you no doubt are and busts you back to the status of a novice.

Within these first three months you and your partner will face a bewildering barrage of situations for which you can call on very few frames of reference.

Whether it's seeing your baby smile for the first time (and wanting to strangle the fifth person to tell you that it's just wind) or changing a nappy that looks like there's an alien lifeform in it, it's safe to say that this is a period in your life when new things will happen to you on an almost daily basis.

The first big cry

Chances are your baby will have cried in hospital, she may have even cried the moment her little head hit the air. But there is often a moment once you've got home when for the very first time you and your partner are witness to your immediate future.

'Wow, she's got a great set of lungs on her,' you'll say nervously. Inwardly you'll be thinking, 'I can't take that, that's not a cry, it's an artillery onslaught, a non-stop barrage of noise sharper and more penetrating than any bullet.'

'Hasn't she just?' your partner will say, inwardly smiling as you get to hear what she had to deal with on her own in hospital for the past few nights.

Crying is designed solely to grab your attention, and evolution has engineered it so the noise is as effective as possible at doing just that. In fact it is so powerful that some women can lactate just by hearing a cry and it doesn't even have to emanate from their own baby.

So don't worry if crying gets to you, it's meant to.

Your part of the bargain as parent and protector is to try and work out what has caused the cry and remedy it. The term 'easier said than done' could well have been coined in response to this very situation.

The perceived wisdom is that they are either hungry, tired, lonely or uncomfortable – the latter covering anything from a dirty nappy to wind and temperature.

In recent years the 'science' of interpreting what each type of cry means has moved from the realms of mother's intuition to big business. There are even iPhone apps that purport to tell you what your baby wants.

The Dunstan Baby Language system, for instance, claims to have isolated each cry to a remarkable degree and lists the different sounds as:

- Neh I'm hungry
- Owh I'm sleepy
- Heh I'm experiencing discomfort
- Eh I have wind
- Eairh I have lower wind
- Ey Wassup I've been allowed to watch too much telly.

While I may well have misremembered the final one, they are big claims, although not ones that have been scientifically verified in any significant way.

Even if you can speak fluent baby, you'll still no doubt find yourself in a situation where sating your relentlessly crying child is seemingly impossible. The stress this can cause, especially when you throw in chronic fatigue, is not to be underestimated. Working as a team to help each other out is crucial, but if you are on your own, take deep breaths, remember that your baby is doing all it knows how to do and that it will pass.

Honestly.

The first nasty nappy change

Whoever does the PR for nappy changing needs a talking to, it's just not that bad.

All right, on occasions you'll put your finger in something disagreeable, but at least it's your baby's disagreeable produce. If, by some freak of nature, you are unlucky enough to find yourself changing the nappy of someone else's child you will come to see your own offspring's excrement in a whole new and favourable light.

Technique-wise, disposable nappies are as straightforward as it gets and gone are the days when you needed advanced origami to pin a towelling nappy together. (If you are planning to go with the old-style nappies by the way, I doff my cap to you and also say a little prayer.)

A few little tips are worth knowing. First there are the three Ps – Preparation Prevents Pootastrophy. A fully stocked changing table is a beautiful thing. Once you open the Pandora's Box of a full nappy, putting a lid back on it again while you try and find some baby wipes is not an easy thing to do.

Likewise if you are doing a change on the hoof, have the essential kit within arm's length or woe betide both you and that nice clean T-shirt you've got on.

When you do open things up, try and use the inside front part of the nappy to get the first wipe in. It will collect a very decent amount of poo from the soft little bottom of your cherub and will leave you just the detritus to deal with. Graphic, I know, but you'll be thankful of it.

As babies get a bit older, they often don't like having their nappy changed and distraction is the key here. The fear of your little one getting her hands in her own doings as you clean up, lives with all of us at every nappy change. If it happens, you are in the lap of the gods, as what is essentially a dirty protest unfolds before your very eyes. Perhaps the best thing to do is just revel in your baby's creativity as she cavè paints all over your white wall or — especially if you have a boy — creates a charming water feature right there in your living room.

You're not truly a dad until you have a face full of something nasty.

The first smile

Your baby's first proper social smile can occur as early as four weeks post-birth — and after the month or so you and your partner will likely have had, a little bit of a reward will be gratefully received.

As ever, the timings of this joyous happening can vary a lot, so don't worry that you have spawned a mini Morrissey if you don't get belly laughs when you're expecting them.

If you are lucky enough to see a smile even earlier than the four-week mark, don't let any sour-faced fool dismiss it as wind — smile right back and let the love in.

As well as being a beautiful thing to witness, early smiles play a big part in your baby's seemingly innate desire to communicate with the two most important people in its life. From very early on they can imitate the facial gestures of their parents — try sticking your tongue out, even to a newborn.

Your little one is programmed to hold your gaze and engage you in a social tête à tête — which has you hooked right from the off.

The time you spend gazing into your baby's eyes won't just lower your stress levels, but will be a key part of the development of your baby and the bond you share with her.

The first bath

Nervy one this, and definitely a team sport – the four hands that you and your partner can muster hardly seem enough in the early days.

Getting the temperature right is crucial and not that easy first up. So petrified was I of putting our beautiful baby into scalding hot water that I had the tendency to put him in what was essentially an ice bath instead. An experience he did not enjoy.

Spending a few quid on a little plastic thermometer which tells you when it is spot on is a good move, if you don't trust the age-old trick of testing the temperature with your elbow.

Even when the water is perfect, the first few bathtimes can still be a little unsettling for all concerned. Strangely enough newborn babies don't always react well to either being naked and exposed, or being lowered back first into a strange wet bowl.

So with a hand to support the neck and head and the other one under the body the trick is to slide the baby as gently as gently can be into the water, feet first. Once she is in, you become acutely aware that you are essentially holding a live salmon in your hands. Coupled with the frighteningly painful position you have put your back into as you leant over the bath, you begin to wonder if you will ever move again.

Once you do bring the event to a close, you'll immediately be grateful that your partner remembered to lay out the 23 individual items you will now instantly need to keep your baby warm and very quickly get them dry and dressed.

A palaver, yes, but fast forward a month or two and bathtimes will be a doddle, such a well-seasoned dunker will you have become.

The first cold

Babies are full of snot.

For what seems like months, they snort and snuffle their way through the night and make you sit bolt upright time after time as they seemingly struggle to breathe.

Then they get a cold.

What you thought was bad, was in fact nasal normality and now they have the snuffles plus an infection and it knocks them for six. You watch helplessly as their tiny nose streams, their little pigeon chest heaves and they even go off their beloved milk.

Because her immune system is still developing, the chances are your baby could get lots of colds in her first year alone. This amounts to an awful lot of disturbed nights for everyone. But strangely enough, she probably won't get a cold until after three months, as up until then, she is protected by maternal antibodies that are still in her system from pregnancy.

Given that a nipper's cold can hang around for up to two weeks before it gets fought off, you'll soon begin to wonder if anything other than mucus actually exists in the world, as one infection rolls inexorably into the next. A big problem lies in the fact that babies can't actually breathe through their mouths, but only through their noses for the first five months or so.

And what can you do to help? Not much, unfortunately. When they get past three months you too will worship at the altar of infant painkillers which can bring down fever and make them generally feel less shit. Keeping them hydrated is important, too, so if they struggle to feed for the normal length of time because of breathing issues, offer it to them as little and often if possible.

Actually shifting the mucus is tricky. Saline drops squirted up the nose work well, and are used regularly in hospitals, but to say babies hate having them applied would be a substantial understatement. There are also aspirators on the market which claim to be able to remove the excess snot by the power of suction – essentially reverse bogie bellows. Almost everyone seems to buy one, but few have the heart to use them.

Plug-in vaporisers, liquid capsules and chest rubs all come in to play past three months, but for now the biggest thing you've got to offer your little one as they struggle through is love and cuddles.

If at any point you are even mildly worried go and see your GP. Not wanting to trouble anyone isn't an option when they are this small, especially if it's your first and you've not got anything to compare it to.

The first travel-cot battle

Just to get this straight, every time is like the first time you put a travel cot up.

When it works well, life is good, when it goes off on one of its illogical and infuriating wanderings, the Marx Brothers in their pomp couldn't have choreographed a more farcical scene.

This side stays up, that one doesn't. That one stays up, this one doesn't.

After much push-me-pull-you nonsense and with your baby's bedtime approaching at a frightening speed you gird your loins, pull up the middle and launch a surprise attack on the insurgent outer arms.

Nothing.

The situation is critical and you are sweating and swearing in a way not befitting either a new father or a guest in someone else's home.

Reinforcements are needed – don't worry who, anyone in the house will do. The moment your ally approaches, your travel cot enemy will sense that humiliation is almost complete and will become putty in their hands, gently complying with their every movement.

Swines.

Words from your fellow fathers:

Tom, father of two: *I think the hardest thing early on is working out what to do when they make noises you can't possibly identify – it's like looking under the car bonnet, realising you need a mechanic, then it dawning on you that you have to take responsibility to sort it yourself.*

Marcus, father of four: *The travel cot was the most challenging piece of equipment. In truth I've never managed it and it's still my wife's job.*

Suki, father of three: *The biggest shock was probably that first explosive nappy and the thought that the only way to deal with the situation was to plonk the baby into the bath.*

These are the times you have to stay calm and rely on a plentiful supply of wet wipes.

Rob, father of two: *I remember throwing the travel cot across the room at one point because it was so difficult to put up.*

The baby wasn't in it at the time, of course.

LOOKING AFTER THE GROWN-UPS

It's hard to imagine another area of life when something so fundamentally and earth-shatteringly draining as delivering a baby would be followed immediately by another happening that in many ways is even more taxing.

But that's what your partner is facing as she arrives home from hospital. Regardless of whether the birth went without a hitch or a stitch, under any other circumstances it would be bed rest, book reading and back rubs all round for the recovering patient.

That kind of recuperation is a very hard trick to pull off when there's a newborn politely letting you know in their own inimitable way that they are feeling hungry or have an air bubble trapped inside them that feels the size of a Ford Galaxy.

Which is where you come in.

Physical recovery

There's no nice way of saying this, but new mothers bleed a lot after they have given birth.

It's not the sort of thing that mums say to mums-to-be, it's not even the sort of thing fathers of a different generation may have been aware of – but it happens and you should be ready for it.

No matter if she's had a vaginal or caesarean birth, this bleeding, called lochia, is how the body gets rid of the lining of the womb after birth.

The blood may come out in gushes and include clots or flow more evenly like a heavy period. More often than not, it will change colour from the initial bright red and become lighter as the uterus heals and returns to its normal size.

Your partner may bleed for as little as two to three weeks or as long as six weeks after having the baby. Generally, other than taking it easy, keeping an eye on the colour and amount of the flow and stocking up on maternity pads (tampons are a no-no, as they can cause infection) it's just a case of waiting for it to finish.

It's far from plain sailing, though. You should call the midwife or doctor immediately if your partner:

- has a tender tummy
- has a fever or a chill
- passes clots bigger than a 50p piece
- has bleeding that stays heavy and red for more than the first week
- has bleeding with an unpleasant smell

Occasionally, bleeding that's much heavier than normal can occur between 24 hours and six weeks after birth. It is called secondary postpartum haemorrhage and it's thought that fewer than one new mum in 100 experiences it.

Your partner could also have a wound between her vagina and back passage, an area called the perineum. She will need to keep this part of her body clean to prevent infection there, too, and although they sound painful, salt baths can do a world of good and can actually be soothing.

While bleeding is a very common and widespread postnatal issue, there are a whole host of others that can make an appearance too, just when your partner could do without them, such as constipation, skin problems and incontinence.

She's been in the wars in a big way and a big part of your new dad duties are to be there to make like as easy and pain-free as possible for her as she gets to grips with the gargantuan job of being a mother. If she is recovering from a caesarean delivery, you are going to be a very busy boy indeed.

C-section births

Even though it is quite obvious that a caesarean is major surgery in every sense of the word, the after-effects and the pain it causes can still take a newly babied couple by surprise.

It can hurt to cough, to laugh, to shuffle around in bed, to do almost anything in fact. Thank goodness your partner can recover properly with lots of stress-free rest and blissful peace and quiet.

Ah.

Just because your partner didn't have a vaginal birth, it doesn't mean she won't have heavy vaginal bleeding after the birth. If it was an emergency C-section there's a good chance ventouse or forceps were given a go first too, which may mean further stitches in the perineum.

It's tough and it's down to you to help make it better by taking some of the strain of new motherhood on your broad shoulders, even if they are hunched through fatigue.

First things first, your partner needs to eat and drink well and keep her wound clean and safe. Despite what her body may be telling her, she needs to get up and take the first ginger steps toward mobility as often as she feels able.

Breastfeeding is a hard enough skill to crack without being wracked with pain every time you move. The good news is that once they start, women are just as likely to breastfeed their baby successfully after a C-section as they are after having had a vaginal birth. Helping her to get comfortable before she starts a feed is your job. It's a vital one, given that the first few days and weeks of breastfeeding are critical to establishing a pattern and environment that will work for both mother and baby.

Lifting of any sort is out, including lifting older children. Any jobs that involve stretching are also off limits as is being too proud to accept help. If friends or family offer, accept it. If they don't, offer for them.

Keeping visitors down to a minimum for this first week or two – except for those who will pull their weight and come armed with a shepherd's pie so large it could have its own postcode – is another very smart thing for you to take control of. As much as you want to show off what is undoubtedly the most beautiful baby ever born, it will be even more beautiful the following week so try and resist the temptation to have a totally open house – your partner, despite in some cases what she might be saying, really does need to rest and get to know the new person in her life.

As the days and weeks go by, things get easier and as far as driving is concerned, despite reports to the contrary, very few motor insurance policies stipulate the need for post C-section women to take a set amount of time off the road. It's down to how she feels she would cope with the likes of an emergency stop and the view of her doctor or midwife.

Your partner may be up and at 'em within a few days of being home, but for many women the post-caesarean spell is a difficult time when they rely heavily on their partners and other kith and kin to help them through.

The emotional recovery

After such a crescendo of emotions and hormonal upheaval suffered by your partner, it's inevitable that there will be, for want of a better phrase, a come-down after the birth.

The 'baby blues' is the name given to that process and the often weepy and irritable mood which it brings about. It's estimated that something like 80% of new mothers experience this crash back down to earth. It's thought to be linked to hormonal adjustments the body makes two to four days after the baby is born.

Add in an often daunting new sense of responsibility, post-birth pain, fear of failure and a nice dollop of dog-tiredness and you've got the potential to feel tremendously overwhelmed.

Your first role is as bouncer to keep visitor numbers down. But perhaps the most vital thing for you to do through this spell is listen and be there for her to cry on or rage at if she needs to. In most cases, the baby blues pass as quick as they arrived and are a necessary, if intense, part of the healing process.

If things persist, though, or baby blues symptoms reoccur much past a month after having the baby, something more serious could be afoot.

Postnatal depression

It wasn't too long ago that postnatal depression (PND) was seen as a rarity among mothers.

The figure that was bandied around of one in 10 mums suffering has since been revised to more like one in four.

As the stigma around mental illness is slowly dismantled piece by piece, more mothers are recognising the symptoms and, crucially, seeking help. Rather than seeing the statistical change as proof of an epidemic, perhaps we should give thanks that at least now far fewer women are suffering in silence.

As with all mental health issues, spotting the relevant symptoms either in oneself or in someone you are close to can be a fiendishly complex area. To add to the difficulty, the existence of the baby blues muddies the waters slightly, but the medical advice is clear when it comes to distinguishing between the two. While the baby blues are short-lived and often disappear without treatment, the opposite is true of PND.

Tell-tale signs and symptoms are different for every mother, which is why your role and that of your close family and friends is crucial in identifying behaviour or feelings that are unusual for the person you know so well.

Broadly speaking, a real sense of hopelessness, anxiety, guilt or loneliness can all be key signs. Exhaustion and a feeling of being trapped are also symptomatic and given the lack of sleep and huge life change new mothers go through these can often be put down to something other than genuine mental distress. But if you sense your partner is overwhelmed by any of these feelings and that the black cloud just isn't shifting, it could well be PND.

The illness often creeps up on mothers around four to six weeks after the birth of the baby, but it can and does come out of nowhere months afterwards, too.

The reasons why PND strikes and why some people are more vulnerable to it than others are largely unknown. Brain chemistry, genetics, reaction to hormonal changes, diet – they've all been postulated and researched but as yet no real answers have been found. What's for sure is that isolation when coping with a new baby, being away from family and friends, can be an enormous factor, as can the strain an awful lot of women find trying to breastfeed.

If you are worried that your partner is suffering from PND, you need to come to the party in a big way.

First, gently encouraging her to speak to a health visitor or GP about how she is feeling is crucial. If she's nervous or scared, offer to go with her if it helps – and keep reassuring about just how common and beatable PND is.

You'll also need to take a lot of the strain off her and may well need some time away from work to make that possible. Take care you don't charge in and take over, that will only make her feel worse. Offer to take on jobs and help her to prioritise what she is taking on.

Exercise is increasingly seen as a key tool in beating depression, so make time for her to go to the gym, walk or swim or whatever she fancies. If she's not been finding the time to eat well, you can help to put that right too.

But perhaps the most important thing of all is that you listen to her and reassure her that she's a great mum, and that you love her very much.

Be under no illusion, though, supporting someone with PND is tough and you'll need to take care of yourself, too. Organisations such as the Association for Postnatal Illness (http://apni.org) can help you help your partner through what can be a frightening and bewildering time.

Once a diagnosis has been made, there are a lot of treatment options on offer and with the right help it is a very beatable illness, despite how your partner may feel while she is in its grip.

Most GPs can refer sufferers to support groups, counsellors or psychotherapists. Cognitive behavioural therapy (CBT), which teaches everyday coping strategies, is becoming a popular route.

Antidepressants are the other option. These work by raising the levels of the hormone serotonin. Between five and seven out of every 10 women who take antidepressants report that their symptoms lessen within a few weeks of taking them.

However, these drugs have been shown to pass into breastmilk, although in very small amounts – so it's far from an easy choice.

Speaking to your GP to get a clear assessment of the risks and benefits involved is vital.

As is, if recent studies are anything to go by, your own mental health; because it seems that men get postnatal depression too.

Men and postnatal depression

There's a growing body of thought that suggests that many new fathers have been experiencing PND, with scores of cases going undetected. A US study put the number of cases at around one in 10 (the same number that female PND was thought to be prevalent at for many years).

Life changes, new responsibilities, lack of sleep or supporting a wife with postnatal depression were cited as the potential triggers by the Eastern Virginia Medical School academics. The research also found that new fathers tended to be happiest in the first few weeks after the baby was born, with depression taking hold after three to six months.

These are extreme cases, but don't underestimate the potential impact having a baby will have on you mentally. We want to be involved and engaged, to play a big part in bringing up our children as well as providing for them.

And it can take its toll.

Men and women tend to react differently to stress and it's said that men with depression get mad, while women get sad.

While this is a generalisation, an increase in alcohol consumption, or self-medicating can all be signs of mental anxiety and disquiet in men. Becoming a father is a big deal and it's all too easy for men to ignore their own health when pride and the stiff upper lip kicks in.

Just as air safety announcements tell us to apply our own mask before helping others, taking the time to look after yourself isn't a selfish act, it's the exact opposite.

Words from your fellow fathers:

Ben, father of two: *Once your wife has a baby I don't think any rational man can look at the fairer sex again without thinking 'Hats off to you'.*

If men had children, caesarean sections would have been invented before the wheel.

Rob, father of two: *The recovery period was very tough because my wife had an operation to deliver the baby.*

I helped her with feeds, changing nappies and waking in the night to attend to the baby. I also cooked throughout that period – so I think I was brilliant!

Jason, father of two: *Second time around was a C-section so six weeks of taking it easy means Dad has his hands full. Initially we did consider getting her a bell to ring for my service. I really enjoyed looking after her and the boys, though.*

Marcus, father of four: *Looking back I think my wife did suffer from postnatal depression, although I doubt she would admit it today.*

Winston, father of two: *I wasn't depressed, I think I might have mourned my previous, happy-go-lucky life but I wasn't depressed. Fortunately, I was a happy dad in a stable relationship and always felt lucky.*

Colin, father of two: *I don't think I suffered from depression, but can quite believe dads can get it.*

Such highs and lows of emotions – stress, elation, pressure, fear, pride, guilt – are all experienced in a very short space of time with very little sleep, so it must affect some people that way.

PROGRESS REPORT, 0–3 MONTHS

Your baby

As we've seen, your baby is making remarkable progress before your very eyes on a daily basis during the first three months – with brain development leading the way.

Over this period your little one will change from a watery-eyed, floppy-limbed alien-like creature to being capable of holding her head up, tracking objects with her eyes and even smiling at you.

Never again will she learn so much so fast – she'll even begin to recognise you and your partner from the seven billion other people on the planet – clever.

Sleeping could also start to take a semblance, by which I mean not very much 'blance' at all, of regularity and order, and you'll also start to see a schedule of sorts around eating and pooing.

What I'm trying to say is that your tiny little tot, all innocent and sweet, will throughout these three months begin to enforce their routine on you, your home and your entire life. Muahahhhhhha

Your partner

We've seen in detail what a tough time this can be for your partner, from recovering after the birth to the trials of breastfeeding and the spectre of postnatal depression.

But let's not get too carried away with the black paintbrush, shall we? Many new mothers, while it's undoubtedly a tough sleep-deprived time, are also experiencing the most intense and emotionally powerful period of their lives as they bond in quite spectacular fashion with their child.

This bonding process can be amazing to watch and be around, although some dads do report feeling a touch left out as a love affair unfolds in front of them – which leads us on to . . .

You

If you do feel your nose being put slightly out of joint by the closeness of the bond between mother and child know this; your time will come.

In this initial spell it's easy to feel a bit of a spare part where the baby is concerned. Remember that every cuddle you give and every gaze you hold is working to cement you as one of the two most important people in this little person's life.

If you possibly can just revel in the moment, embrace every 3am wake-up, relish every nuzzle, soak it up and file it away. The first three months are rock hard for sure, but they are also magical, unique and fleeting.

GETTING DOWN TO BUSINESS

You've been a dad for more than 12 weeks now – that's over 80 consecutive days of fatherhood under your belt.

You are a master.

Kind of.

After a while the visitors stop coming, the giant lasagnas cease to materialise and you and your partner are often left relatively well alone to enjoy your baby.

While everyone's experiences will be different, there are three key things that, more likely than not, will be true about your life during the next three months.

- You'll be back at work and the 'but I've just had a baby' line will be wearing pretty thin as an excuse for your tardiness and all-round poor showing.
- Your baby will almost certainly be waking up at least once a night.
- Your tiny new arrival will have generated more jobs to do in your home than you ever dreamed possible.

This tricky triumvirate combines to create what politicians call a 'challenging environment', when what they actually mean is a living nightmare.

I'm painting an overly dark picture, but there is no denying that you will become very interested indeed in the answer to a few fundamental questions. How can you get your little angel to sleep in a way which allows you to feel like card-carrying members of the human race, if not actually looking like one?

How can we do what needs to be done at home without tearing each other limb from limb in indignant rage as we lay side by side in bed thinking 'Surely you can't think it's MY turn!?'

And how can we both weave the very occasional conversation with friends, fellow parents and even, heaven forbid, people without children into our chaotic lives to help keep us sane?

Tricky questions one and all. Let's go for the big one first, sleep.

THE S WORD: PART 2

Once your baby has adjusted to being on planet Earth over the course of its first few months, you stand a chance of establishing a semblance of a sleep routine back into your domestic world.

As you've probably noticed, on average a three-month-old baby will sleep twice as much as their parents, but half of this will be in the daytime. On average your baby will sleep for blocks of about two hours in the day, and four to six hours at night.

Just like us grown-ups, babies fluctuate between deep and light sleep all night; in fact from six months onwards your baby was establishing sleep patterns while they were still in the womb.

Babies do some serious dreaming too, spending almost half of their kip time in the REM state that leads to it. With dreamtime seen as vital for filing away and making sense of our experiences, you can see why a baby, for whom almost every waking second represents a discovery of mind-blowing magnitude, would need more than its fair share of the stuff.

As your little one grows she will gradually sleep more during the night and less in the day. At this stage, on average, she will be sleeping twice as long at night as in the day – or so the story goes.

These daytime naps gradually coalesce to become a bit longer and less frequent by the six-month mark. By the time they reach 12 months, most babies will have one or two daytime naps before eventually these sleeps are dropped as they move through toddler-dom and only sleep at night.

Way before that milestone is reached, though, balancing the daytime naps against the night-time sleep is the game you'll be playing. Obvious as it sounds, the more your baby sleeps during the day the less she will sleep at night – worth considering as you luxuriate during that three-hour lunchtime nap – you may pay later! But don't go too far the other way: babies need sleep in the day; otherwise they will get too, or even the dreaded over, tired and then not sleep well anyway. It's a fine line.

Another tricky area revolves around the classic vision of parents dismantling the doorbell, manoeuvring round the squeaky floorboard and tiptoeing up the stairs to ensure junior isn't disturbed one iota. When you consider that all babies have essentially been listening to the sounds of your home through the thin wall of the womb for at least a couple of months before they arrived, you begin to realise that a relatively normal noise level is the way to go.

This is borne out by just how quickly an awful lot of babies are soothed or even drop off when they hear the sound of the extractor fan in the kitchen or the vacuum cleaner in the lounge. So potent are these white noises that you can download entire concept albums of household implement racket so you can use them to induce sleep wherever you are, without turning your baby's nursery into a Currys showroom.

Despite this novel little trick, your baby's need for constant feeding, her propensity to be disturbed by wind in a quite extraordinary way and the fact that her sleep patterns will mean she enters light sleep up to five times a night, all mean that a decent night's sleep will be a rarity at best and a fleeting memory at worst.

An often controversial little device that parents have turned to for many a long year can help.

To do the dummy?

Few things are as divisive in the world of parenting as the dummy. Some swear by them, some loathe them, some do both and are driven to use them behind closed doors, keeping them from public view like a dirty little secret.

What's for sure is that they have been around for donkey's years and they work as a way of getting your baby to ease themselves into the land of nod as they soothe themselves via the action of sucking.

As well as the obvious advantages of dummy use, there's some evidence that they can help to prevent cot death by preventing the airway being blocked. However, putting your baby on her back and not smoking anywhere near her remain by far and away the most important prevention methods.

On the negative side, prolonged use of a dummy is said to increase the risk of ear, chest and stomach infections. Also, the longer your baby uses a dummy, especially if they are still using it past the age of three, the more likely it is to cause changes in the way their teeth grow – which can result in an over- or crossbite.

Using a dummy could also affect your baby's speech development a little further down the line for the simple reason that they have their mouth full a lot of the time. The recommendation is that you use a dummy only for settling your baby to sleep and not during the day.

All in all, dummies, when used sparingly, are a viable and sometimes much-needed option that can give you and your partner a well-earned break as well as helping to calm a distressed baby. However, do weigh up the pros and cons before embarking on the dummy, and if you can cope without it, health professionals will applaud you.

As with breast vs bottle, once you've made your decision, try to avoid beating yourself to a pulp about it. In life's rich tapestry it is but a trifling thing really. If you do decide to go down the dummy route, try and use an orthodontic or flat dummy which can help the mouth develop more naturally than the traditional rounded ones.

Keep the dummy as clean and sterile as possible, change it regularly and don't dip it in sugar or whisky no matter what any older relatives may suggest.

For many, getting rid of the dummy happens naturally before the first birthday is reached as the baby begins to spit it out and get themselves back to sleep without it.

But some youngsters can grow to love their dummy for a long time and the longer you wait to get shot of it the more of a palaver and emotional tug of war it can become – but we will deal with that further down the line.

Aside from the soother, is there anything else you can do to make your baby more content, sleep better and develop a routine that fits hand in glove with your idea of a perfect day and night?

You had to go and ask didn't you?

The Baby Wars

Having a strategy to help you cope with bringing up a baby is nothing new. The long bracing walk in the perambulator, the journey in the car or the lullaby – have all been popular and passed on down the years.

What has changed is the proliferation of working mums, their time stretched to the limit and also the ability of tens of thousands of people to gather together online and essentially beat the virtual meconium out of each other over what the best way to bring up baby really is.

The chances are your partner's bedside table will be heaving under the weight of a goodly number of books, all of which outline a different route to baby happiness. There's one approach in particular that has caused more debate than all the rest combined, Gina Ford's *The Contented Little Baby Book* (Vermilion).

First published in 1999, it has sold by the carry-cot load and has established its author as the undisputed queen of routine. Ford advises new parents to break down their day into five-minute slots, with the baby being woken and fed by 7am. Subsequent feeds and naps are slotted in at set times up until the final feed of the day, during which parents should not make eye contact with their baby in case it gets excited before bedtime.

The endgame of all of this is to deliver not just a contented baby, but one who sleeps through the night like a dream.

To say that this method produces Marmite reactions in parents would be doing this book's impact a severe disservice. For those who love her methods, Ford is a heroine, a woman who has singlehandedly given them back their lives and their sanity, restored order and calm to their household and allowed them to retain at least a semblance of their former lives.

For working mums in particular it has been a boon, it seems, meaning the sleep they need to juggle their two jobs is on tap and their baby can be minded by someone else with ease as long as they watch the clock and follow the plan.

For those who disagree with her approach, Ford has been labelled Public Enemy Number One. Such is the venom with which some of her detractors have a swipe at Ford's techniques, she took legal action against the website Mumsnet in 2006 and in 2010 even the Deputy Prime Minister Nick Clegg had a pop, calling her approach 'absolute nonsense'.

Out of the smoky battlefield there does seem to be a middle way emerging, though. There's little doubt that babies seem happier when their day follows some sort of semi-regular pattern – your first overnight stay in a strange house will probably demonstrate that to you pretty well. Whether or not that routine needs to be drilled to the nearest five minutes is a moot point. While the online battle still rages about the Fordian approach, there are also plenty of people prepared to admit they subscribe to the routine approach, but not necessarily with as much military vim and vigour as is suggested by some.

One area that seems to have gathered controversial steam rather than shed it, is the notion of letting the baby 'cry it out' as they attempt to drop off or wake during a sleep.

Controlled crying

As you or your partner haul your sorry backsides out of bed for the fourth time in as many hours to rock your baby to sleep, life can seem really quite bleak.

Will this ever end? Will I make it through a day at work without curling up in the corner of a crowded lift and drifting into blissful rest? Will we ever find a way to crack the sleep problem?

Or perhaps getting up is long gone, perhaps you find yourself ousted from your own bed, your baby having moved in on a semi-permanent basis, feeding on demand from dusk till dawn.

Whatever your scenario, if you and your partner are consistently denied the kip you need, there's a very good chance you will have the 'controlled crying' conversation. While there are many controlled crying methods, the general gist is that you leave your baby to cry for slightly increasing spells which are punctuated by you entering the room and either physically comforting them or just verbally reassuring them before leaving again.

When it works, parents can find that after just a handful of admittedly often horrendous days they have a baby who settles herself to sleep and stays asleep – or at least drops back off on her own when and if she wakes.

But at what cost?

Research suggesting long-term behavioural damage can be caused by the crying baby's brain being flooded with the stress hormone cortisol can be found side-by-side with other studies which suggest nothing of the sort takes place. Not particularly helpful at 3.47am when you have discussed the merits of letting her cry for the third time that night.

There are no clear-cut answers, I'm afraid, but what is for certain is that listening to your baby cry out and resisting the urge to go to them is one of the toughest things you'll ever attempt.

If you find yourself with a baby who has become thoroughly used to being rocked to sleep and screams like a banshee at the merest hint of a cot sheet coming into contact with their soft little cheek, one alternative to controlled crying is the pick up/put down method.

Initially championed by the late Tracy Hogg in her popular *Baby Whisperer* books, it involves picking the crying baby up, comforting her until she is calm and then putting her down again.

Then repeat ad infinitum until baby gets herself to sleep.

Hogg reckons this procedure takes 20 minutes on average, although admits it can run over the hour mark, by which time not only will your baby be asleep, you will have pecs like a super steroidal bodybuilder.

However, health professionals now only advocate controlled crying for babies over four months old, and recommend that you do not pick your baby up, but comfort her in her cot.

Whatever way you choose to try and crack the sleep problem – and there are no quick fixes – the most important thing is that you and your partner both support each other and try, try like the wind, to retain even a semblance of a sense of humour as you battle through. Not easy, I know, but laughing hysterically in the wee small hours is a much better option than adding to your wretchedness by having an argument as the sun comes up on another busy day.

Talking of which, have you noticed that there's rather a lot to do now you have a baby in the house?

Words from your fellow fathers:

Steve, father of two: *We got ourselves into quite a bizarre routine with our eldest. We would stroke her forehead until she fell asleep, sometimes in the* room for an hour or so, then creep out of the room on our hands and knees backwards.

This was fine apart from we had ONE squeaky floorboard that we would always crawl onto. We'd scrunch our faces up and pray this wouldn't wake her up, but it always did.

'RIGHT' I snapped one night, we are doing this controlled crying thing.

My wife couldn't cope with this and went downstairs so she couldn't hear Olivia cry (and also turned music on VERY loud to drown out the noise, oblivious to the fact this rock concert in the room underneath was not aiding the sleep process).

I left Olivia and said good night. She went crazy because she wasn't getting the princess treatment of head stroking. I waited a minute outside. Went back in, acknowledged I was still there and left for two minutes. The noise out of my little girl's mouth still amazes me to this very day. She was quite clearly unhappy with my new approach to parenting.

After eight attempts, she finally fell asleep from pure exhaustion. I repeated this for the next five days. The sixth day onwards, our lives changed for the better and she was able to fall asleep without thinking she was Victoria Beckham.

Nick, father of two: We felt that we had to give controlled crying a go. Once you get in to picking them up, you are on the back foot. And front foot is everything in this game.

Ben, father of two: You have got to try controlled crying at some point in my opinion. Unless you are given a real sleeper how do babies know what to do?

Try it when you are both feeling good, as it can be full-on. Don't wait until you both are frazzled and feel you have no choice. You'll be crying as much as the baby.

Simon, father of one: In the end we opted for a bit of controlled crying.

In fairness you shouldn't use our experience as any kind of guide, our son rarely sleeps through the night still.

Yes, we could leave him crying in his cot, in the dark, on his own at 3am but as far I'm concerned that would just make us a couple of bastards.

RETURN OF THE BABY BOMB

We touched on it earlier, but it bears a second visit now you're in the thick of it – the baby bomb is here.

The effects of the Baby Bomb certainly aren't confined to these three months, nor even the three years this entire book covers. You'll feel them throughout your parenting life, if you haven't already.

You see, your relationship with your partner changes forever when you have a child. The terms of reference, the environment, the communication, the priorities, everything alters overnight.

This change doesn't necessarily signal the end of companionship, love and togetherness – often quite the opposite in fact – but imagining that 'and baby makes three' is the beginning, middle and end of it can lead to quite a shock for a couple of big reasons.

Equality

By and large, the modern relationship has enjoyed a period of equilibrium-inducing change over the past 30 years. A hideous generalisation, I know, but on the whole, life's decisions get made as a couple much more than they used to in our parents' or grandparents' age.

The earning stats back this change up too: in 1968–9 just 5% of women brought home more money than their partner; in 2010 that figure was shown to be 44% and rising fast. The breadwinning woman is a new and powerful phenomenon.

Then suddenly into this fluid, egalitarian and gender-role-blurring reality comes a newborn child and in the time it takes to pack a baby bag women often find themselves feeling like they have been unceremoniously yanked back to 1953.

Put simply, babies are to working women what dog turds are to street performance.

While we may have changed, evolved, progressed, whatever you want to call it, at lightning pace these past 40 years, a new-born baby's raison d'être is identical to what it was centuries ago.

They aren't going to adapt to our world; we – initially at least – have to move very much towards theirs. With the average age of mothers giving birth having steadily risen to 29.2 years, for most women, that is a lot of adjustment – especially as careers and entire ways of life are put on hold or irrevocably altered.

It's a big deal and is something to be both aware and sympathetic of. The initial shock of becoming a mum seems to be becoming more seismic for many women because of the perceived loss of equality and hard-fought-for independence they have to seemingly cede, at least temporarily. Readjustment can take a good while. You have a big part to play in making it as smooth a journey as possible and ensuring it feels like a change you'll both embrace together.

Not that you'll have bundles of time on your hands to make this happen, because the second effect of the Baby Bomb is to create more work to be taken on, a lot more work.

The division of labour

Pre-children, friction about who pulls the most weight around the home may well exist, but it is as nothing compared to what it becomes when children arrive. There's lots and lots to do, and it never ends.

Within this environment it is incredibly easy to fall into a tit-for-tat war where keeping score is endemic on both sides.

'I've been up with the baby every night this week' 'You've not done bathtime since the weekend' 'It's your turn to do breakfast'

'I've been at work all week' (Never, ever say that, ever)

Then there's the issue of not what you do, but how you do it.

Nappy needs changing you say? Not an issue, all clean and ready to rock in the blink of an eye. OK, so I may have changed her on the sofa to save my back or a trip upstairs to the changing table and the dirty nappy may well be left on the floor for the next six hours, but no one can deny that the original problem was sorted very quickly indeed.

In a survey by US broadcaster MSNBC, respondents were asked if the chores in their households were performed by just one person or if they were shared. A nice chunky 74% of men said jobs were done as a team, but just 51% of women said the same.

Let's be honest – this disparity probably doesn't surprise either of us does it? We do have a tendency to exaggerate our efforts just a smidgen and out of the three words 'job half done', the middle one, can, on occasion, be completely invisible to an awful lot of us.

So is that it? Are we destined to argue and mither our way through the next 18 years of our lives, both feeling underappreciated, undervalued and under the cosh?

Not necessarily. Harmony and enjoyment can flourish with the help of a few changes that – while looking simple written down here – take a goodly amount of fortitude and resolve to make happen.

First, regularly remind each other what a great job you're doing of raising your youngster and validate the feelings of exhaustion, frustration and even boredom that you both may have at different times. This is a smart move for obvious reasons. Being a parent is a remarkable thing to do, but it's real life, not a commercial. Shit stuff will happen and tedious jobs will need to be done. Occasionally feeling like you'd rather be anywhere else isn't cause for shame or finger pointing, it's cause for a hug.

Second, there's an element of giving in to be done here. For you that may mean getting off your arse a bit more and chipping in. You need to come to terms with the fact that your life really has changed, rather than trying to fight the fact tooth and nail. For your partner it could mean acknowledging the fact that the house may never truly be as she likes it again, or that her way may not always be the only way to get things done.

Finally, finding the time amidst all the work and the upheaval to enjoy what's happening right in front of you can bring some much-needed perspective to proceedings as you argue for the third time in a week about the best way to sterilise a teat.

Missing your children growing and developing in a blur of disinfectant wipes, frozen purée trays and games of chicken where you hope your partner will be the one to blink first and get up to see to the baby is to miss the point entirely.

We've all done it – and no one more so than me – but just occasionally if you can both agree that the washing and the emails can wait and having an hour on the floor with your beautiful baby is the way to go, you'll find that things won't seem quite so tough after all.

Told you it sounds simple. If you crack it, please let me know how.

Words from your fellow fathers:

Suki, father of three: *I would be surprised if my father ever changed a nappy!*

In those days the roles of mother and father were much more clearly defined. Now, not only are fathers expected to be much more involved in bringing up their children, they also want to be more involved and part of the whole experience and to build a relationship with their children from a young age.

The maxim 'you get out what you put in' does truly apply here.

Rob, father of two: *I think gender roles were much more defined 30–40 years ago. Nowadays both partners pitch in with all responsibilities. Or is that just in my house!?*

Murray, father of two: *We had our disagreements on the way things should be done, for sure, but I felt it was such a personal experience for my wife giving birth that she should be as comfortable as possible with all the decisions that were made.*

I think looking back she would have liked more opinions from me, but luckily we both have a similar philosophy which is largely instinctive although pretty rigid routine-wise.

Name withheld!: *Somewhere in the late 70s/early 80s a generation of men stitched us all up and caved in. One minute we are having cigars in the pub being treated to brandies while waiting for our wives to come back from the maternity hospital to cook tea. The next we are getting up to feed children in the middle of the night before going to work and coming back to change nappies.*

Winston, father of two: *My dad would come home too late from work to get stuck into bathtime or feeding us. He was a more remote figure than I hope I am for my children. But he was still a great dad, it perhaps took me longer to find out.*

I think it's true that mums initially scrutinise your every movement, which is fair dos considering how much bother they have been to in acquiring the child, but my wife learnt to let me get on with things, otherwise I would never have gained the experience and knowledge of how to go about things.

Simon, father of one: *I felt the pressure. My wife was always casting a critical eye over everything I did. There were many mistakes. At which point she'd just take over and tell me to get out of the way.*

PROGRESS REPORT, 4–6 MONTHS

Your baby

As well as the all-consuming business of feeding and sleeping, this three-month spell sees some real spatial awareness and body control being introduced to your baby's repertoire.

She may be strong enough to roll over from her back to her front or vice versa – which will come as a shock if she does it while you happen to be looking away. She may even start to bear her weight on those lovely little legs when you hold her arms – she's a good few months away from walking – but you are watching the very first signs of her wanting to take her first steps.

As well as general chattering and babbling on the increase, you might think you even hear the odd ma-ma and da-da, too. It's a bit early for her to be necessarily connecting them with you yet, but it still sends a tingle up your spine even if you may have imagined it from the gobbledygook of sounds.

She might start to grasp toys at this stage, too, and even pass them between her hands. She could also begin to give faces she hasn't seen before a funny look. Even the early onset of teething might rear its ugly head – all pretty impressive stuff for someone who just eight weeks ago was a floppy, cross-eyed little dot.

Your partner

In between feeling exhausted and drained of all vitality as she feeds and nurtures what still is a very young baby, your partner might just be thinking or dreaming about starting to exercise and getting her pre-birth strength back.

Getting back in shape after a pregnancy is a notoriously difficult thing to do. Your help in creating the time for her to do some exercise will be enormously well received. Be careful how you phrase things, mind you – 'Isn't it time you went to the gym?' could land you in a world of trouble.

The psychological and physical benefits of exercise are well documented and it's a great next step on the road to recovering from the shock of the birth.

Another milestone on that road could well be the return of her periods during this spell. Occasionally this can happen even if she is still breastfeeding, but more often than not her cycle will begin when she reduces feeds or stops altogether.

You

As outlined in the Baby Bomb section earlier in this chapter, approaching the six-month mark can be when relationship issues surface, especially around childcare.

Quite often men want to and are requested to take a more active role in looking after baby by their partner – which is all good. What's not so great is the sense many men soon get as they get more involved that nothing they do is right.

From the woman's point of view you can see how this comes about – they have spent every waking moment with their baby since its birth, they know its moods, they know its cries, they know everything. Handing the responsibility for that precious thing over to dad, even just for an hour, can be an extremely tense and nerve-wracking thing to do. The temptation for the mother to give advice and micro-manage the father as he tends to his baby is enormous. Coping with what in bad cases can feel like an under-mining barrage of criticism can be incredibly tough. You need to learn in your own way, too, and your instincts need nurturing not crushing. If you'd have stood over your partner for the first six weeks passing negative comment on her mothering skills you'd have been a very bad man indeed.

The key to working through it, rather than hitting a stalemate that helps no one, is well-thought-out communication on your part.

Trying to have the 'please trust me to do it my way' debate in the middle of an incident where you may have been pulled up by your part-ner never, ever works. Emotions are running too high to have a calm, rational and open discussion so if you can, curb your instinct and address it at a neutral time with her. You'll probably find a much more sympa-thetic audience to your plight.

What's key to remember is that at this stage of the game you are still very much in the trenches. It might feel like after six months you should be home and hosed with this baby malarkey but that's just not the case – especially when it's your first.

You'll be doing a much better job as a couple than it may seem. If you have friends with a similar-aged tot who project an image of calm and serenity, know this – behind closed doors they will be paddling just as hard as you are to stay afloat.

THE FOG BEGINS TO LIFT

Don't even begin to think, not even for a moment, that you are somehow out of the woods, but . . . things do begin to get a little bit more recognisable, a little bit more manageable and often a lot more enjoyable during this spell.

Don't misunderstand me, you enjoy every waking moment of being a father. Of course you do, no one is suggesting otherwise, honestly. But as your baby grows and begins to take in the world around her, you might just begin to enjoy her a little bit more, that's all.

The combination of baby starting to try something other than milk as her source of energy and even beginning to move around under her own steam somehow makes more of a difference than simply having to give her food and make sure the house is safe for her to roam. They represent the first tangible signs, albeit fledgling ones, of independence.

You can even start reading to her now, too – you could have read to her from day dot, but from now there may well be visible, even audible signs that she is enjoying it and absorbing it, which she is, by the bucketful.

Then there's the outside chance if the battle against the axis of evil that is sleep deprivation and fatigue is being at least waged, that you and your partner might actually stay awake long enough to have your first non-baby-related conversation in months. You may even rekindle a little of the fairy dust in your relationship that brought the little one into being in the first place.

Unbridled joy and happiness abounds. Until the teeth come along, that is.

Teething is a world of pain for you and your often red-cheeked, furiously irritable, endlessly drooling little soldier – and it lasts for about two-and-a-half years.

Let's not dwell on that just yet though. Chin up! Your baby will soon be able to eat a banana on the move!

So proud.

WEANING, CRAWLING AND TEETHING: YOUR BUSY BABY

Weaning

Weaning is another of those areas, like the best way to put your baby to sleep, where the advice given to you as parents has shifted around over the years.

The official line from the Department of Health now says that while it's best to exclusively breastfeed a baby until she is six months old, from that point on a milk-only diet doesn't give her everything she needs to thrive, with iron the main thing missing.

Until relatively recently, guidelines advised introducing babies to solid food at four months. But it's now thought that waiting those extra eight weeks reduces the baby's chance of either picking up an infection from food because her digestive system is immature or becoming poorly because her immune system isn't quite up to speed yet.

It's possible you might have a baby who just isn't satisfied with milk, even lots and lots of milk. When they begin to eat the furniture, turning to solids may be unavoidable – although the advice is to avoid solids under all circumstances before the fourth month. If you do have a ravenous tot on your hands and decide to make the move between four and six months, avoid foods such as dairy products, citrus fruits and juices, eggs and shellfish. Foods that contain gluten are also worth avoiding, too, as there is some evidence that early exposure can cause coeliac disease.

Other than chewing their own fingers down to the elbow the signs that your baby is ready for some proper grub are the ability to hold their head up well, sit up when they are supported, and roughly doubling their birth weight. Perhaps most telling of all, she isn't just curious about what you've got on your plate but actively tries to grab at your food – the little tinker.

Puréed or very well mashed foods like mashed spud, cooked carrots, parsnips, banana, stewed apple or pear are a great way to start. As are baby cereal or rice mixes which you can stir into their milk as a gentle introduction to something a bit more substantial.

Gently does it. Be careful not to fall into the clean plate trap – the amount you make as a portion doesn't tally perfectly with the amount that will fill them up – why would it? They have tiny stomachs at this stage and offering a spoonful or two can often be enough.

There's no hard or fast rule about when to try them out on their first solids, before a milk feed, after or even during, whatever works best for your child. Don't be surprised if whatever you lovingly serve up gets spat right back at you – new flavours and especially textures take some getting used to. The trick is to keep trying and not brand a food or taste as something she doesn't like and never will.

As your baby slowly starts to develop a more recognisable grinding motion with her mouth you can gradually add less liquid to her food and introduce a slightly thicker texture – we're not talking beef wellington here, just soft lumps so your baby can practise her gummy chew and swallow movement and work on those jaw muscles. This will become crucial when talking becomes the next thing on her development menu in a few months' time.

By the time your little one is about seven or eight months old, its recommended that she should be eating mushy solids about three times a day – but do keep an eye out for signs she's full. Just like you or me, some days she'll be hungrier than others and if she refuses to open her mouth, pulls her head away or bangs the high chair and screams 'FOR GOD'S SAKE MAN I'VE HAD ENOUGH!' – she's probably done.

Developing good eating habits from day one is a great idea and can avoid all sorts of fussy eater shenanigans later on, so it's worth offering up a real variety of foods, including thoroughly deboned fish. You should be avoiding all added salt and sugar for the first year, and it's best to give mega fatty foods the swerve too.

A sip of water from a beaker at mealtimes is also a very good thing. Hard as it may be, try not to get into the habit of using food as a reward or threat – it's very easy to back yourself into a Percy Pig-shaped corner further down the line where just getting out of the front door requires a lorry load of sweets.

Within the wide world of weaning there's been something of a finger food revolution of late. Often termed 'baby-led weaning', it revolves around encouraging babies to feed themselves with safe soft finger foods rather than being spoon-fed. A finger of buttered toast here, a peeled pear there help to promote independence and confidence, and crucially to help to build up your little one's speech muscles right from the off. Finger food is also the cheapest route to an avant-garde redecoration of your kitchen as there is to be found anywhere.

If you go down this route be absolutely sure to stay with your baby when she is feeding herself in case she bites off more than she can chew.

As ever, there's a dazzling array of specialist equipment you can shell out for to help make weaning easier and your wallet lighter, but outside of rubber spoons, a highchair and maybe a suction bowl that will stay put all you need is patience, a sense of humour, and a fluid colour scheme in your home.

There's something very rewarding about watching your baby munching her way through real food, it's a big step and the start of lifelong refuelling. A word of warning, though, when your baby starts to eat more like an adult they start to poo more like an adult. Prepare yourself for a change in colour and smell and when meat is introduced to the mealtimes you'll essentially be changing a baby lion.

Enjoy.

Crawling

As if learning to eat isn't enough of a challenge for your little one to take on, it's highly likely they will also tackle mobility in these few months, too.

There's some evidence that because babies aren't sleeping on their fronts and so strengthening their arms and neck muscles anywhere near as much as they used to, crawling is on its way out. Despite that fact being trotted out a lot by all and sundry, the chances still are you will have a crawler roaming around your living room sometime soon.

Crawling may start with your baby balancing on her hands and knees, sometimes accompanied by a comedic rocking back and forth like Usain Bolt on his blocks. Alternatively, you may have a bottom shuffler in the family. This ungainly but surprisingly effective form of transport involves using the backside as the fulcrum and the legs as oar-like appendages.

It might not be a good look, but it works.

Some babies only crawl on hands and feet, others bring their knees into play – in fact it's not the technique that's remotely important, it's getting on the move by hook or by crook that's the big deal. Don't worry if at nine months your baby isn't a speed machine. They are all different. The medical advice is that if they have shown zero interest in moving an inch by the time they are 12 months get them checked out by the GP just in case.

Whenever they do decide to get going you'll need to view your home in a different light – in the words of the legendary consumer broadcaster Lynn Faulds Wood, every nook and cranny is a 'potential death trap'.

All right, that might be a touch alarmist but get down on all fours yourself and have a crawl around. Anything you can swipe, crush, throw or put in your mouth needs moving. Anything you can open, slam, or swing needs securing. Anything you value, even remotely, needs putting at least seven feet off the ground.

'Babyproofing' your house, as it's rather tweely known, is another baby area that has spawned a raft of products and gizmos that will turn your home into a museum of modern plastic if you're not careful.

Some of the kit is vital – try and live without a stairgate and you will be a jabbering, twitching wreck by the end of the week as your baby returns to the forbidden but enticing wooden mountain an astonishing 89 times in a single hour period. You won't talk them out of it, they won't forget, you just need to block it off, no matter how hideous it makes your hall look.

Plug socket blockers, plastic guards for sharp corners, rubber stoppers for heavy doors, clips for forbidden cupboards are all useful too – in fact who am I kidding, the second that you are aware of the existence of a new child safety gadget the pull to buy it is immediately overwhelming. With the Royal Society for the Prevention of Accidents stating that more than 600,000 children aged four or under need hospital treatment each year following accidents in the home, resistance is futile, you'll be urged on by your fear gland to plastic your home to buggery like the rest of us.

Apparently the Royal Society for the Prevention of Accidents lists most accidents as happening in the lounge and dining room, closely followed by the kitchen, bathroom and stairs.

There's also research suggesting that most accidents occur during the day, with the hour between 6pm and 7pm being particularly dangerous when meal and bathtime activity is high and energy reserves are low.

So, little did you know it, but the past six months or so have represented a physically less demanding period than the one you now enter. When your baby moves, so do you, and your baby will want to move a lot in all directions.

If you weren't drinking so much red wine the weight would drop off you.

Teething

The way we humans go about getting teeth is on the face of things pretty dumb.

As you are about to discover, milk teeth cause a disproportionate amount of bother in the short time they are operational.

From around the six-month mark onwards, your baby will start the three-year long journey to push out a set of teeth that will give a year or two's service before they start to fall out and are replaced by the real deal.

The process of cutting these baby teeth is termed 'eruption' by medical folk and never in the field of biological jargon has one word been seen as so apt by so many.

The first series of 10 or so teeth your baby cuts over the next six months have the capability of causing one or all of the following:

- burning cheeks
- red ears
- high temperature
- broken sleep
- an urge to bite everything and everyone within reach
- screams of pain as the jagged demon cuts through soft gum
- cold-like symptoms
- drooling by the bucketful
- and nappies so rancid thanks to the acidic teething saliva being produced that you feel like calling in a UN weapons inspection team to give them the all-clear.

Don't put absolutely everything down to teething – and if you are remotely concerned about your baby's behaviour or health, get her checked out with the doctor as soon as you can.

As a loose guide, these eruptions generally start with the central incisors between 6–12 months, then lateral incisors at 9–16 months, first molars 13–19 months, canine teeth at 16–23 months, and second molars at the 22–33 month mark. It's said that tooth development is hereditary so if you gave your folks hell, it's payback time in a big way.

Other than comforting them, there are a few things you can do to relieve the obvious pain many babies go through during teething. Giving them something cold to chew on like a teething ring kept in the fridge works well, as does a peeled carrot or slice of chilled apple if they are old enough to chew on it.

You'll see homeopathic teething powder in the chemist's and you might as well give it a try. There's next to no evidence it does any good whatsoever but there are parents out there who will wrestle you to the ground rather than concede it's a load of old flowery hokum. At worst they give your teething bub something new to think about for a while once they feel the white granules in their mouth – or should that be a bit of comic relief as they repeatedly push the open packet away leaving you looking like a cack-handed cocaine dealer.

If your baby is older than four months, there are some pretty good gels to rub on their gums – beware once they have already cut the first tooth, they will bite down on you and laugh at your shrieks afterwards.

Then there are the big guns – Calprofen® and Calpol® (infant ibuprofen and paracetamol). Always follow the instructions – and make sure you have some in the house, car and shed at all times for about the next 20 years.

Words from your fellow fathers:

Paul, father of two: *Baby-led weaning might be a bit of a poncy name, but as a strategy it works.*

It's got to be better to let them try all sorts of things in little bits, than to mush everything up into a slop, feed them on that and then suddenly present them with a full roast dinner when they are two and expect them to munch through it.

Marcus, father of four: *Our first baby gave crawling a miss and went straight to walking although we didn't hear the end of it from all the health care professionals.*

Tom, father of two: *Given the midwife described our eldest as a 'lazy boy' for being two weeks overdue, it should have come as no surprise that he was in no hurry to shuffle, let alone walk.*

While frustrating for him (and us when 'other parents' suggested some-thing was wrong) 21 months gave us two summer holidays where he just lay there, which was fairly handy.

As for teething nappies I don't think the word 'rancid' truly does them justice. It's like every bit of evil in the world was popped into a blender and mixed with every bit of roadkill, with the whole cocktail placed into a flimsy excuse for a nappy which then channels it all the way up their back.

Nick, father of two: *I'm not sure teeth coming through are the best design. It went on for a week and then you realise that they have 24 of the things and it seems to go on forever.*

Winston, father of two: *Both mine suffered badly from teething, and your heart goes out to them because it looks so miserable.*

On the plus side, however, teething can be used as an excuse for any sub-par behaviour by your children right up to the age of eight.

GETTING TO KNOW YOU

As you slowly emerge blinking into the sunlight from the first six months of parenthood you may well glance to the side and see a figure that you vaguely recognise.

The rounded shoulders, the pallid skin, the 1,000-yard stare, yes they are all familiar, you've passed those features many a time on the pre-dawn landing, trying to block out the distant tweeting of birds as you hunt for the elusive Calpol® syringe like a crazed paracetamol-pushing junkie.

But it's not those traits that are registering with you just now, it's something far more deep-rooted, like an old memory involuntarily twitching back to life in the recesses of your sleep-deprived brain.

This is your partner, the person who just half a year ago was the ying to your yang, the Bonnie to your Clyde, the Janette to your Ian Krankie – and now as you both surface from the baby bunker it's time to start getting to know each other again.

Jetting off to Venice to relight your fire isn't really an option for most – even a trip to the local multiplex involves logistical preparation on a monumental scale. So what do you do to ensure that you don't just turn into a bottle-sterilising, nappy-bin-emptying robotic nightmare of a couple who haven't only forgotten what drove them to have a baby together, but also how they actually managed to make it happen too?

Romance amidst the reflux

It's surprising how hard it is to be warm and loving in the wee small hours of the morning.

Likewise for the ability to retain anything even approaching a sense of humour.

Hysterical laughing, that shows itself from time to time yes, but water off a duck's back, laugh in the face of life's challenges. Bona fide humour? No, not very much of that knocking around at all.

This environment of hard work and fatigue can be stony ground indeed for love's delicate seeds, but there are things you can do, small things, easy things that keep the flame of romance flickering during the tough times, ready for you to take the bellows to it when the time is right.

First of all try, try, try to keep the little intimate gestures that are the understated lifeblood of any relationship going. I'm not talking about a grope that indicates you may have woken up from your slumber enough to feel fruity (we will be getting on to sex shortly). It's the touch as you pass in the kitchen, a kiss every now and then. It's vital these aren't meant or seen as a big come-on – having an actual conversation to agree that these little things need to be reintroduced for their own merits is a smart move.

I'm aware this sounds hideously contrived and manufactured but the truth is for a lot of us that unless you work, at least initially, at keeping things ticking over on that front, tiredness and even stress will triumph over love – and we can't have that, can we?

As we've already acknowledged, the long weekend away is a big, big ask just now – if breastfeeding is still going on it's almost definitely out unless your partner is an expressing queen. Even when bottle-feeding is the route of choice, many new parents find handing their baby over to even the most trusted and experienced friend or relative incredibly hard to do for more than a night.

But an afternoon or an evening out will do you more good than you can imagine. You might be checking the phone a lot to see if all is well, but getting away, properly away to a nice restaurant or for a film and a pizza is crucial. Don't put it off, organise it now and make it happen, it doesn't have to be flash. Pooh sticks on the river and a picnic will do – you'll be glad you did.

When you've done it the once and the world didn't end, get another date in the diary pronto. It doesn't have to be that soon even, the anticipation of a break can get you both through all sorts of trials.

You're the entertainment officer now as well as the daddy, so crack on.

By the way, don't for a moment think I'm suggesting all this as someone who knows all the answers – my wife will be reading this to a soundtrack of derisive shrieks that will be knocking pictures off walls. No, most of this wisdom is pieced together from the dads I've spoken to, all of whom made mistakes galore, but between them were nestled some real gems to help insulate your relationship in the tough times.

Choosing to spend hours on end writing a book in the first years of parenthood probably wasn't one of them if I'm honest though.

Sex and the newly parented

At the heart of the altered relationship arena for new parents is, of course, sex.

Depending on your respective sex drives, the often-decreasing amount of lovemaking you find the time for can cause obvious and profound problems for how together you feel as a couple and how able you are to cope with all that your new life will throw at you.

In a nutshell, the closer you feel, the more intimate you'll be with each other, the more intimate you are with each other the better able to cope and be tolerant and sympathetic with each other you'll be – and the closer you'll feel.

Catch that number 22.

While it's often the case that the man wants sex and the woman not so much, as with all generalisations there are many, many cases where the opposite is true. Pressure at work and at home may mean the very last thing you feel capable of is performing in the bedroom big top.

Whatever your particular configuration, though, there will need to be, at some point, the first time you make love since baby was born.

Official medical advice suggests around eight weeks or so. For many women the sheer physical upheaval that they have endured is enough to lengthen that time frame by some considerable distance, not to mention how absolutely exhausted the adults in the household are too.

Whenever you both decide to reacquaint yourselves, it's worth remembering that in many ways it's very much like the first time all over again and you'll need to take it nice and slow.

Without getting too graphic, women can be a bit dry during sex, especially if they are breastfeeding. So don't get upset and think she's not turned on, have some personal lubricant to hand and let her choose the position and pace that's right. Also be prepared for things to feel a bit different too – there's been a lot going on down there.

That was quite graphic actually wasn't it? It's best to know, though.

A word of warning: Don't be fooled into thinking that you can do without birth control for a nice long while – it's true that a woman isn't fertile immediately after birth, especially if she's breast-feeding, but guessing how long that spell will last is a game of Russian Roulette you'll not want to lose, unless you are immediately ready for number two (are you mad?). The hormones in most oral contraceptives don't mix with breastfeeding either, so you are looking at some sort of barrier method too – always nice.

As well as the physical elements that make up being ready for bedroom intimacy there's the emotional side, too. There's many a reason why more time and understanding might be needed. Your partner may be seriously apprehensive about pain, she may not feel at her most physically attractive, after the indignity of labour she may not feel quite the same about her most intimate parts for a while and she will definitely be knackered beyond belief.

Space, affection, understanding and compliments are the order of the day – applying even delicate pressure may well start a chain of events which will turn sex into a battleground and bargaining chip – which is deeply unsexy and unfulfilling for everyone involved.

You wouldn't do that, would you?

Your partner may not be the only one who has a few mental scars that need to heal either. Some men have real trouble recovering from the sights they viewed during the labour, especially the gynaecologically graphic moments. As with all these psychological issues, the romancing and the wooing we've already talked about is the way to go. You're both going through an enthralling but exhausting time of your lives where you are essentially falling in love with the new little person in your lives while your partner's body and hormones are still on a massive comedown.

It's tough, so if you can, give yourselves a break and enjoy getting to know each other again.

Words from your fellow fathers:

Nick, father of two: *I think our first overnighter without the baby was at a wedding.*

We completely overplayed our hand, as though the world might never serve us alcohol again, if we didn't show some form.

Regretted that, until the next time.

Stuart, father of two: *We didn't have family close by and didn't know any babysitters we could trust so I think our first night out was months if not over a year after our eldest was born.*

As for an overnighter together with no kids – we're still waiting for that to happen four years in!

Tom, father of two: *Put it this way, I never ever in a million years, thought I'd hear myself saying I'm too tired.*

Paul, father of two: *Sleep is the new sex.*

PROGRESS REPORT, 7–9 MONTHS

Your baby

Given that your clever little tot is learning to crawl, eating solid food and cutting teeth during this three-month spell, you'd imagine she'd have very little time for much else.

Not a bit of it! She is a learning machine, and among other things you might find that she starts to turn towards you when she hears her own name. When you stop to think about that, it is an astonishing achievement. Not only is she picking up that the noises people make mean something, she has even associated one of the thousands of slightly different sounds she has heard so far in her brief life with being something to do with her.

She's a genius. They all are.

She'll also start to imitate you, nodding, shaking her head, sticking her tongue out. The beginnings of an independent spirit – more of which in the next chapter – start to shine through as she grabs at her bottle or spoon and attempts to feed herself.

Peek-a-boo will start to be the most entertaining pastime your household has ever seen at this stage, and it will retain its popularity for months to come.

If you've not taken your little one swimming yet get your trunks on. Getting your baby used to water early doors makes an awful lot of sense from a safety point of view and they have an absolute ball in the water.

You'll need to ensure you have a tonne of kit in the swim bag, from swim nappies and toys to a snack and the ubiquitous changing mat – but it's well worth the rigmarole to see her little face as she splashes around and enjoys a real sense of freedom as she is surrounded by liquid, just like she was less than a year ago!

Your partner

If your partner is still breastfeeding, you may well have to become accustomed to blood-curdling screams from her as your recently betoothed baby bites down on her nipple.

Yikes!

Looking after a baby who moves is unsurprisingly a lot more shattering than keeping an eye on one who helpfully stays exactly where you plonk them. Even when you are in the same room as them the average length of any sit down you may sneak would be, should any academics have measured it, no more than 15 seconds in length, I'll wager.

All of which goes to create a very, very tired person. If you've still not reached a state of 'sleeping through' yet then we are talking some serious fatigue here and you'll have to play a big part in helping run the house and keeping your partner's pecker up.

You

The only trouble with the last sentence above is that you'll be pretty knackered, too – which can lead to some rather fractious conversations.

The classic battleground on this front is the fact that after a long hard day at work you come home and naturally feel the need to relax and unwind. Your partner, after a day feeding, chasing and cleaning a teething, crawling, yoghurt-throwing nipper sees your entrance through the front door as her long-awaited chance to relax and unwind.

There's a problem there, isn't there? But what's the answer?

Please do let me and the rest of parentkind know if you happen to stumble across it.

What's for sure is that clear, unemotional communication can really help avoid flash points and arguments that make already diffi-cult situations much, much worse. In some ways, when to raise an issue is almost more important than how you do it. Choosing a peace-ful, relatively calm moment to discuss something, whether that be about the division of labour, childcare techniques or whatever, is infinitely preferable to letting your hackles rise and spewing out a long list of pent-up frustrations right in the middle of an already stressful moment.

Once you've got things off your chest at the least inflammatory moment possible you'll need a cocktail of compromise, understanding and humility topped up with copious amounts of humour to make a new plan and move on.

YOU'VE COME A LONG WAY, BABY

Pretty soon you'll have been a father for an entire year.

Although you may feel you've aged 10 times that amount and that you've never worked so hard, worried so much or slept so little – the chances are it will shock you just how quickly time has passed and how much your floppy newborn has changed in these 12 months.

As if to rub it in, technically the term 'baby' no longer applies past the first year – you've got an 'infant' on your hands from this point onwards – although no doubt your baby will be called 'your baby' for many years to come yet.

As well as deciding how best to celebrate the year milestone this spell may well also see your little one take an enormous evolutionary step in every sense of the word, as she casts aside her recently acquired skill of crawling in favour of walking.

The development of physical independence is also matched by the mental and emotional strides taken now, too. A real sense of self often becomes apparent and with that comes a sense of others – you and your partner in particular. In a beautifully choreographed piece of psychological learning your baby can almost at a stroke become more independent as she gets to know herself and at the same time more dependent as her recognition of both of you leads to separation anxiety if and when you have to be apart – or even if one of you merely leaves the room.

Separation can be a hot topic for mothers, too, during these few months. Maternity leave often ends for many, with the readjustment back to work and – perhaps more dauntingly – the childcare conundrum all to be tackled.

Meanwhile your baby is as cute as a button in what is a glorious stage of her young life as she continues to explore, grow in confidence and melt your heart with her ever-widening smile.

WALKING

Learning to walk isn't just one of the most impressive things your baby will ever do, it isn't just a huge leap towards independence, it is an anthropological, evolutionary marvel and it'll probably happen right in your front room.

After just 12 months or so on the planet the new little human in your house will be desperate to get in on the act, too.

It's natural, almost inevitable that you'll get a bit twitchy when one of your baby's contemporaries makes one giant leap before your pride and joy does. As the comedian Michael McIntyre wryly points out, you don't often see adults dragging themselves into work because they just never got round to learning the walking thing – so try and relax, if your baby is otherwise physically healthy, it will happen.

Once she moves from crawling to pulling herself up on the furniture and cruising around the joint, it's only a matter of time and confidence. By around the 15-month mark most healthy babies are walking on their own, so have a little patience. Luxuriate in the knowledge that once they do start marching around the place they are even more of a handful until they really master their steps months later.

From cruising they can move into the clean and jerk, where they slowly squat and stand, squat and stand like a lethargic Cossack dancer. Then it's often on to the 'look at me' holding hands stage where with your help they motor around the place sporting an almightily cute grin.

From there they will gradually pluck up the courage to take that first step on their own. While it would be fantastic if it were to happen in front of the two of you with a lighting rig set up and three smartphones recording, don't be too crestfallen if it's just your partner or the childminder or nursery staff who get the privilege of witnessing the golden moment. Just be grateful and proud she has cracked it and know that you have played a massive part in helping her reach that milestone, and every other one along the way, too.

You can certainly help your baby along the way and the toddle truck toys you see are great for encouraging them, although you'll need to be standing nearby for a while. Before you know it, you'll be happily chopping an onion when your lower ankle will be rammed at high speed in a surprise attack.

Baby walkers, the proto Dalek-wheeled chariot that were all the rage a decade ago, have seriously fallen out of favour and are even banned in some countries – it's argued that as well as giving your baby extra height to get at hitherto out of reach danger items on work tops, they can adversely affect your baby's development.

Likewise, baby bouncers that hang from door frames have also become frowned upon. The best bet is to Google them both and read up on the pros and cons before you make your mind up.

As your baby learns to walk, it's best not to truss her feet up in shoes too soon. It's not as if she will be walking on shingle at this stage and the more chance her feet have to grow unfettered, the better. Once she is ready for the great outdoors a qualified fitter is recommended – despite the fact that gram for gram, baby shoes must be the most expensive item on the planet outside of weapons-grade plutonium.

If your baby seems to be really lagging behind and isn't walking by around 18 months, go and see your GP. They'll do some blood tests, to rule out any rare muscle disorders. They say the chances are that if you or your partner were particularly late walkers your children could be too, so a word with the folks could reassure you – or make things a hundred times worse, depending what they are like – bloody parents, eh?

Words from your fellow fathers:

Paul, father of two: *Both of mine have taken their first steps at their grandparents' house. This is either because despite being OAPs they have the energy to cajole it out of them or the fact that they have lovely soft carpet and we have practical, wipe-clean floorboards.*

Mark, father of one: *I missed the first steps but she did them again for me when I came back from work.*

It was truly moving and funny seeing her get some independence but then do a funny waddle across the room.

Winston, father of two: *I might not have seen the very first steps, but certainly among the first.*

The look of achievement on her face was something to behold.

INDEPENDENCE DAYS

Here's a strange thing to consider. It's believed that when your baby is a newborn she thinks she's a part of her mother and, to a lesser degree, you. You only have to watch the look of bemusement bordering on terror when she first discovers her own arms and hands (at around four months) to know that's the case.

As her fleshy appendages flail around in front of her her eyes widen as if she's being teased by a giant squid – if I'm you, Mum, who the hell owns these two things?

At around six months of life, the penny drops and she'll start to realise that she is a person in her own right. Quite how mind-blowing that moment of clarity must be is almost beyond comprehension and it's arguable that as humans we never make a discovery as profound ever again.

Once you realise that you are you and not someone else, the next step is to realise that if you're not particularly liking something, or would rather it done another way – your way – kicking off about it is most definitely an option. This sense of individuality which slowly begins to develop now takes years to develop fully, but what you begin to see now are the seeds of the toddler tantrums you'll encounter soon and also a glimpse into your child's broader personality.

Which is both exciting and fascinating.

The other side of the independence coin is realising that you can be apart from others, and separation anxiety also kicks in around this time, too.

Separation anxiety

Up until the six- or seven-month mark your baby hasn't got time for psycho codswallop like developing a sense of self – she is a survival machine, food and love are what she needs and everything else can form an orderly queue behind Mummy.

But gradually as she discovers that she can do things like smile and get smiles back, cry for attention and get angry at the unspeakable injustices heaped upon her like nappy changing and face washing, she learns that what she does affects these two people who seem to be hanging around a lot, which must mean that she is separate from them.

What a clever little baby.

It's around this point of enlightenment that you'll likely start to notice that either of you, but especially your partner, leaving the room will often result in a sudden bout of tears. Trouble is, she doesn't yet realise that when you nip to the loo, you'll be back.

Sneaking out so she doesn't see you leave isn't advisable, according to some child psychologists (although you may well find yourself instinctively doing it to avoid upset) because it can make her even more afraid when she suddenly notices you've gone.

Interestingly, games such as peek-a-boo and later hide-and-seek can help develop an understanding of separation and return. If you disappear under a blanket and then come back you'll do the same when you leave the room or the house. The reason she laughs at peck-a-boo is because the laugh and the cry are very close bedfellows, indeed even in adults – the scream on the rollercoaster is perhaps the absolute middle ground between the two, titillation and excitement when fear of the unknown is close at hand.

Your baby might still be getting upset at being left at nursery when she is two or more so this is a long-term process. What's vital is that throughout it she is becoming slowly more secure, more content that you will come back. This trust is built up by the love and care you show for her. As her memory develops, she taps into that more and more in her moments of anxiety when one or both of you aren't there.

This is pretty deep-rooted stuff and you can see as clear as day how a repeatedly insecure existence at this tender age can have major implications later down the line. What's equally important is that you don't castigate yourselves for having to go to work – it's a fact of life in our society where a single income often doesn't even come close to covering a mortgage.

What's also a fact of life is that children absolutely need to develop a strong sense of independence and be secure enough to step out on their own. As ever in parenthood, especially when both parents work, it's about striking a tricky balance between keeping your children safe and letting them explore, running a household and spending time with your children, comforting them and keeping them close while encouraging them to develop and learn on their own.

In many ways, this is one of the most central challenges any parent ever faces and it's true to say men and women approach it differently. Just as it's been noted that women tend to hold their youngsters into them to protect and men outwards so they can observe, both you and your partner will bring different skills to the table where independence and separation is concerned. You may allow them to take a few more supervised risks or, on the flip side, become more impatient further down the line when they seek comfort when you may think they should pick themselves up and dust themselves off.

Both approaches are valid and needed, it's down to you and your partner to create the right blend of the two for your child – and that blending starts now.

Within all of this, what is irrefutable is that your baby and later toddler needs a rock-solid attachment to you and your partner so that she can begin to explore the world securely and test her developing skills – safe in the knowledge that she can always return to you.

Giving her consistent love, engagement and confidence-building encouragement is key to creating that attachment, that trust. As your baby moves into toddlerhood, ensuring there is a safe environment for her to explore at home is also a key factor, meaning she won't constantly hear 'no' when she is trying to strike out and learn.

Later on, when she is striding forth ready to take on the world as a three-, four- or five-year-old, she will still need to know that you are there when needed, uncritical, loving and warm. When you think about your relationship with your own parents as I've just done writing that, the need for that safe haven from the people who were there in your most formative years never really fully leaves us does it?

With all that in mind, it's obvious to see why providing your child with the best possible environment when you can't be with them at this early stage in their lives becomes such an all-consuming issue for parents everywhere.

WORK AND THE MODERN FAMILY: WELCOME TO THE CHILDCARE CARNIVAL

Across the globe, more mothers than ever before are working – and nowhere is this trend more prevalent than here in the UK.

Half of British mums go back to work before their child's first birthday, according to a worldwide report by the Organisation for Economic Co-operation and Development (OECD) – with more than a quarter of them in paid work before their child is six months old.

When you consider that in 1968 only 18% of women earned the same or more than their male partners and that today that is the case in 44% of households, you can see just how integral woman's earning power has become to both the national and domestic purse.

This profound shift in the economic fabric has led to a rise in the stay-at-home dad, with research suggesting that the number of fathers acting as the primary carer now stands at around 600,000 – a tenfold increase over the last decade.

With the introduction of joint parental leave that can be shared between both parents, even more fathers will be able to spend time with their children. The stay-at-home dad may become a permanent fixture in our society and an increasingly large and vociferous group capable of making its own views known.

Childcare

Plenty of parents are more than happy with a situation which allows them to both achieve fulfilment through their respective careers while enjoying a family too.

There are also those who post-maternity/paternity leave would love nothing more than to spend some or all of the week with their young ones, but whose finances dictate that they both need to work every hour they can just to keep the wolf from the door.

What these groups share is a reliance on childcare in some shape or form – and, as you may have already found out, this is an incredibly expensive and complex area. The OECD report mentioned earlier went as far as to say that quality childcare in the UK was among the most expensive in the Western world. In fact it's a multi-billion pound industry in the UK and with a number of options open to parents there's a lot to get your head around.

Childminders

Childminders have become a hugely popular childcare option over the past 30 years or so, with registered childminders being regulated by Ofsted in England and the relevant bodies in Scotland, Wales and Northern Ireland, to look after babies and older children.

As well as the Ofsted checks, which mean that they must attend a registration and first aid course within six months of enlisting, all childminders must be Disclosure and Barring Service (DBS) checked, as must all adult members of their family who share their home.

In the main, children are looked after at the childminder's home, which itself has to be inspected regularly by Ofsted, but some can offer their services based in your home rather than theirs.

Finding a childminder you, your partner and your child likes is vital and tricky in equal measure. You need to seek someone out who has a good reputation, can deal equally with their own children, if they have any, and those in their care and can be firm and fair without scaring the bejesus out of either you or your kids.

It goes without saying that a childminder who doesn't enjoy being with children is to be avoided, as is someone who you sense will reach for the TV remote or dish out the iPads the moment they need to keep the kids occupied. As with all childminding options, the chances are your little ones will be spending some serious time in the company of this person and if they have some creative ways to engage their happy gaggle everyone will benefit.

Knowing that your tot is being looked after in a warm, friendly home by someone you trust and like is worth an awful lot – which is precisely what you'll be paying for it.

Nurseries

Nurseries employ a combination of qualified and unqualified staff to look after children from as young as four months old up to five years of age.

Open for anything up to 11 hours per day, the modern nursery works hard to accommodate parents' work situations and although many close for a short break in the summer they tend to be open pretty much across the board.

Choosing a nursery takes time, and asking around in the local area even before you have children can be very worthwhile as many places at the best nurseries are booked up months in advance. The average nursery place will set you back £131 a week so it's reckoned, but you can easily find yourself paying much, much more, with prices reaching £300 per week not unheard of.

Less intimate than the childminder or nanny option, what they do offer is a real sense of socialisation for your little one, if that's what you think they will need and thrive on.

Nannies

For the most part when people say they have a nanny they have an arrangement with someone who looks after their children in their own home, has a recognised childcare qualification and is responsible for duties including planning activities, assisting in the child's development, shopping for and preparing the youngster's meals, keeping the child's areas of the house clean and tidy and doing the child's laundry.

That's quite a list and even more of a responsibility.

Nannies are an attractive option for many who can afford them – as well as offering one-to-one care, the disruption to your child's routine is minimised because the care takes place for the most part in the familiar surroundings of your home.

If you've ever seen *Mary Poppins*, you'll know all too well that finding the right nanny is a tricky and time-consuming business. Notwithstanding having your ideal candidate floating in on an umbrella you'll have to place ads, use agencies and keep your ear to the ground to be able to snare the right one for you and your family.

The cost?

Well before we talk about anything as grubby as money bear in mind that when you hire a nanny you become an employer. It's down to you to sort out paying tax and National Insurance and then there's sick and holiday pay.

And what perks can you offer? Use of the car, private health care, gym membership? We might be looking toward the top end with these kinds of sweeteners, but increasingly the market is becoming a cut-throat world – which is why the average nanny takes home between £350 and £450 a week with supercalifragilistic ones pocketing much, much more than that.

Au pairs

I have news. Au pairs exist in real life and not just in 70s sitcoms.

An au pair is a foreign national who in exchange for the opportunity to learn another language and a spot of board and lodging at your place will do some housework and childcare duties.

Most au pairs aren't strictly trained in childcare and most agencies who hook them up with prospective parents suggest that they are best used for older children, but the prospect of an au pair to help around the house, babysit and look after the children during the day has its obvious appeal. But things can and do on occasion go a bit pear-shaped.

The language barrier might be too much, the lack of genuine childcare experience and training may not sit well with you in reality, perhaps you'll go power mad and ask them to do way too much or maybe they just won't fit in with family life in your house for one of a million reasons.

Whatever the reason may be, because there is no real contract as such they can simply leave without notice if they wish. The agency can often help resolve some of these issues, but it's important not to be blinded by the benefits of an au pair and ignore the potential pitfalls.

Financially, au pairs offer serious value for money. They are generally expected to work for five days a week, up to a maximum of five hours per day and be available to babysit for two nights a week.

Family members

Despite the proliferation in other childcare options, informal arrangements with relatives still make up most childcare arrangements in the UK.

Whether it's reciprocal arrangements between two related part-time workers or a mother/mother-in-law tag team of fearsome proportions, family members can offer low- or no-cost, flexible and ultra-secure childcare, just as they have for millennia.

As well as the obvious positives there are some equally obvious pitfalls too.

'Mum, we'd just like a word about the knife-throwing game you are playing with them.'

Just as going into business with a relative can be a recipe for unhappy families, so childcare can generate some intergenerational heat when it comes to delivering friendly tips and suggestions.

But if you've got a relative with whom you have a good honest relationship and who shares your general philosophy on bringing up children, then as well as being quids in and a lucky bugger you will also be giving your child perhaps the most loving and secure childcare option of them all.

Flexible working

As well as carefully choosing which childcare route works best for you, your partner and your infant, there are two things you can try to wheedle out of your employers which could help in different ways.

Flexible working is simply the act of finding a way of working which suits both you and your employer.

Whoever set up the whole Monday to Friday nine to five thing obviously didn't have a daily school run to squeeze in, so increasingly flexible working patterns are being agreed across a range of industries ranging from part-time working, to flexi-time days or job shares.

What's more, you, as a father, are just as entitled to have a flexible working request considered as mothers are. If it's refused, there must be valid reasons for saying no. 'Don't be daft, you're a man' won't cut it.

So, if you have a child under the age of six and have been employed for six months by the time you apply, you can put in a serious request and expect serious consideration – the trick is to do some real planning and research before you put your request together. Are there any other fathers and mothers who have had flexible working sanctioned where you work? If so, how? What could your employer's objections be and how can you mitigate them?

Also make sure you put some effort into your presentation and show your boss that you've not only taken this very seriously, but that it also means a great deal to you. On your part you need to be sure that if as part of your plan you are suggesting a drop in hours you can really cope with the subsequent drop in salary. Trying to undo it can be very tricky.

But if you are sure you can cope financially, flexible working can be a real bonus for you and your partner and as well as potentially reducing your childcare bill you can get to spend some proper time with your child during the week, rather than flying in the door at five to seven only to find you've missed bathtime again.

Of course, post-pandemic working from home has taken a giant leap into the mainstream with huge numbers of us now taking up the option to split our time between in person and on laptop. Dovetailing with your partner so the week's pick-ups and drop-offs are covered can be a real boon. Anyone trying to actually work from home with a baby or toddler in tow has both my admiration and sympathy.

Childcare vouchers

Equally as helpful, although nowhere near as exciting, are childcare voucher schemes. These allow you to ring-fence a stipulated part of your salary to pay for childcare. You don't pay tax or National Insurance on that slice of what you earn, so you get more bang for your buck and can save hundreds of pounds a year.

Your employer needs to be signed up to the scheme for you to be able to benefit, but if they're not, point out to them that it also means they can reduce the size of their payroll costs and increase staff satisfaction levels to boot.

If that doesn't work, erect a tented village outside the Human Resources director's office until they capitulate.

Words from your fellow fathers:

Nick, father of two: *We tried an au pair. She was terrible.*

We knew it was bad when our boy would walk in the room and just look at his shoes when she was there. She ended up sleeping in our bed when we went away for a weekend. She left soon afterwards.

My wife is freelance and we found this great woman who is really flexible, the children love and can turn up at the drop of a hat. If not we begged grandparents.

Colin, father of two: *We were lucky – we found a childminder a minute away from my wife's work and she was flexible so when I wasn't* *working we didn't have to pay for childcare and I could look after our daughter.*

Ben, father of two: *Find a very earnest friend who has a slightly older child than you who has vetted all the local nurseries first and then just copy them.*

Stuart, father of two: *As soon as we got pregnant we knew that once my partner's maternity leave was up I would leave my job as a graphic designer (as I could continue doing little jobs from home) and become a stay-at-home dad. So from our point of view it was pretty straightforward.*

BABY IS ONE!

Congratulations! An entire year has passed since you first became a dad and you have survived – let's celebrate.

In all honesty your baby's first birthday is more for you and your partner than it is for your little one – and there's nothing wrong with that is there?

Negotiating the first year is something you should be rightly proud of because between the three of you an awful lot has been learnt. Tears have been shed, foul smells have been emitted and smiles abound from your beautiful bairn.

But it's not all about you – what do you give to the one-year-old who has everything, if by everything you mean an old telly remote and half a biscuit from under the highchair?

The answer is that presents don't matter a jot, the chances are she's already inundated with plastic toys that are magnetically attracted to the underside of your feet the minute the lights are off.

The best present they could get is you having a day off work and playing on the carpet with them for five hours solid.

Another good thing to do is take a picture on the big day and then on each birthday subsequently. As well as being a really lovely memento and memory jogger (the amount you seem to forget as a parent and the speed at which you forget it never fails to amaze and disturb me) it will also act as ideal embarrassment fodder should you wish to plaster the entire reception venue with them when their wedding comes around.

But if a shedload of presents is a waste of cash, a party, a gathering, a get-together, a shindig, a bit of a do, most certainly isn't – you all deserve it!

Party time

As we've seen, one-year-olds aren't necessarily the biggest socialisers in the world. The guest list, if they were in charge, might just about stretch to mum, dad, grandparents . . . and, er . . . that's it. A houseful of strange faces all chanting a weird song at you while flashing lights go off and tiny sticks are set on fire sounds like something that just missed the final cut of the *Wicker Man*. If you get carried away and plan too big, you could well have a tearful tot on your hands.

Some youngsters love other babies, others couldn't be more indifferent towards them if they wore a jumper saying 'DO I KNOW YOU?' – so it's down to you and your partner to set the level just right. The antenatal class crowd is often a good bet, with joint parties a good option given the proximity of the birthdays, or maybe just keep it to a bit of a family do?

A couple of hours for the kids is way long enough, but if you want to make it a bit of a let-your-hair-down session for all the parents in the house, make sure you do your maths and take naps into account to avoid a cacophony of cries drowning out the sound of popping corks.

Cake? Of course.

Party bags? Give yourselves a break. Theme? Absolutely not.

Restock the changing table? Good idea. Double-check stair-gates? You bet your ass.

At the end of the day, when the house is quiet, the cake has been trodden firmly into the carpet and the cat has been peeled off the ceiling, make sure you share a glass of something nice (it'll be cold by now!) with your partner, take a look at the pictures from the day and even a few from the year you've just completed together and toast yourselves – you did it.

Words from your fellow fathers:

Ben, father of two: *Kept it all very low key. Small family tea party. Only mentalists and very rich stay-at-home mums have big parties before children are three and even then they ALWAYS end in tears.*

Jason, father of two: *We had the two families round. Could have been disastrous but went quite well. Babies do positive things.*

Winston, father of two: *We had lots of family, mums and dads and babies and my daughter cried when everyone sang Happy Birthday because she didn't like the tune.*

You want to celebrate for getting through it and we ended up pissed as loons at the end.

Simon, father of one: *Coincidentally, our son shares his birthday with my dad, so we had a joint celebration. Low key – a few friends and family, a few beers, a few rows.*

PROGRESS REPORT, 10–12 MONTHS

Your baby

Your standing, cruising and potentially walking miracle of a baby can also start to develop a taste for some very light rough play around now.

It's a funny thing, rough play. On one hand it's as stereotypical as it gets, exactly what people would expect a lumbering dad to do with their delicate and precious babies – spin them around a bit in an oafish display of chimp-like exuberance. But guess what, in the last few years research has started to unearth just how important the more roughhouse type of play is in young children's development.

At this tender age the utmost care must be taken when playing. Oversized heads and still under-strength necks must be treated with absolute caution, but it's at about this time that you and your little one will begin a physical interaction that will carry on for many years and, according to scientists at the University of Newcastle in Australia, deliver some profound benefits.

The researchers believe that this kind of play creates a sense of achievement when the child 'defeats' a more powerful adult, which in turn builds their self-confidence and concentration.

As well as letting them win, though, when dads resist their children in rough play the crucial lesson that we don't always triumph in life is also communicated in a powerful and real way. The researchers even went on to suggest that the very act of a stronger adult holding back that strength also helps to build deep-rooted trust between father and child.

So maybe the apes know what they are doing after all?

You might also start to notice the beginnings of a vocabulary at this stage, the 'da-das' and 'ma-mas' might be more detectable, and there might even be an odd 'ow' or a 'meow' knocking about too. In the next chapter we will look at how your baby learns in such a scarily impressive way.

Your partner

The end of the first year can be a tough time for your partner – it may be the point she stops breastfeeding, goes back to work or both. Together with your baby walking and even starting to talk, all this can culminate in a real sense of time passing incredibly quickly, of your little one growing up before your eyes.

Luckily your partner will still be so exhausted that any feelings of loss or wistfulness will be edged out by bone-crunching fatigue and a constant worry that the last person who went up the stairs (you) didn't close the gate.

She might not have lost all the weight she wanted, she may not be able to remember the days when going to bed at 8.30 on a Saturday night would have seemed sad rather than exciting and she may never have thought that having an uninterrupted shower would seem the very height of luxury – but your partner has been a mum for a whole year and she's changed and grown in ways she never dreamed possible.

A little gift for her to celebrate what she has achieved in these past 12 months would be, I'm sure you'd agree, richly deserved, not to mention going down really rather well.

You

Did the things you were worried about before the baby arrived pan out, or were you broadsided by stuff that simply hadn't occurred to you?

Have you developed a new appreciation or understanding for your own father, or have the strength of your new-found paternal feelings simply generated more questions in your mind about the relationship you have with him?

Being a dad brings some serious emotional stuff to the surface on a regular basis. While it's tempting to beat it back down again with the thick end of a packet of wet wipes, if you can air some of it with your partner you will reap the benefits on all sorts of levels. There's much more to come, when your toddler tries your patience and you feel anger towards them for the first time. When someone else's child is mean or even violent towards your little angel you'll be tested – my, how you'll be tested – but you can handle it, grow from it even, because along with the trials will come moments of joy and pride that will swell your chest to bursting point.

But for now, let's just say well done on the first year and assume the brace position for toddlerhood.

YOUR BABY: THE INFORMATION JUNKIE

Your baby enters her second year having learnt to smile, interact, eat, move and make your heart disintegrate with the merest wave of the hand or point of the finger.

Chances are she will also be starting to turn her babbling into the basis of coherent words. As she sits in the highchair and fixes you in her cheeky gaze you might find that the traditional dropping of the broccoli floret on the floor will be accompanied by a beautifully delivered 'Uh-oh'.

This is seriously impressive stuff, but just you wait, she's only just beginning and will soon start to pick up words, intonation and expression at a frightening rate. Before you know where you are you'll have a three-year-old who sits in the back of the car and asks if you are lost, when you frankly have no idea where you are. But just how do they do it? How do they suck up information so quickly given that adulthood renders the remembering of more than one password for your laptop all but an impossibility?

What's more, what can you do to encourage, facilitate and help them learn without turning into the kind of 'show them how you can count to 50 in French' parent you have always wanted to resist becoming?

What toys are best to buy? Is putting them in front of the TV even remotely educational or is it simply the only way you know to buy the time needed to empty the dishwasher?

There are many more questions too, some of them so new that finding answers to them is tough – notably around the digital revolution we are in the midst of – do apps teach them anything or just make your car journey easier? Should you encourage them to use a computer or discourage it and get a Victorian spinning top out?

As you may imagine, hard and fast rules are thin on the ground, but these are all issues that will run and run throughout your parenting career and you'll be amazed at how quickly you are forced to address them. All the evidence, as we will see, points to the fact that the earlier you get a handle on things in this realm as a parent, the more your child will benefit.

The reality is, your infant, not even 18 months old yet, will almost certainly be irresistibly drawn to not just books, but the goggle box in the corner of the room and any digital device they see you using. Then it's only a matter of time before they will make you look like a leaden-fingered Luddite as they master them in ways you never knew existed.

Let's start this journey by looking at how your baby's brain manages to pull the great learning trick off.

HOW BABIES LEARN

It's pretty clear that the first three years of life are a period of incredible and never-to-be-repeated growth and development.

At birth, a baby's brain is about 25% of its approximate adult weight, but by the age of three it has spurted in dramatic fashion and produced billions of cells and trillions of communication routes called synapses that link the cells together and form the network of all networks. This makes the internet look as complex and technically impressive as a pushbike in comparison.

While it's true that the young brain's development takes years to complete and indeed that our grey matter shapes and reshapes itself throughout our lives to adapt and cope with new challenges and experiences, it's becoming increasingly clear that what youngsters encounter and engage with from the very start of their existence has a huge part to play in laying the right foundations for learning right through their lives.

What's more, what a child experiences in its early days profoundly influences how that development will take place and the way they interact with the world throughout their lives.

They might not to be able to remember a single thing you've done for them in these early years and months but, my goodness, it will have an effect on them.

According to the World Health Organization, a startling array of challenges in adulthood, such as mental health issues, obesity, heart disease, criminality as well as the perhaps more obvious instances of poor literacy and numeracy, can be traced back to early childhood and the environment children learn from.

In the relatively recent past, extended family members were often close by, offering us advice and being the role models for us newbie parents – but with the change in the way we live and work, that isn't the case for a growing number of us anymore.

Which all amounts to the reality that as if keeping them away from the stairs, out of the fire and off the M6 wasn't responsibility enough, you and your partner are also very much in charge of the brain department, too.

Perhaps the most stark way your baby's experiences shape their brain growth is the way in which they learn language.

Language and literacy

By the time an infant is just three months old her brain can distinguish several hundred different spoken sounds rather than words; that's comfortably more than exist in her native language.

As the months move on, though, she will filter out the sounds she doesn't need and recognise only those that are part of the language she regularly hears. The brain doesn't discard this astonishing skill completely though, oh no, during early childhood it stores the ability to re-learn sounds it has discarded at the drop of a linguist's hat.

This smart move explains why young children typically learn new languages in a way that makes us adults feel like we will be stuck asking the way to the station when we actually want the beach, for the rest of our days. From about the age of 10 onwards kids finally begin to lose this ability, just in time for most of them to begin being taught French at secondary school.

Merde.

Leaving this educational anomaly aside, it's obvious that very early experiences play an enormous role in how well a child will not only speak, but also read and write in their native language. Research has found that parents who spoke to their infants regularly enabled their little ones to learn almost 300 more words by the time they were two than children who were rarely spoken to.

Other studies have also found that just being exposed to language by, let's say, listening to the television (more of which later) adds very little indeed. What children need, it seems, is direct interaction with real, proper, actually standing-there-in–front-of-them human beings.

Which raises two questions – how should I speak to my baby and how the hell can I find the time to do it more?

First, the 'to baby talk or not to baby talk' debate is an interesting one. You may have already come across the school of thought that subscribes to the 'talk to them like an infant and they will always talk like an infant'.

It's normally trotted out by quite annoying people for some reason.

Likewise, you may also have been witness to the other extreme – a language so gooey, so dripping with squeaks, raspberries and truncated words that you worry if the deliverer isn't having some sort of breakdown.

The best practice it seems, as is so often the case, lies somewhere in the middle of the two with something called infant directed speech (IDS).

Acting like a Victorian workhouse owner and talking to an 18-month-old like she's a fully grown adult isn't conducive to optimal language learning for the same reasons thrashing your youngster 23-nil at garden football probably won't plant within them the seeds of a lifelong love of the beautiful game.

Infants need to be given a chance to differentiate between the words they are hearing, so using a more melodic tone with shorter, simpler phrasing gives them that chance.

Using IDS means using many of the same words that come up in everyday speech but in a slightly more stretched-out way that elongates the pronunciation of vowel sounds. As well as slowing things down, this also has the effect of sounding more emotionally exaggerated, a way which also seems to help the little listeners comprehend the emotional intentions of what's being said.

If you are struggling to hear this happy medium approach in your head, a clever experiment may help you nail it.

In 2007 a team of language and psychology experts found that the way we speak to infants using their first language has some striking similarities to the way we speak to people in their second or third language – we slow things down and extend our vowels a bit.

What we don't do is repeatedly say 'nana' instead of banana or 'time for a liddle nappy nap to bye byes land?' instead of 'would you like to have a rest?'

Using a soupçon of baby language and nonsense talk never hurt anyone and if you're anything like me your heart will break just a tiny bit every time your child leaves behind one of her sweet verbal affectations, but it does seem that to help them the most we should leave what we say pretty much the same but adapt how we say it.

The second question of how you make more time to speak to your child is fiendishly complicated on one hand and the picture of simplicity on the other.

The tricky bit goes back to our look at the importance of child-care. Whoever looks after your child while you and/or your partner are at work has a big role to play in this early literacy development. They will more likely than not be spending a very healthy chunk of the week with your little one, which makes it all the more important to try and find someone who shares the approach of you and your partner – which isn't always easy to pull off at all.

What's more straightforward is to make sure you talk directly to your baby whenever you are doing something together. Commentate on the nappy change, point out the trees and flowers in the park, take them through the Indian menu, anything – just talk to them.

It sounds obvious and indeed is, but children who receive thoughtful, responsive care and attention from their parents and other carers in the first years of life get a serious head start – and we aren't just talking academically here, their emotional well-being has as much to gain too.

When researchers examined the life histories of children who have succeeded against the odds – their surroundings stacked against them achieving – they consistently found a common thread throughout most of the stories; they each had at least one supportive, rock-solid relationship with an adult in their lives that began in the very early years.

Which means it's equally as obvious to state that children who don't often get spoken to or indeed are denied the regular opportunity to explore and play won't just get bored, they will run a serious risk of feeling the ramifications of that rather lonely start in life for an awfully long time.

So we know that talking to our babies and toddlers is a very good idea indeed, all that remains to do now is work out how's best to play with them and which toys will not only keep them amused, but help them develop too.

Simple?

No, not really.

Words from your fellow fathers:

Paul, father of two: *I think that the oldest children in a family get spoken to in baby talk and then as people have more kids and less time they ditch it* *and just talk to them normally – which is part of the reason why youngest children are often so advanced.*

Well that's my theory anyway.

Stuart, father of two: *Apart from the 'mama', 'papa' type words one of the earliest ones that stuck in my mind was during a walk in the park and my daughter shouted out 'ree roll' – which after a while I understood as squirrel.*

Nick, father of two: *'mama' was our son's first word but he went on to the use the word 'fuck' instead of 'help'. A lot of problems with that, especially when you consider how many times they ask for help or when they become more independent and let you know they don't want it.*

TOYS AND THE IMPORTANCE OF PLAY

You and your partner aren't the only ones who work every day in your house. There is another determined, conscientious and driven individual who puts the hours in at the coal face, come rain or shine.

Play is your baby's work. Yes it's fun, but in terms of development, when the toys come out your child couldn't be doing more of a job if she demanded a one-to-one, told you she was feeling undervalued and threw the odd sickie.

Through play, babies and toddlers explore, innovate, experiment and create – whether it's rolling a car back and forth or looking through an old kitchen roll tube, they will be learning multiple new skills and honing old ones at every turn.

What's more, you and your partner hold the truly great honour of being their first and absolute favourite playmates – a position that in a decade or so's time you will no doubt be clinging onto as they grow closer to their friends and viewing you as a cardigan-wearing fuddy-duddy.

But for now and a good while longer you are the coolest person to muck about with ever – so how do you make the most of it?

Taking it nice and slowly is a pretty good place to start. Show them how to get started but resist the temptation to do it for them while simultaneously helping them enough to keep frustration at bay.

Theirs, not yours, I mean. Then there's repetition. Then there's repetition.

You will need to get used to doing things over and over again, clapping and cheering with renewed vigour every single time an action is repeated because what you are witnessing is your baby practising and repractising her new-found talents and absolutely loving her own work – and if that's not worth a round of applause, I don't know what is.

As your child grows, her play will become more complex and what she learns from it will become equally as impressive – she will pretend, role-playing herself to a standstill in the process; she will recreate scenes from your very house, mortifying you as she tells off her teddy in the exact same way you have chided her.

Striking the right balance between interacting with and guiding them and just letting them get on with the serious business of play-ing is important – as is resisting the temptation to see play as some-how a waste of time compared to 'structured learning'.

Playing is learning.

All of which feeds into a much wider debate that will come to impact you in a few years' time – do British children stop playing and start school too early?

A lot of the evidence says they do.

Finnish pupils, for instance, start formal education at seven, enjoy mammoth summer holidays and end up with the highest educational standards on the continent.

In the UK our children are among a handful of European kids who start formal school at four and also have some of the shortest holidays to be found anywhere – and yet we languish in mid-table when it comes to the achievement rankings.

What's more, introduced in 1870, this early start had very little to do with educational benefits in the first place, according to the Cambridge Primary Review report, but rather it was seen as a way of actively reducing the time children spent with their feckless parents.

That wasn't even the half of it. A secondary reason was to keep nervous employers happy – an early start meant an early leaving age and more young workers for the sweatshops.

Let's focus on how you can help your baby and toddler play, what toys are best and which ones are just enormous pieces of garish plastic tat that will not only survive longer on this earth than our entire species, but will spend most of that time in your loft or garage.

Toys

The international toy market is worth around £50 billion every single year. That's a lot of Sticklebricks by anyone's standards – especially given the old cliché that children are more likely to play with the box than what's in it.

As we've seen, the modern parent has realised that these toys aren't just handy ways of keeping the kids quiet, they are essential tools in the physical, emotional and social development of their children.

And don't the marketeers know it.

There are still toys out there that are focused solely on fun, but more and more toy brands are tapping into the growing awareness that every second of play is a learning process.

One of the most globally predominant of these brands, Baby Einstein, has been at the centre of a heated legal and media battle over what it claims, or is seen to claim, its huge range of toys can help achieve.

It's incredibly easy to get sucked into this world of guilt purchasing, the guilt deriving from the fact that you are somehow denying your pride and joy a vital and irreplaceable developmental boost by not buying the fully interactive ergonomically centred sensory suite with free 'plot your child's manual dexterity' wallchart.

There's no doubting that some new toys are nothing short of brilliant, but don't beat yourself up if you can't afford to buy them all. A well-thought out, well-researched single purchase is often greeted with much more enthusiasm and engagement than a wheelbarrow full of swag. Present occasions are also the perfect time for your child to receive that fun, educational toy from grandpa or aunty. You will probably shy away from secondhand toys first-off – namely because you'll be given many as gifts, but also to put your mind at rest hygiene-wise. However, there's nothing wrong with a well-loved, very well-washed toy!

As a rough rule of thumb, from birth to six months toys that stimulate sensory and motor development are the best bet – that's rattles and the like in English. Up to the 18-month mark experimenting and achieving goals is what your child loves to do so the building block, jack-in-the-box toys hit the mark, as do very simple musical instruments.

As they head towards their second birthday, children often engage in make believe and problem-solving play and can match objects by shape and colour. Their vocabulary tends to explode into a riot of new words – so your house will be awash with costumes, puppets, dolls, toddler trucks and bikes.

The third year is when your little genius really starts to hone and master the skills they have been practising, so you move into the arts and crafts phase. Simple board games may make an appearance and if you've not already been drawn into the world of cars, trains and dolls' houses you probably will be now – not to mention toy cookers, vacuum cleaners and washing machines as your little one wants to act as grown-up as they feel.

So as you can see, you'll get through a few toys! Some items remain firm favourites throughout, some never capture the imagination, others benefit from a spell in the cupboard under the stairs and reappear triumphantly like returning gladiators.

Whatever the particular toy-box ups and downs in your house, it's wise to take advantage of charity shops, eBay and local second-hand sales if you want to avoid having to sell your actual kitchen appliances to afford the pretend ones.

There's one toy that I've deliberately passed over so far, because despite being simple, relatively inexpensive and as old as the hills, it deserves to be looked at in isolation, such an all-round star is it.

I give you, the humble book.

Books

We already know that early language and literacy development starts in the first three years of life, but what is perhaps more surprising in some senses is just how closely linked that progress is to the child's earliest experiences with books.

Way before actual reading is on the agenda, babies and toddlers soak up literacy learning by the mere physical interactions they have with books, paper and crayons.

Before school appears on the horizon, children are learning to talk, read, and even write by using books and other literacy materials such as magazines and newspapers. They essentially enter the world of words from the very start of their lives and the more they encounter the tools of reading and writing, the more they learn.

In her book *So Much More than the ABCs*, Judith Schickedanz outlines categories that can be used to understand the book behaviours of very young children. These categories help us as parents to recognise what's happening in front of our tired little eyes.

Schickedanz highlights the fact that even something as seemingly innocent and simple as your baby handling a book is increasingly being seen as a key building block for adult literacy. Turning the pages, chewing the corners, even throwing books around is all grist to a very important mill.

As your tot grows, how they pay attention to the actual content also becomes key. From gazing at the pictures, chuckling at a favourite page and then pointing to characters or feeling different textures in some of the excellent touchy-feely baby books around, it all represents the next stage.

While this kind of activity has always taken place, what's new is the importance that is being attributed to it.

Next comes a level of understanding and comprehension of what they are looking at, basic imitation of what's on the page and even the beginnings of verbal recounting of the story. If your child starts to babble as you read to them, they aren't bored, they are recognising what reading is, what it sounds like.

Stunning stuff!

By making books part of your child's everyday life and not just a bedtime treat you can really help to increase her exposure and therefore rate of learning. Anything and everything from reading the bus ticket out loud to making them their own little shopping list as you go round the supermarket, all counts and all helps – and costs next to nothing.

What's key is that whatever you do is fun and remains fun. A couple of minutes reading at tender ages is fine and it matters not one jot if they skip pages or want to return again and again to a particular page they have grown fond of. They aren't going to be examined on the content, it's the act of reading and enjoying it that is the developmental goldmine.

Likewise if it's initially the pictures they are drawn to, rather than the words, talk or sing about them rather than slavishly reading the text. Love of the narrative will come later. Babies respond to the rhythm of the spoken word, so keep at it. If they want to turn the pages themselves encourage them to, safe in the knowledge that rather than having an impatient terror on your lap you have a reader in training strutting their stuff.

When they do become more interested in the story itself, running your finger along the words and bringing the story and characters to life with voices and noises will only increase their love of reading with you. It can be amazing how something as simple as a book can help to pacify a grouchy toddler – you don't necessarily need an increasingly exotic array of flashing toys.

Once you are really properly reading to them and can tell they are engrossed in the story they are hearing and seeing, you can really go to town. Make it personal and relevant to them – 'doesn't that elephant look like Nana?' You can also begin to use the story as a springboard to conversations about familiar objects, situations and people in their lives.

As they approach three you'll find them memorising their favourite stories and even making up their own endings and asking you to do the same.

From the early stages of chewing and banging books up and down you will have, in very short order, fostered in them a real love of words and pictures that will see them move through interest to recognition and into creativity.

All through little old books.

If in doubt, shout

As time goes on, you may become worried about your baby's language development – the official guidance says that most children have learnt to say at least one word by the time they reach their first birthday and it's relatively unusual for a child to not be speaking at all by the 18-month mark.

As ever, these pesky infants have a real habit of disregarding official guidelines like a half-chewed carrot, tossing them aside with wilful abandon. You may have a tot who can do the 100 metres in just under 10 seconds by the time they are a year and a half, but who has barely uttered a word yet.

Typically, boys tend to develop language skills more slowly than girls, especially when they are under two. Also if your baby is a little more cautious they may hold back with the chatter until they feel they can do themselves justice and talk on more of a level playing field. This can be particularly true of younger siblings as they gather words in their heads ready for launching a verbal onslaught of Shakepearean proportions when the time is right.

If you are really worried, you've got nothing to lose by mentioning it to your health visitor or GP and getting things checked out – the earlier any issues are picked up the easier it will be to get your little one back on track.

So we've pretty much nailed that as developmental toys go, books are pretty hard to beat, but I'm sure you've noticed that we are slap bang in the middle of an information revolution that asks interesting questions of parents in general and often gadget-obsessed fathers in particular.

How does the onslaught of electronic and digital media change how we should be playing with and teaching our infants?

Words from your fellow fathers:

Winston, father of two: *For all the interactive shape sorters and role-play toys, you'll go a long way before you find something more popular than a humble balloon.*

Tom, father of two: *And we wonder how China is suddenly calling all the economic shots?*

You also realise why batteries are always 50% extra free. It's a sad day when you're nicking some triple As from a noisy spinny thing to make the TV remote work. 'Must have stopped working, darling.'

Nick, father of two: *We tried to go wooden when we could but you can't avoid the plastic. So much rubbish but we had to get something. When he was about eight months my wife and I were looking around the house and* *thinking that we didn't have many toys, which was great as it meant that it wasn't cluttered. We then saw him pulling the cap off the radiator and putting it back on again – doing it over and over again. We jumped into the car and loaded it with plastic – you are responsible for their sanity and development.*

Paul, father of two: *Buy them a balance bike, a cheap one will do, as soon as you can. They basically ride around on it and then hop on a pedal bike and off they go, no problems at all.*

I mean, why wasn't that invented decades ago? All the stabiliser trauma we had to go through could have been avoided!

THE DIGITAL BABY

There was a time, not that long ago, when the only mobile that was relevant to your infant was the one hanging above her cot.

But no longer.

From on-demand TV, a gaming sector than turns over more than Hollywood and Bollywood combined and smartphones and tablets which seem to act as a toddler magnet, our children have been born into a digital world that will be second nature to them, but which at times leaves us agog at its sheer innovation and pace.

But should we be encouraging our kids to engage fully into this new world they will eventually inherit or is it to be avoided at all costs, put out of reach in favour of a trip to the park and a pop-up book?

Let's take the oldest, biggest and still (for now) reigning champion of the heavyweight information division first shall we, television.

Television: friend or foe?

The chances are you watched a fair bit of telly when you were a child.

Your memory banks are almost certainly flooded with televisual moments and if you were required to sing the theme tunes to at least some of your all-time faves I'm sure you'd make a good fist of it.

In our day (cue Hovis music) we had to make do with an hour or two of kids' TV in the morning and an hour or two in the late afternoon – if we were lucky.

Bye but we had it tough.

Nowadays our offspring can choose from 12 hours of wall-to-wall brilliance from CBeebies, to name but one outlet – with seemingly infinite hours on demand. So successful is the BBC's consistently impressive infant channel that it spawns live stage shows and enough magazines each and every week to wallpaper your entire house many times over. I often wonder, in fact, if push came to shove and the Beeb's licence fee really did come under threat, whether the nation's parents would club together and sub the Director General themselves, just to keep *In the Night Garden* on air.

But is all this TV good for them? Is even the likes of CBeebies (meticulously researched, carefully produced and advert-free as it is) a purely benevolent force – how much TV is OK for our children?

Well, one major industrial nation recommends that absolutely no TV is best for children under two and that those older than two should watch no more than two hours a day of quality programming.

And which nation do these seemingly draconian guidelines originate from? Finland maybe? Sweden, or any of the other Scandinavian countries that always seem way ahead of the curve on issues like this?

No, this advice comes from none other than the American Academy of Paediatrics. The reality in the USA, however, is somewhat different, as you may imagine. A sizeable 43% of children under the age of two watch bagfuls of TV every day and nearly one in five watches videos or DVDs every day.

According to data gurus Nielsen, the average US household has 2.24 televisions, with the average child spending 1,680 minutes watching television each week, and over 70% of daycare centres having the television on for at least part of the day.

All of which equates to the typical American youth spending around 900 hours in school each year, but watching 1,500 hours of television over the same period (during which time they view an estimated 20,000 30-second commercials).

As far as younger children are concerned, Nielsen estimates that American kids between the ages of two or five years spend on average 21.8 hours each week in front of the TV, that's approximately three hours each day, or a quarter of the time they spend awake.

What are our children's viewing habits in the UK? While the stats aren't quite as wide-ranging, the picture that's painted from what we do know is equally as stark.

On average British children spend five hours and 18 minutes either watching television, playing computer games or online each day, which equates to 2,000 hours a year in front of a screen of some sort, compared with 900 hours in school and 1,270 hours spent with their parents.

And that, it has to be said, feels like a conservative figure.

So what effect is all this TV watching having on the development of the very young?

For starters, a 2008 US study by *The Journal of Pediatrics* carried out at the Center on Media and Child Health at Children's Hospital in Boston, and Harvard University, concluded that television viewing is, 'neither beneficial nor deleterious to child cognitive and language abilities' for children under two.

That's pretty clear then . . .

A further study by the University of Washington Child Health Institute supports a connection between TV viewing and attention problems. A three-year-old who watches two hours of TV per day is 20% more likely to have attention problems by the time they are seven, compared with a child who watches no television.

OK, anything else?

Well, yes, I'm afraid there is. A study of more than 10,000 people carried out at University College London found that the risk of becoming an obese adult increased by 7% for every hour of TV watched at weekends at the age of five.

So, just to recap, watching TV doesn't help children read; has a detrimental effect on their ability to focus and makes them fat.

The reasons TV is suspected of having such a seemingly catastrophic impact on our young are manifold – first, time spent watching TV means less time doing other more productive things, like creative and imaginative play and physical activity. TV is essentially a one-way street flooding information towards the sofa, and not generating much else. When a child is watching TV they aren't socialising or receiving the vital feedback to their actions and behaviour they need to grow and develop.

When you put exposure to advertising into the mix, things get worse still. As well as encouraging demand for material possessions, it's also been linked to the rise in obesity, thanks not only to the sedentary nature of the viewer but also the exposure to junk food that some adverts bring.

The UK's National Literacy Trust, which among other things campaigns to raise awareness of how to regulate a toddler's viewing habits, suggests that rather than switching on the box, parents should:

'Limit exposure and encourage other one-to-one language-enhancing activities that centre on talk at mealtime, bathtime, shared reading and imaginative play.'

So then, to the recycling plant we go, TV sets strapped down to our roof racks like the peddlers of evil they are. The trouble is that television is as much a part of our culture as the motor car we'd use to drive them to their deaths and we all know what a world-ending thug that four-wheeled hunk of metal is.

It takes a family of extraordinary fortitude to completely banish the telly from their lives – and while these families do exist, they represent a tiny percentage of the parental herd of which we are a part.

So what do we do?

The obvious answer is to take a keen interest in exactly what and how much programming our children imbibe, rather than constantly using TV as a cheap childcare option, guaranteed to keep the kids glued to the sofa when we need time to clean up, or try one final time to find the house keys.

While highlighting the negative impact of television on children, the National Literacy Trust are smart enough to recognise that a blanket ban just isn't going to happen and so their advice is to:

'Encourage exposure to some high-quality, age-appropriate educational television for children aged two to five.'

The quality of the output really does matter it seems. Dorothy Singer, co-director of Yale University's Family Television Research and Consultation Center, states that:

'Children who are watching good programs do make gains, both cognitively and socially.'

What constitutes a 'good' programme is down to your judgement as parents. As are decisions later down the line as to whether a TV in the bedroom is a good idea for your children.

But what about computers in the bedroom when your kid's older? What about iPhones in the back of the car right now; what about computer games for infants?

Oh God, why is everything so bloody complicated?

The rise of the i-baby

I remember as a cocky primary school pupil telling one particularly exasperated teacher who was trying to get me to practise and re-practise my absolutely woeful handwriting that it wouldn't matter anyway because I'd be typing everything when I was a grown-up.

What an annoying little bugger.

I wasn't far off, mind you, and as for our children, who knows what the world will look like by the time they are adults, given how quickly things have changed in just the last five years?

But what's the deal with computers and smartphones and iPads? It wasn't that long ago that playing video games was seen as classic couch-potato activity. But now it's accessible everywhere and anywhere, should we now be encouraging our infants to soak up as much new technology as they can, as early as they can, or put this area in the box marked 'when you get older'?

Not only is that a complicated question, it's one that has parents, academics, and medical experts floundering to keep up, not only with the expansion of new technology, its benefits and drawbacks, but also with the rate at which children are becoming exposed to it environmentally.

One of the few bodies looking into this area is the Joan Ganz Cooney Center, named after the driving force behind *Sesame Street*. A report from the organisation called 'Always Connected: The new digital media habits of young children' focuses on the rare studies that do exist about young children and digital media – as opposed to the hundreds on how teenagers interact with it – and it makes for interesting reading.

It seems that even in America, which as ever (or maybe that should be for now) is at the vanguard of this phenomenon, there are few hard and fast conclusions, let alone guidelines, being drawn up on what's best to do. Instead there is debate – and much of it.

To put it very simply, in one corner you have the increasingly sedentary lives of the children who are exposed to digital media and the negative physical and psychological impacts they can have on them.

In the other, you have emerging evidence that 'well-deployed' digital media can generate fresh skills, higher levels of achievement and allow children from different backgrounds, creeds and even continents to make connections in ways never before dreamed about.

As you may have guessed, what 'well-deployed' actually means is pretty much down to you as a parent. With almost all the research available focusing on children of eight years or above, your guess really is as good as anyone's on whether letting your two-year-old play around on your iPad is a good thing or not.

While the report makes the oft-stated point that platforms and outlets themselves aren't the issue and the actual content they are exposed to is where the hub of the 'digital media good or bad for kids' debate sits, it also concludes that what research there is provides strong evidence that the media habits of children are seriously out of whack.

It recommends that:

'We need higher-quality educational offerings to promote critical thinking for children and adults in their selection and use of media. While we can imagine a day when young children themselves will produce their own media, for the time being they are still counting on us!'

Then there is the rampant commercialism at play. In their book *Consumer Kids* Ed Mayo and Agnes Nairn paint a picture that makes televisual advertising targeted at children seem positively benign.

They argue that while parents seem to have registered the threat of sexual predators who make use of the power of the digital space, they have no clue how their children are groomed for profit. They say:

'The screen can no longer be classed as an electronic babysitter that keeps children occupied. It is a whole electronic world in which they are immersed and which is underpinned firmly and securely by a profit motive. It's the commercial world that dominates the time of today's children.'

Right, that's it, never mind the telly, every digital device in the house is going in the bin first thing in the morning.

Be still my beating reactionary heart. Although there's precious little research out there to tell us if the other side of the coin actually exists, there is one report, carried out by the same people who drew together the 'Always Connected' paper mentioned earlier.

'Learning – is there an app for that?' looks at what it calls the 'pass-back effect', a term which beautifully captures the moment you may well soon recognise – if you don't already – when you pass your mobile device, children's app already loaded up, to the back of the car.

The report found that – surprise, surprise – even very, very young children picked up the skills needed to use these devices at an almost indecent speed – especially when it comes to the mega-intuitive, touchscreen kings such as the iPhone.

And do they actually learn and develop by using these apps? The report, albeit slightly hesitatingly, says yes, early evidence suggests so and what's more it goes on to recommend that American educationalists should 'optimise children's time with mobile devices' and even 'use mobile devices as supplemental tools.'

But what about you and me? What does it say our role should be in this new era of the pass-back? Well apart from the almost obligatory statement that it's basically all down to us to regulate and balance exposure to mobile devices and specifically the content on them, it goes on to add that:

'When it comes to smart mobile devices, many parents do not yet view them as potential learning tools – and thus restrict how their children use them.'

Which sounds a lot like 'get with it, Granddad' to me.

So all in all it's safe to say that the jury isn't just out on this whole digital/kids debate, the courtroom hasn't even been built yet. As with television exposure, keeping a very close eye on the amount and quality of your child's interaction with digital media feels like the smartest route we can take in lieu of any cast-iron evidence either way.

One thing is for sure though; if you've ever seen the way a toddler grasps touchscreen technology within seconds, you'll know it's built with them in mind much more than us.

AI AI Oh

What impact will the recent explosion of AI language models such as ChatGPT, Bard and Sage have on how we interact with our young children, how we should educate them as they grow and what the job market will look like for them in a world where finding the right prompt is more important than finding the right answer?

God knows.

Or perhaps the AI knows.

One thing seems for certain, this genius-like genie seems very unlikely to be going back in the bottle, so just as our parents had to find their own way with the increasingly ubiquitous presence of TV, it's now down to us to find a way through this new technological maze – even though it's changing on a daily basis.

All I can assure you is that it really is me writing this.

Although I would say that wouldn't I?

Words from your fellow fathers:

Winston, father of two: *Television is a necessary evil where parenting is concerned. There is a lot of interesting stuff on the BBC, and Mr Tumble is a genuine star, of course.*

Tom, father of two: *Pingu should be part of everyone's life. Question is how much and what constitutes too much TV.*

It's always when you've had a 'DIY' weekend where you've used TV to occupy them a little more than you should have, you feel guilty and then the first thing you read in the Metro is yet another bloody UN report on how bad TV is for kids!

The spectre of advertising to kids is only just coming into effect as we're moving away from the mothership of CBeebies to the commercial channels.

It completely sucks, there is so much of it and the kids seem to treat them like programmes. I would love it to be banned.

Chris, father of two: *All advertising annoys me and having worked in the media I am very sceptical of it. I hope to instill that scepticism – or at least questioning nature – in my kids when it comes to ads.*

Paul, father of two: *I'm constantly torn between thinking that allowing my youngsters to play on the iPad is a good or a bad thing. Instinctively it feels lazy and a waste of time they could be spending running round outside. A nagging voice in my head tells me that this is the kind of technology (and way beyond) that they are going to live with their entire lives and they should get on board as early as possible.*

The deciding factor is often that it keeps them incredibly quiet and entertained!

PROGRESS REPORT, 13–16 MONTHS

Your baby

So what else are these cute little learning machines up to during these few months then?

A lot.

They could well be drinking from a cup like a seasoned pro by now and a fork and spoon could be a big part of the mealtime routines, too. Still lots of food on the floor and walls, but there will be an increasing panache to the way they catapult that ravioli square gracefully through the air.

New words appear at a dazzling rate now, too – go out in the rain and the chances are they will come out saying a baby version of umbrella and melting your soggy heart.

Walking increasingly becomes more doddle than toddle as they gain confidence with every step, amazing you and your partner as they stop, bend, pick something up and move on – a skill you would probably struggle to replicate given how knackered you are and how creaky your back is.

Don't worry if it feels on occasion like the progression you expect is interrupted with your little one becoming scared of things that they used to take in their stride, like the vacuum cleaner or even the bath. Much the same as with separation anxiety, this is progression, as their senses unfurl and their independence grows they will take against things hither and thither just because they bloody well can.

You'll probably find yourself saying 'Where's your nose? Where's your nose?' and other body part location-finding questions a lot now, too, as they revel in their ability to find them. The more fuss you make when they point to the right area, the more they will want to do it and the more you will fall in love with them.

Glory days, soak up every second you can.

Your partner

If your partner's back at work, the childcare carousel will be in full spin. As we've touched on, when childcare is good, it's a relief. When, for whatever reason, it's a cause for anxiety it can consume every waking parental moment. If that's the case for you, the chances are you can multiply the worries you have by a factor of 10 when it comes to your partner.

There's little more unsettling and upsetting for a mother than having to leave their baby somewhere they are less than 100% happy about. Perfection, as we all know, is pretty thin on the ground in any walk of life, so try your best to be alive to any childcare worries your partner may be having.

If you have the beginnings of a fussy eater on your hands, this too can be a huge angst generator. We will look at this in detail a bit further down the track but it's worth remembering that where toddlers are concerned tomorrow is most definitely another day. What gets hurled on the floor one day may be ravenously devoured by the end of the following week. Help your partner not to overly fret as your little one is sure to pick up on her stress and dig her heels in even more. Keep persevering with different foods.

You

How are you, love?

No really, how are you?

Worried about work, about the mortgage, about not being at home enough, of supporting your frazzled partner in the way you'd like to? Or just loving every single second of being a dad so far?

The answer is you're probably all of those things before you've managed to put on your socks of a morning.

We can be awfully tough on ourselves and each other as new parents and the truth is we are learning constantly. When and if number two comes along, a whole new set of challenges and questions arrives too and I've a feeling they just keep on coming in different guises for good now.

Having someone you love and care for more than anything else in the world changes you for good, and almost always for the better in every direction – so give yourself a break and enjoy it.

As we've been talking about all things technological, the digital world has made it shockingly easy to bring work home nowadays and the new post-pandemic work-from-home revolution, for all the flexibility it's delivered can also bring an 'always on' feeling with it.

I'd love to be able to help you out with how to switch off, but as a major culprit myself I'm in need of assistance, too. What I do know is that in years to come, the chances of me remembering that staggeringly annoying email I just had to respond to at 7.15 on a Tuesday evening is minuscule compared to the time my daughter finally caught her first ball and ran round the garden like an Ashes winner.

GETTING AWAY FROM IT ALL

As you begin to really settle in to your new life as a father and at least a semblance of normality returns – or a new version of normality – you might just find yourself contemplating all sorts of things that just 12 months ago seemed unthinkable.

We're not necessarily talking about that John O'Groats to Land's End bike ride you've always half-fancied in a not very serious sort of way, and that extension to the kitchen can wait a little while longer too, but it feels like your robust, inquisitive little youngster is ready for a holiday.

Lord knows, you and your partner could do with some sun on your backs and a little reward for the stunning child-rearing job you have been doing thus far too – so that's it settled then – we're all going on a family holiday.

As with much – well everything really – in your life now, your considerations when deciding where to go and how to get there have changed somewhat. So in this chapter we'll take a guided tour through the whys, wherefores and WTFs of getting away from it all with a wee one in tow.

Hopefully unrelated to your travels, (but often not) your toddler's ever-growing pioneer spirit not only keeps you on your toes and helps her learn and develop in all sorts of ways, it occasionally results in her putting herself in harm's way – which often leaves you and your partner as the first line of medical support.

Unless you're a doctor, nurse or health professional yourself (in which case you couldn't have a quick look at my ankle could you?) the chances are your first aid skills amount to a dog-eared card in your wallet which proudly states that you undertook basic training in 2016.

Now is a very good time to brush up, and we'll look at some of the most common things you could be called on to deal with.

Not that you should live in a constant state of bowel-opening worry of some hideous fate befalling the most precious thing in your world. But let's be honest, even the most confident and gung-ho among us occasionally succumb to a phenomenon that seems to have arrived in spades at roughly the same time as your child did – fear.

Where your children are concerned, love and fear are two sides of the same coin, increasingly so in a world where we are constantly reminded of the threats and risks that seemingly lurk like smirking traffic wardens around every corner.

How do you keep fear in check while the love you feel climbs ever skyward as your relationship with your child grows by the day?

In short I don't know, and I don't think anyone else does either, but let's delve into the issue and see if we can't make ourselves feel a bit better about it, shall we?

HAVE CHILD, WILL TRAVEL

You've seen off the tough early days; family bliss has broken out all around and you fancy a break, no not a break, what you fancy is a family holiday – the very words turning you into your parents the instant they pop into your head.

Getting away from work, away from the house, away from those black bits that seem to be coming out of the bath toys – all these things are good.

God knows your partner would appreciate a change of scenery, having you around 24/7 to share the load, you might even be able to reacquaint yourselves with one another as the holiday spirit takes hold and the day-to-day duties of parenthood take a back seat for a while.

Your adventurous little one would love it too, new terrain to cover, new faces to frown and then smile at, new cupboards to open.

Let's go.

The only tiny thing is, parenthood doesn't stop just because you are on your holidays, and that new terrain your baby will relish needs to be chosen with care. These aren't big issues, though. We can do this, all it takes is a bit of planning.

WHERE TO GO

Home

Babies and toddlers get to every corner of our green and pleasant land on their jollies nowadays it seems.

Such is the scramble to get hold of parental disposable income 'family-friendly' is replacing 'no football coaches' as the sign you are most likely to see on your holidays in the UK. Stacks of high-chairs can be found in restaurants far and wide and soft play areas now live where the pool table used to in lots of pubs.

Holidaying in the UK with your kids has never been more popular, primarily, it has to be said, because of the economic climate rather than a positive change in the meteorological one.

But there's no doubt holidaying in the UK has improved as an experience since our day. Facilities are better; there's more to do when the heavens open and businesses of all hues are practically yanking you and your buggy off the street to relieve you of your spending money.

Yes the weather has gone nuts, lurching from sun that we can't deal with to rainfall that flash floods the bejesus out of us before lunch time, but you can't have it all, can you? You know the lingo, you know the food and you know the water's safe to drink – and for many parents embarking on their first holiday, this is all that counts.

Then there's the fact that your little one can do the whole thing in the comfort of her own car seat. Of course, six hours to Cornwall is a bit different to a jaunt to Sainsbury's, so more food, more liquid, more wipes, more everything is needed, including – as you'll find as you are forced to weld the boot shut – more car.

What's really essential is a flexible attitude. A seemingly enormous six-hour on-the-road allocation might seem generous, extravagant even, before you set off, but a baby crying in the back of the car isn't only tough on the eardrums, it is also dripping with so much argument-producing venom that it beggars belief.

Add in a spot of satnav shenanigans and the baby monitor beeping in the boot like R2D2 and you've got yourself a holiday hydrogen bomb. Best to take it nice and slow, plan some stop-offs on the way to really stagger the journey or even stay really local to up the holiday and cut the travel time.

Away

Going overseas with a little one used to be a relative rarity, but not anymore.

The travel magazine *Family Traveller* says it has seen a rise in pre-schooler-specific holidays and destinations, driven primarily by the fact that travelling during term time when there's a lot more availability and everything is considerably cheaper makes an awful lot of sense.

Of course, choosing your destination with care is recommended. The obvious health risks that apply to you when you spend two weeks somewhere unfamiliar are magnified many times for your baby. Extremes of temperature, ropey sanitation and just general culture shock can turn your holiday into a nightmare for all concerned and a jet-lagged toddler is a sight to behold.

Sunburn early in life, for instance, is more likely to cause skin cancer later on, so a constant round of factor 50 application, shade hunting and hat replacing will be called for if you choose somewhere that's baking.

People do it, though, for some it's to see family, for others a statement of intent that their pre-family wanderlust shall remain. Eyes wide open and meticulous planning is the way to go if you take it on.

For most, though, a trip abroad with a small child means Europe or, at a push, the US. Thousands upon thousands of families head for Spain, Portugal, France, Italy and, increasingly it seems, Turkey every year. Many of these destinations enjoy a well-earned reputation for being brilliantly child-friendly, the locals whipping your children from your arms to coo over them in a way that would have you screaming the place down back home.

Ferries full of top-box carrying cars make the journey to mainland Europe every summer, others take the Channel Tunnel and yet more take to the air.

Children on aeroplanes – now there's a thorny little issue. Cast your mind back, if you will, to your pre-fatherhood days. You take to your seat, glance left and see an already rampant toddler yanking at the hair of the woman in front, as the mortified parents apologise at the rate of a sorry every nine seconds while still managing to fit in the time to tear strips out of each other about who forgot to pack the raisins.

Let's hope for your sake that you showed these poor people kindness – because if you didn't the forces of kiddiewinkle karma will in all probability smite you down with such vengeance that you'll wish you had opted for two weeks under your kitchen table.

Small babies can be a doddle on flights – they just sleep, eat, smile, sleep. It's when they start to move and wriggle and attempt to open the doors that the fun really starts. But hey, it's only a few hours isn't it and if people imagined there'd be no children on a holiday flight they'd obviously started on the ouzo before they left.

Hand luggage crammed full of nice food, copious drinks and as many books and toys as you can jimmy in will serve you well. Producing a never-before-seen item can also be a boon and as we've already discussed they bloody love your smartphone, don't they?

Where to stay

Where's best to lay your hat for a fortnight with a little one in tow?

Hotels are an obvious option. Many offer kids' clubs that you can take advantage of during the day if you are so inclined, so for a few hours at least you and your partner can really unwind and talk to each other about something other than centile lines, teething gel and why your bubba isn't clapping hands, pointing and playing the tambourine like the high achiever from the NCT group.

You'll probably end up talking about all that anyway, but you'll just be able to do it while reclining on a sun lounger with a cheeky cocktail in your hand.

Where hotels can start to lose their lustre somewhat is in the evening. Unless you are comfortable taking advantage of any babysitting facility that's on offer, you'll probably end up staying in your room – which is great if you are flush enough to book a suite, or even somewhere with a decent balcony. If you can't, you might find yourself playing cards by head torch in a pitch-black room and trying to eat crisps in silence.

Funny and sweet and romantic for about 25 seconds then actually quite rubbish.

Also don't worry if you start to wonder if the travel cot will fit in the bathroom, you're not evil, we've all had those thoughts and some of us have even carried them through.

Then you need a wee at midnight.

Hiring your own pad is another route – whether that be a cottage, villa or apartment.

The benefits here are obvious, you have more than one bedroom – unless you have booked spectacularly badly – and a kitchen to cook for yourselves and baby.

Asking for highchairs and travel cots to be provided is a good idea as is requesting a stairgate. What a website will describe as child-friendly can often be anything but when you arrive. And for the love of God don't rely on the photos, they lie. Childproofing an entire holiday cottage isn't on so you might need to be canny about where the baby zones are and shut off the jagged, super slippy marble staircase with a strategically placed armchair.

Whatever bricks and mortar accommodation route you go for, one thing you must never, ever, forget to take with you is some sort of light blackout material or blind. Many a curtain rail has been yanked from its moorings by desperate dads as they perch on a chair and attempt to attach a three-tonne blanket to the window using stolen pegs, some plasters and a size 4 nappy.

Which leaves us with the king of family holiday environments, a double-edged world where when it's good it's very good, but when it's bad it's wetter – camping.

Many people can't abide the very idea and would rather spend a week on hold to BT.

For others, the pull of the open air and the whistle of a camp stove kettle is irresistible, and campsites, especially in the UK, have never been better equipped or more numerous.

Likewise for tents, the new-fangled materials they use to make them mean they rarely let in water and no longer require a doctorate in engineering to put them up – a mere diploma in hydraulics for the fancy new air ones will suffice nowadays.

Get the right weather and your toddler will be in heaven, roaming around without a care in the world and taking in so much fresh air that bedtime is embraced like an old friend.

Then it's onto the deckchairs and hello to the sauvignon blanc.

Get the wrong weather and you are just a tent peg or two away from hell. Monopoly and Bop-It might keep older kids happy, but a wet toddler, in a wet field, with wet parents is hard for even the most annoyingly enthusiastic among us to pull from the doldrums.

If you get lucky you'll have a ball and you'll wish you'd invited your friends and family – or maybe you did?

Who to go with

You're a ready-made family unit now so why on earth would you need anyone else on your holidays?

Well, not to beat around the bush, there's babysitting. Taking Nana and Granddad doesn't just mean they get to spend some quality time with the apple of their eye, but you just might get some time alone, too.

As for holidaying with friends I'm sure there are parents out there who have been away with pals who don't themselves have small children, but I'd put a small wager on them never having done it twice. Feeling guilty about broken nights, heinously early mornings and the inability to indulge in the vacation antics of the childless must weigh heavy on that kind of arrangement.

Or maybe that's just me being too much of a weak-willed wuss, maybe these people need to know the reality of the parental situation, maybe they need to see for themselves the hard work that parents put in, maybe they need to do alternate mornings.

Maybe not.

There is another option, that you get together with people in the same boat as you. You can all do the mornings, share the bathtimes, keep an eye on each other's nippers, who in turn have a playmate – and the grown-ups might even have a night out each.

What's not to love about that?

In my experience very little, sharing the load and a few laughs with parents of children around the same age as yours can be a great way to do things. Yet there seems to have been an awful lot written recently about the pitfalls of such arrangements, especially when it comes to taking infants it seems.

First of all, you've got the fact that people have the habit of going away with a couple they only know because they happen to have a baby the same age and have perhaps only met in an NCT-type environment. I can see how this could unravel in quite spectacular fashion.

A spot of lunch in the local pub surrounded by a wagon train of buggies is very different to a fortnight getting to know someone else's parenting foibles. It may seem perfectly natural to you that your child needs to fall asleep to the digitally remastered version of 'Stairway to Heaven' every single night – to your vacation companions this may, alas, appear a little strange and even, whisper it, annoying in the extreme.

Perhaps worst of all, though, so the horror story articles go, you've got the exposure to other people's relationships as seen through the parental prism. What if the other father doesn't pull his weight in anywhere near the same way that you do? What if he is an unreconstructed non-dad who barely notices his child, let alone the mountain of jobs that need doing to keep it alive on a daily basis?

Awkward!

I say awkward when what I really mean is 'get in'. You will be in so much clover as you feed, bath, entertain and soothe your toddler, while simultaneously administering an Olympic-standard foot massage to the mother of your child, that you could rip your flight ticket asunder and float home.

But what if, pity me no, but what if you are put in the shade by your opposite number? What if your fatherly efforts, hitherto in your mind's eye worthy of some sort of humanitarian award, are eclipsed by the picture of paternal perfection you have foolishly chosen to entrap yourself with?

That's never going to happen, is it – you are untouchable, hear me, untouchable.

Pick the right people, don't be afraid to go off and do your own thing and you'll be fine, honest. Who knows you might end up with holiday buddies for life which will mean one thing for sure, the kids will always have a ball.

DON'T PANIC: FIRST AID FOR PARENTS

It's no coincidence that we turn to first aid straight after family holidays. The change of terrain and climate has a nasty habit of throwing up a minor emergency or two.

In reality, it's your home where the danger lurks and it's a good idea to be prepared.

Baby first aid courses exist and are worth doing, but if something happens to a newborn you hit the phones to medical experts pretty quick.

It's when toddlerdom starts to beckon that a whole host of relatively minor injuries and conditions can and do crop up that are still quite painful for them and frightening for you.

Trained medical help should still be your default setting if you are at all worried or feel out of your depth. When my son beat the unbeatable child lock on a kitchen cupboard and mistook a Fairy Liquitab for a bright blue marshmallow he did what any of us would do in that situation and took a lovely big bite out of it.

DON'T PANIC! I just about managed to blurt out through the blind panic I was feeling.

A call to the much-maligned NHS Direct saw me transferred straight to a nurse and then speedily onwards to the National Poisons Information Service (who knew we had one?) who looked up what a liquitab lunch would do to an 18-month-old and gave me the appropriate advice, all within 10 minutes of the call being put in.

You can't knock it, no matter how much we all do.

Aside from instances like that when nothing but expert help will do, there are a whole host of situations where knowing some good basic first aid procedures will serve you and your new family very well indeed – here are some of the more common ones.

Cuts, scrapes, bumps and bruises

As well as the really minor and incredibly frequent knocks that your toddler will pick up you may well need to give some TLC for slightly more hefty knocks.

Knowing when expert help is needed is half the battle in the first place. The advice is that if the injury is less than half an inch around, there's little or no bleeding and once the initial shock has died down they don't seem to be in excessive pain, you can deal with it yourself.

Other than that – and especially if it's a bump to the head or if you're just not sure – get it checked out.

If it's a cut, it's worth remembering that things almost always seem worse than they are when blood is around, so keep calm, take a good look at the wound with clean hands before deciding if you can deal with it.

If you think you have it covered, rinse the area by holding it under the tap and dab it dry with a sterile swab if you have one (a decent first aid kit is a purchase worth making, for sure).

Then you can put on a spot of antiseptic cream if you like and finally pop on a Mr Bump plaster. It doesn't have to be Mr Bump but his backstory can help to make your injured little soldier feel in good company.

If there's bruising, you can try applying a cold compress to reduce the pain and swelling. Bruises are blood clots and the worse a bruise looks the more it's clotting and healing.

That's right, your mother wasn't lying to you.

If the bruising is really severe, covers a large area and doesn't show signs of getting better after a day or so, it's another trip to the GP surgery for you. If only they gave Nectar points.

You can try arnica to reduce the swelling too, if you fancy. As with almost all homeopathic remedies, some people swear by it while others swear at the very mention of it.

Choking and swallowing things they shouldn't

My God, it's scary when a child chokes on something. In fact they don't even have to choke, just a splutter while finishing off an apple juice will have parents lurching towards their offspring in full 'ready to react' mode.

If something serious happens on the choking front, it's really worth knowing your first aid onions because time is very much of the essence. No one wants to think they might be put in a position where they have to save their child's life, but it happens every day.

Now I could try to explain the dislodging and resuscitation procedures here, or you could even buy a specialist first aid book. But by far your best option is to book yourself on a toddler cardio-pulmonary resuscitation (CPR) course pronto (the NCT run a good one) and get some hands-on practice at what you need to do.

It's incredibly easy to mean to do something like that and forget, but it's a skill you may need in a very big way one day soon, so it's worth making the time and doing it.

As you'll no doubt know by now, babies and toddlers learn about the world around them by touch and taste and if it fits in the mouth it will jolly well go in the mouth.

It's for this reason that more than 500 under-fives are rushed to casualty each week in the UK because it's thought they may have been accidently poisoned.

Yikes.

Medicines are the most common culprit, with everyday pain-killers top of the list, presumably because we parents are much more lax in terms of locking them away safely. That, and the fact that we always have a bloody headache.

Although more and more detergent nasties are being made with bittering agents that make them taste so immediately foul that kids spit them straight out, it's far from being a universal practice – so the obvious safety precautions need to be taken to keep dangerous items well out of reach at all times.

Including liquitabs.

Heat stroke and dehydration

Heat stroke is a life-threatening condition and children are especially prone to it.

It occurs when the body's temperature rises while its ability to cool off shuts down, and nippers don't need to be in tropical climes to get it. Playing outside in hot weather coupled with not getting enough liquid down them can be all it takes. It can also happen if they are overdressed or left in a parked car where temperatures can rise much higher than those outside.

Your toddler may well first show signs of heat exhaustion, like thirst, fatigue, leg or stomach cramps, and cool, claggy skin.

If not addressed, they may then develop any of the following symptoms: hot, red and dry skin, a rapid pulse, confusion, dizziness, headache, vomiting and eventually unconsciousness.

It's not pretty, this.

Dehydration also has tell-tale signs, such as your child going six to eight hours without a wet nappy, lethargy or even a lack of tears when crying, which sounds so tragic it's almost beyond belief. If dehydration worsens, you could see much worse, such as sunken eyes.

If you even half suspect heat stroke you need to first call 999 and then bring your toddler's internal temperature down as quickly as possible before they slip into unconsciousness. You can do this by undressing her completely and laying her down in a cool area. While the ambulance is on its way sponge down the body with a sponge dipped in cool, not cold, water and fan her, too.

With dehydration it's best not to faff about, either. If you suspect it's reached serious levels make the call, as your child may need to be given fluids intravenously. While you are waiting, try and get an electrolyte drink such as Dioralyte down them.

Burns

Burns! Man alive, we're getting heavy now aren't we? Well yes and no.

We're not necessarily talking house fires here – hot drinks are the number one cause of scalds amongst the under-fives. A youngster's skin can be anything up to 15 times thinner than an adult's and hundreds of children are admitted to hospital with burns or scalds every week.

For less serious burns you should cool the area by submerging it in cold water rather than under a running tap, which can be too abrasive. Leave it there for at least five minutes, preferably 10. Then gently dry the area with a clean towel and cover it with a sterile bandage.

Much like bruising, blisters are a good sign that the healing process is under way, so don't pop them, just add a little antiseptic cream and cover the area loosely with a clean non-stick bandage.

Even if the burn itself doesn't seem too serious, if it's larger than two inches across or on your child's face, hands, or genitals, or if it has been caused in any way by electricity or chemicals, seek medical help immediately.

Aside from those exceptions, mild first-degree burns like this may well heal in a few days, but anything more serious needs immediate medical attention too. Don't attempt to treat a more serious burn yourself, just place a clean sterile cloth over the area to keep germs out while the medics arrive.

Whatever the cause, whatever the damage, witnessing an injury to your child will shake you to the core. Try to keep a cool head and resist the urge to shriek like a banshee. You will be of more use to your poorly child, who is so attuned to your behaviour and feelings. So count to 10, and do it for the kids; if you panic and appear anxious they can easily become even more distressed.

As well as how you react during and after an event like this, an interesting thing tends to happen to a lot of men when they become dads – the love they feel for their children, combined with the primeval duty they feel to keep them safe, come together to create fatherhood fear – and lots of it.

Words from your fellow fathers:

Marcus, father of four: *With the second and third ones, casualty was like our second home.*

We are still in the habit of arriving anywhere (on holiday, family visits, etc.) and checking out where the nearest casualty department is before we do anything else. We have visited casualties in Spain, France, Italy, USA, Germany, in fact every country we have ever been to. And babyproofing has never been any help.

Colin, father of two: *Our daughter broke her leg when she was 18 months . . . it was awful. She stepped off the bottom step of the stairs (4 inches) and twisted her ankle. It was missed by the X-ray and wasn't diagnosed until two days later . . . rubbish time.*

Nick, father of two: *A few falling off beds, etc., but no great dramas with the first one. My second couldn't spend enough time in casualty – or so it seemed. It looked like her every action was designed to get her there as quickly as possible.*

Ben, father of two: *Our son fell off the changing table, while under the control of my wife. We rushed him off to casualty and he was given the once over and was fine.*

My wife has never forgiven herself, mainly because the doctor was a stunning young blonde who laughed at all my rubbish new dad jokes.

Needless to say I got up that night to do the late feed.

LOVE AND FEAR

The love

It's often said that fathers truly fall in love with their children a bit later down the line than mothers.

The theory goes that newborns only really have eyes for their mums and the bond between the two is often so instant and strong that as men we only really get the chance to feel the full force of parental love when our little ones begin to show their personality and engage more with the world around them.

There's also the claim that babies tend to be born looking more like their fathers than they do their mothers to give us an instant and needed physical sign that the little person who has just been born really is our progeny – evolution's very own instant paternity test.

A couple of studies even back this hypothesis up with test groups having significantly more success matching photos of babies and their fathers together than with shots of the mothers.

Whether or not there's any truth in both of these thoughts, once the love drug properly kicks in for you, whenever it happens, you'll certainly know about it because there's nothing else quite like it.

Even the most narcissistic, self-absorbed and selfish among our number tend to be gripped eventually by a feeling so deep in the chest, so adept at flooding our systems with potent hormonal narcotics that it can stop our egos dead in their tracks.

The first time you see your toddler's innocent interest and friendly advances towards a slightly older child spurned, you will almost certainly feel like someone has yanked your heart from its protective rib cage, placed the still-beating lump of muscle in a blender and made a smoothie out of it.

How could that big brute dismiss my sweet, well-meaning naïve little one like that? You'll want to scoop her up and smother her in a blanket of affection and love, hoping that the cruelty of the outside world is kept at bay for a little while longer at least.

In a year or two's time it will be your baby that's dishing out the brush-offs to the younger set as they get in the way of the stairs to the slide – but that doesn't figure right now – what gets you is the rejection they've suffered, even though they know very little about it and continue to totter around in blissful innocence.

It's getting me going and I wasn't even there.

That's just one of a million instances that can and will make you realise that you don't control the love for your child, it controls you. Just wait until your son or daughter comes home from nursery with a tiny bite mark on their arm. Plans for fiendish and satanic revenge attacks will pop into your mind and you'll temporarily shock yourself with just how emotional you become.

Most of us manage to tame these reactions though, thank goodness, and sure as eggs is eggs, the bitee has a good chance of becoming the biter at some later stage.

The strength of your feelings doesn't just demonstrate itself when injustice and retribution rear their ugly heads. The overwhelming pride we feel as parents at the progress our offspring make also has the power to leave us acting in a very different way from our pre-parenthood days.

Even if you are acutely aware of the pitfalls of becoming a baby bore, even if you have almost melted with embarrassment and annoyance in the face of a father telling you in great detail that their cherub not only eats broccoli by the field load, she does so mostly with a knife and fork and on the odd occasion chopsticks – you, too, will fall foul.

It's impossible not to at some point – even if it's just to yourself in the mirror – and there's nothing wrong with it. The ultimate paradox of parenthood is that on a macro level 250 babies are born every single minute of every single day somewhere on the planet – it's nothing special, in fact in many ways it's perhaps one of the most inevitable and everyday things we ever do as animals, next to sneezing and eating too much cheese.

Yet on the micro level it dwarfs all the other things we treat as important to us, it makes us think, act and feel differently and often with more intensity than anything else we ever experience – it makes us really love.

So if you feel like telling the world how bloody great your child is, you go right ahead. Just don't overdo it, all right? The rest of us have just eaten and besides we know for a fact that it's our own babies that are the real stars of the show.

So we've established that, as Wet Wet Wet suggested, love is indeed all around when you become a dad, but it's not alone. It has a shadowy, unpredictable but no less powerful brother: fear.

The Fear

It stands to reason, really.

When you love something so very much you also become apprehensive, worried, even paranoid about bad stuff happening to it.

On its most basic level there are physical threats, such as cars.

If I think too long about roads and traffic and parcel delivery vans driving down residential streets as if they are planning to take off at the end of them, I get an urge to weld my jack-in-the-box son's bedroom door shut.

I will only release him, I think to myself, when he has

demonstrated by way of a series of independently verified examinations and vivas that he has developed the wherewithal to convince me that he is among the safest and most conscientious pedestrians in the country.

How he will gain this knowledge confined to his bedroom I'm unclear on, but it is a trifling problem compared to the dire alternative.

The fact that the UK has one of the best road safety records in the world is immaterial to me when I am in this state; it appears to my fearful mind as positive propaganda pumped out by the evil cartels of motor manufacturers, tarmac layers and bone-idle lollipop operatives hoping for an afternoon or two off work.

It's easy to get carried away when the fear grips, you see. Then there's stranger danger.

On average 11 children are killed by a stranger each year (compared to 124 child road deaths in 2008) and statistically children are at a much higher risk of abuse from someone they know. Yet despite the stats, the news coverage that these utterly tragic stranger abductions and deaths create, precisely because they are so unusual, instils what looks on paper like a disproportionate level of fear in parents.

Our fear glands aren't made of paper, and the sheer horror of contemplating even for a nanosecond that something like that could happen to your child has curbed the freedom we afford our kids, especially where outdoor play is concerned.

This fear-driven change is increasingly seen by some as playing its part in the increase in social disorders and behavioural difficulties that is being seen in the country's children.

A combination of fear of the bogeyman and the risk-assessment culture that we increasingly live in is cutting back on the opportunity our children have of developing in the time-honoured way of learning from their mistakes.

As Sue Palmer, author of *Toxic Childhood* puts it:

> All real children's play involves an element of risk, and the more real play children are allowed the better they become at analysing and managing those risks.
>
> If, on the other hand, adults try to eliminate risk from their lives they're likely to grow up either unduly reckless or hopelessly timid.

And so it is that just as love generates fear, so fear begets guilt, guilt that you are being over-protective, or too reckless, or, as we shall discuss later, focusing too much on the need to be the provider that you spend all your time working and not enough playing.

It's a decidedly complex balance to strike for the modern parent and it's made even harder by the fact that as a couple you and your partner must work to find a common approach to fear and risk with which to bring your children up.

You may be petrified of the roads; she may be more concerned with the effect TV adverts are having on your little one. You might think your toddler should be allowed to climb to the top of the big slide; your partner may think you have lost control of your senses.

Having the courage to overcome your fears and anxieties and let your cherished child explore and learn, while keeping them safe and secure, is truly one of the most important and difficult of all the skills you need to perfect as a modern parent.

The nature and form of the way you set boundaries and instill discipline soon enters into the equation too – but that is another issue for another chapter. For now, as you begin to refine and redefine your approach to loving them so much on one side of your brain and being petrified of something happening to them on the other, rest assured that every other parent on the planet is wrestling with the same dilemma as well.

Know too that it will never, ever end.

Once your fear of parked cars has eased it will be replaced instantaneously with anxiety about exams, then alcohol, then killer drugs masquerading as plant food, then your child's job security and enormous mortgage and then, well then it will begin all over again when you wonder if your grandchildren are being kept inside too much.

Yes indeed, the love and the fear are part of the long-term parenting package and as you will have no doubt found already it isn't just mums who worry, not by a long chalk.

Words from your fellow fathers:

Winston, father of two: *You become more fearful of accidents when you become a parent, not just to your kids but to yourself and your partner too.*

Chris, father of two: *I'm not an anxious person and I always believe things will work out, so I don't have that over-riding fear that I see in a lot of parents. In fact I believe that fear is a negative thing that is harmful to children. I worry like any parent about them being good people, being nice people, and enjoying life . . . I guess I just have to show them that life can be joyful, that anything is possible and I realise the rest is up to them.*

I think the only thing that really scares me is the harm the world can bring unexpectedly – but if I teach my girls NOT to get in a car with a young drunk male, then things will be OK. I know that my kids need to know risk, they need to be in risky situations, and hopefully I can equip them with the notions of how best to deal with those situations.

And in a way I think (minor) bad things happening is part of life and that's how we grow. So if they don't make friends instantly at playschool, that's fine . . . that's life . . . I am confident that my kids will be able to move on and deal with it.

Paul, father of two: *The more you grow to love them the more you worry about them. As I'm dropping off to sleep I'll sometimes replay stuff that has happened during the day and start to play out all of the 'what ifs' – what if I'd not got him before he climbed the stairs, what if she'd have pulled the kettle off the worktop.*

If I go too far my eyes open automatically as if my brain is saying, 'stop this you fool'. It's a powerful thing indeed.

PROGRESS REPORT, 17–20 MONTHS

Your baby

We're about halfway on the road to your nipper celebrating her third birthday – but as we stand here proudly at the midpoint, jam on our shirt, two giant Duplo blocks in our work bag and the whereabouts of the back door key still unknown, we can see that our 18-month-old is much more of a toddler than she is a baby.

Yes indeed, she has come a long way from the startled little extra-terrestrial we brought home from the hospital. For starters she has a grasp on the language which could at this stage even constitute combining two or even three of her newly learnt words together to form rudimentary but surprisingly efficient sentences – 'more grape Daddy' certainly does the job for instance. By 20 months, she could even be stringing two sentences together.

You might also notice that she's beginning to recognise that some things are different and some the same, you might stumble across – or more likely into – a pile of toys clumped cleverly into groups of all the same colour or shape.

This may not be the most spectacular development you'll witness but when you think how important the basic skill of being able to differentiate is to us you can see why it's a milestone in its own right. Living in Britain as we do it's important to us as parents to instill into our children the custom of saying 'please' at least three times when requesting something and firing at least five 'thank-yous' out on receipt of said item. As for 'sorry', well you just can't say too many of those can you – preferably before, during and after an event that almost certainly wasn't your doing anyway.

Well, the good news is that your child can now begin the process of being inducted into our politeness club and by far the best way to make that happen is by being polite when you ask her to do something.

Your partner

Whether your partner is at home, at work or a mixture of both, she will be putting in what contemporary football managers seem to refer to as a 'shift'.

Or put another way, working her arse off.

Toddlers are demanding little beasts both physically and mentally. They are sometimes still seriously attached to their mums and often don't like it when mum dares to go somewhere else and increasingly have the tools to let her know their displeasure in the most vocal way possible.

We'll be looking at tantrums, discipline and all things terrible-two in the next chapter but for now be aware that toddler-wrangling is tough work and your partner needs all the support she can get from you

– especially if she's trying to juggle a job and worrying about childcare at the same time.

There's a chance that rather than having a toddler of the clingy and screamy variety, you have a super independent little person on your hands – which is great, but can leave some mums wondering where their little baby has gone all of a sudden. This in turn can trigger thoughts and conversations about doubling the number of children in your house.

More on which later.

Finally, take a good look at your partner the next time you get the chance. She has carried, delivered, nurtured and loved your child these past 29 months or so and if she's anything like most other mums on the planet, she'll have done it all brilliantly. It's astonishing to behold but tragically easy to miss in the heat of the family furnace just what a formidable feat this is.

It's the size of the achievement that can also sometimes see new mothers at this stage struggle to remember who they were before they became an expert on the merits of Bugaboos over Maclarens. So enveloping is early motherhood that recalling that other things, other people and other places once existed or even just vaguely remembering that the sofa wasn't just for wiping clean, but actually sitting on, isn't a given by any means.

Letting her know what a great job she's doing, what a great mother she has become and that over these next 18 months you'll do everything you can to help her experience a life outside motherhood, would be a very nice thing to do indeed.

You

Been to the gym lately? Or for a run? Thought not.

Finding the time to exercise as a new dad – and mum for that matter – can be a nightmare. Spending all day at work means you want to get home PDQ to see your family before the small one goes to bed and the bigger one dreams of doing the same.

Taking the time to exercise in this world can feel like the height of self-indulgence – 'shan't be home for bathtime tonight, off for a work-out, sauna and long hot shower' isn't a note you want to leave on the kitchen table.

The paradox is that if ever there was a time in your life that you needed the manifold mental and physical boosts that a spot of regular exercise can bring, it's now.

So what to do?

Better to try and squeeze the time from your employers than from your family, so is a lunchtime run a possibility, or a bike ride to work? If not then at the weekend why not turn the lunchtime nap into a proper walk for you and your partner. Not a stroll round the block, a long pacey walk for a good hour or so that can blow the cobwebs away and get your endorphins flowing.

Although it might feel like the very last thing you feel like doing you know deep, deep down in your weary mind that you'll feel better for it.

What's more, the post-bathtime beer or glass of wine that has become like an old trusty friend to you these past months will taste all the sweeter knowing you have burnt at least 8% of its calorific value off earlier that day.

Whoop!

THE TWOS: JUST HOW TERRIBLE ARE THEY?

As you approach the completion of your second year as a father there's much to be proud of.

Your walking, talking little wonder is a credit to you and your partner – you've nurtured, loved and guided her to this point and as you sit and watch her play, a warm feeling of pride and contentment will no doubt wash over you.

And then, from nowhere, your cherub will take a cup from a shelf you didn't think they could reach and throw it with unerring accuracy and admirable power into the very heart of your TV.

Yes that most hackneyed of all child-related phrases the 'terrible twos' will soon start to be uttered to you knowingly by those further down the parental line as you attempt to cope with a tantrum so explosive, so volcanic, that Sky News are running it as a breaking story.

Meltdowns, biting, hitting, pushing – all of these things will need dealing with to varying degrees. In this chapter we will delve into the world of discipline and look at the different approaches and techniques employed so you can choose the one that fits you, your partner and your toddler.

Wrapped up in the discipline debate can often be the 'wait till your father gets home' syndrome that exacerbates the situation in which many men find themselves.

If this applies to you, you'll know that the grown-up thing to do is shrug it off, trot out the line about it being a phase and suck it up. But we both know that when it happens it hurts, so seeing as we are among friends, let's see what can be done.

At this stage of your nipper's life there are also often some big girl/boy moves to be made too – firstly there's the shift from the cot to the bed and then, if you employed it in your battle against sleep deprivation months back, there's ditching the dummy.

As if that wasn't enough at this two-year mark, depending on where you are in the country there's also a health visitor check-up to gauge your little one's growth and development.

DISCIPLINE: SURVIVING THE TERRIBLE TWOS AND BEYOND

Discipline.

It's an ugly word isn't it, dripping with undertones of the cane, the headmaster's office or the Sergeant Major's growl.

Not a word we should be letting within a mile of our beautiful little bubbas, with their smiles, their innocence, and their sweet naïveté.

The thing is, though, all the developmental milestones we cheer at, all the new skills we proudly tell everyone we know about in minute detail, all of these things represent another step towards your child becoming independent, becoming a person.

And we all know what people are like. They have an annoying

habit of seeing things in their own way, of making choices we wouldn't, of loving what we loathe and loathing what we love.

So as your baby grows – even in their first year of life – they begin to understand that they have the power to make decisions, to register displeasure, to disregard advice and to do what they bloody well want.

It just so happens that for many youngsters this realisation first dawns at around the end of their second year, hence the terrible twos. Your child isn't being terrible, though, she's just doing what you would do if you thought you could get away with it, if you hadn't been socially conditioned and handed the fig leaf of embarrassment to hold.

With younger siblings this 'spirited' enlightenment often kicks in earlier thanks to the role model they have who sussed out that 'no' was a small but powerful word many moons ago.

Don't misunderstand me, I'm not non-conformist or stupid enough to be suggesting that the world would be a better place if we ditched discipline and let the children run free to grow up without boundaries.

That world would need to be transformed into a vast soft play area to cope with the fighting and biting we'd all indulge in when some other bugger has stolen 'MY' parking space.

But seeing it in these terms helped my tiny brain to stop chucking out empty phrases like 'why can't you just listen?' and 'I've already told you' when all the irate toddler before me was really doing was flexing their new-found 'me, me, me' muscles.

You need a bit more than just an holistic outlook to help you cope with a supermarket tantrum or a bite mark so deep in the flesh of a fellow nursery goer that you wonder if there's not a big cat living under the sand pit.

There are techniques and tips to help you and your partner dispense discipline when you see fit, but understanding what's behind it is a big help. As well as just the natural exuberance that boundary-pushing creates, there could be a whole host of other factors at play, too.

Young children are remarkably sensitive to change, for instance, be that moving house, an alteration in their daily routine or losing attention to a sibling – and this unsettling change can often lead to testing behaviour.

Then there are the old familiar factors that used to generate a cry in the early months – tiredness, hunger, boredom, frustration – but which now produce so much more colourful a reaction. I mean, why merely cry when you can throw a fully loaded yoghurt pot at a fully loaded clothes horse?

Then there's personality and character. Are you a bit of a one? Do you throw the odd wobbler? Well, chances are your little mirror-image might have a dash of that fighting spirit in them too – which you'll admire and despair of in equal measure.

Whatever the underlying reasons, there will be times from this point onwards when you will need to get across the message to your toddler that painting cats is never OK – or that taking from them the lethal glass photo frame they are holding is actually an act of love, rather than the act of war their resulting meltdown seems to suggest they regard it as.

Tactics and techniques

Before we look at ways that you can communicate with and calm a toddler who is in full furious flow it's interesting to look at why and when your child's behaviour presses your buttons.

Some things are a no-brainer; anything that is potentially harmful to them or others lands right on your fear gland and triggers an immediate response.

But what about the more borderline stuff – do other factors affect when and how you respond?

Most of us, it seems, tend to chide our children more when we are in front of others – especially other parents or our own parents – than when we are alone at home. It somehow feels a very British thing to do, not just because our child's behaviour could directly affect the people we are with, but because our parental credentials somehow feel under scrutiny, because we and our offspring could be judged and marked down as bad eggs.

It takes courage to go against the wisdom of the group and either refuse to pick your child up on what others see as beyond the pale, or reprimand them for something you see as wholly unacceptable, despite it being the norm for the rest.

That interesting little phenomenon aside, here are a few of the key areas to think about when you begin to try and tame your toddler.

Make sure it feels right and that you are both water-tight.

The absolutely key thing is not only to do what feels right for your child, but also to form as super strong an alliance with your partner as you possibly can. A child, even a very young one, can identify a wafer-thin fissure in your approach to discipline from 30 paces and in time they will turn it into a yawning great chasm between the two of you – which isn't good for anyone.

Talk with your partner and try and find a way you both believe in. Honesty is key too. If you are trying to live by a set of rules or a philosophy that you don't believe in, children, like dogs smelling fear, will spot you a mile off. If you don't mean what you are saying, don't say it.

Be persistent and consistent

Disciplining your children is a pain, pure and simple.

It's much easier to let it be and ignore it than it is to stick to a route, saying the same lines over and over and over again – but that's exactly what you have to do.

This stuff takes time – even the fabled 'naughty step', still the discipline destination of choice for millions of parents, is far from a quick fix. No, it takes dedication, determination and patience to follow your plan through, whatever it may be.

Also, with childcare playing an increasingly large role in our lives as parents it's also worth speaking to whoever looks after your child to make sure you are all at least reading the same book, if not on exactly the same page of it.

Avoid over-reaction, encourage conversation

Easier said than done, this. When your child does something irritating for the 23rd time that hour even the more saintly among us is tempted to press the nuclear button. Likewise, when they do something that puts them in serious harm's way and shocks the living daylights out of you it takes real resolve not to let your feelings flood out.

I'm useless when it comes to this last one – especially where roads and cars are concerned as I perhaps gave away a smidgen when we discussed fear. All of my well-thought-through discipline techniques momentarily go out of the window such is the liquid anxiety coursing through my veins, when there is even a hint of traffic danger.

Do my histrionics freeze my son's feet to the pavement? Yes! Do they teach him the Green Cross Code? No.

Talking to our children to explain why we don't want them to do a particular thing is a far more preferable and profitable route to go, as is encouraging them to explain their frustrations or thoughts. Even at this age it's worth doing; more will stick in both directions than you think.

Again in my case that reasonable approach escapes me momentarily after what I perceive to be a near-miss because at that precise moment I seem to be watching a disaster movie in my head which has my little one as the main character.

Don't forget the good times

When you are going through a difficult spell with your child and you and your partner begin to have coded 'We Need to Talk About Kevin' conversations, it's incredibly easy to overlook all the good positive little things that are happening before your eyes.

If anything, the praise volume needs to be turned right up during a tough behavioural time, not down. Letting them know that a lot of what they do makes you happy and crucially gets your attention will encourage them to do more of it.

If the only time they seem to get attention is when they draw a 15ft purple line on your kitchen wall you could soon have a matching one in every room.

Rewards

What's the difference between a reward and a bribe? The academic answer to that question lies in the presence of prior knowledge.

The practical parenting answer is based more around who cares.

Rewarding people for good behaviour works. We all know that to be true, that's why we turn up or log on for work each morning and praise our boss for their foresight, vision and gravitas.

Remember to be specific if you use rewards. Just handing out Percy Pigs without linking them to a very recent action will leave you with an empty bag and very little else. (On that front, handing out sweet treats as a reward is rapidly being viewed the same way as PE teachers using ten press-ups as a punishment – a tad counterintuitive.)

Be warned, though, you have a finite amount of rewards at your disposal before you reach what is known as 'peak reward' – the point where the number of times per day that your child thinks they deserve a reward totals more than the number of Percy Pigs in the supply chain.

This is a dark place to find yourself and, as we will see, with potty training potentially around the corner you may want to keep some of your reward powder dry to help you out.

Distraction

Look, there's a fox in the garden!

Those seven words served my sister remarkably well throughout the bringing up of her four daughters. All of the girls turned out exceptionally well and only two of them have a thing about foxes.

Distraction is the thinking parent's way to avoid or curtail a tantrum. On its own it doesn't teach them the difference between right or wrong, or that roads are dangerous (have I mentioned how dangerous they are?) but it's a very useful thing to have in your tantrum tool kit.

As your kids get older, the equivalent of the fox line will need some creative work doing to it – 'Look! There are two foxes in the garden!' – that kind of thing, but the chances are distraction will become like an old friend by the time you are the age where you are the one who can't remember what you went upstairs to do.

The Voice and The Look

Everyone raises their voice to their children at some point or another – everyone.

Even the couple you know who seem to have the patience of Job and the resourcefulness of Mary Poppins will lose it once in a while and give it some verbal revs to get their point across.

But while everyone does it, no one really likes doing it, or enjoys it – I mean what kind of beast would you need to be to take real enjoyment from rendering your children petrified by bellowing at them?

Nevertheless, shouting is a dirty little secret we all occasionally share, but what can we do to minimise it?

Meet tone. Tone is shouting's smarter, less socially awkward and better-looking little brother. If you can master the use of the tone of your voice as a register of either your displeasure or alarm at your little one's antics you can save shouting for those rare moments when absolutely nothing else will do.

Then, if you are really talented and you can combine tone with The Look – well you are almost home and hosed. An infrequently used, well-delivered and unmistakable look can be a very powerful thing and has the capacity to silently communicate all you need to get across without making everyone else in the room know about it.

It takes practice to perfect The Look, so you'll need to spend some time in front of the mirror until you can really get through to yourself.

Mind your language

I don't mean swearing, swearing is fine, swear away. Kids never ever repeat your profanities, especially not out loud in the middle of nursery, or in front of the doctor and they absolutely never say 'Fuck It' when they drop something while being looked after by your mother.

Never.

No, what I mean is that the language you use plays a key part.

First, there's overuse. If you repeatedly use the threat of a consequence to stop your toddler doing something, you will have to either be prepared to carry that threat out at some point or take the phrase out of circulation once it's become redundant.

And it will become redundant sooner than you think, because you will use it hundreds of times more frequently than you realise.

'If you don't behave we will go home right now,' I say for the 14th time that week.

'No we won't' – thinks the bright little person before me, 'Not once have those words ever been followed by an immediate return to our house. Besides, I didn't ask to come to this supermarket/ wedding/job interview, you brought me here. I'd quite like to go home, actually, there are toys there and what's more when we are at home you at least stop threatening me with immediate return to the bloody place.'

Then there's the altogether more murky issue of the actual words you use. Annette Mountford, chief executive of the parenting organisation Family Links, ran into a storm of political-correctness-gone-mad flak when she suggested that calling children 'naughty' damages their self-confidence. She also suggested the naughty step should be renamed to avoid children thinking it meant they themselves were naughty.

She also made the point that saying 'what you did was naughty' rather than 'you are naughty' sent out a very different message.

Mmmm. Tricky one.

Whatever your take on this, an interesting exercise is to replace the word naughty with stupid. Children do naughty things and children do stupid things, but actively telling them that they are stupid feels wrong on a lot of levels. If you've ever heard a stressed and harassed parent do just that, or if you've been that parent, you'll know that it just intrinsically feels like a very bad thing to do.

A smart technique that a lot of nurseries seem to use is not to tell the children what they are or how they should be feeling after they have done something obviously wrong, but rather to let them know that their actions have made the teacher feel 'sad'.

Yes there's an element of emotional blackmail in that, but for my money given how important it is for children to feel like they are gaining praise and acceptance, that is a powerful method of registering displeasure which avoids the need to repeatedly tell the child that they are in some way substandard or different.

If that's a controversial issue, this final one is the daddy, mummy and primary caregiver of all discipline debating points.

To smack or not to smack?

UK law currently states that parents can smack their children, but it is illegal for them to leave any mark or bruise. The smacking of children in schools, both state and private is illegal, although nannies and babysitters can be given permission by parents to administer 'reasonable chastisement'.

A study conducted by the National Society for the Prevention of Cruelty to Children (NSPCC) in 2019 found that 77% of parents in the UK believed that smacking children is not an effective form of discipline. The study also found that 42% of parents reported having smacked their child at least once in the past year, but only 11% said they used physical punishment as their primary form of discipline.

It's worth noting that attitudes towards physical punishment have been changing in the UK, and there is a growing awareness of the potential harm that smacking can cause. In 2020, Scotland became the first part of the UK to ban the physical punishment of children, and similar legislation has been proposed in other parts of the country.

Does smacking actually work to instill discipline? Well, on one level we all know it does – smack a child hard on their bare legs and they won't only stop what they are doing, they will remember the pain and try and avoid feeling it again.

But what about the long-term effects and consequences? Does the often-repeated paradox of punishing a child for hitting some-one by hitting them really present a long-term problem?

Well let's just say it's a confused picture.

On the one hand we have surveys which seem to show that children spanked frequently at age three are much more likely to be aggressive by the time they are five. And others that even suggest that children who are smacked end up with a lower IQ.

Then we have research which finds that youngsters smacked up to the age of six do better at school, are keener to attend university and even do more voluntary work!

Just to confuse things further, the very same paper also found that if you continue to smack children after they are six it has significant negative effects.

All clear? Good.

The truth is, no one knows – and ultimately for as long as some form of corporal punishment is available to parents it is up to their gut instincts as to whether they resort to it. As of 2021 more than 60 countries worldwide had banned smacking outright and that number is on a seemingly inexorable rise.

One thing is for sure, though: if you and your partner hold concrete but differing views around the smacking debate you need to talk and iron them out pronto, having the conversation after corporal punishment has already been meted out will make a tough issue even harder to resolve.

Up until now we've focused on your reaction to your child's behaviour rather than the behaviour itself. That is primarily because young children can find so many ways to test you that it's hardly worth beginning to list them.

But there is one area that is worth touching on because not only do most of us have to deal with it as parents in some shape or form, but it also happens to be uniquely disconcerting when our angelic tot begins to indulge in it.

Hitting, biting, pushing and kicking

Most young children occasionally bite, hit or push another child – although hopefully not at the same time.

Many even go through spells where they regularly dispense violent retribution like a vigilante cop operating on the margins of the law. While these periods are generally and thankfully short-lived, they can seem to go on for eons, such is the perturbation they cause the mortified parents.

I remember my son pushing a fellow toddler clean off a stage area at a christening once. Such was the force of the shove that the boy seemed to travel a good six feet laterally before gravity was even aware of what was going on and intervened to bring him back to earth with a painful-looking bump.

'Oh my God, we've spawned a monster' I remember thinking as I took him outside for a talking-to. What could he be thinking; did he not know that kind of behaviour could seriously hurt someone?

In a word, no, he didn't know that. In fact he also didn't know what would happen if he pushed someone off a raised surface. So he tried it and as experiments go it garnered pleasing and relatively spectacular results.

Until told otherwise, everything is play to young children, including what happens when you sink teeth into a fleshy arm. This behaviour doesn't mean they will grow up to be aggressive but it is your job to get the message through to them that this particular set of games is not good.

From the strictly logical perspective, the most straightforward way to demonstrate just how much a bite hurts is to have a nibble on your child. This is a very bad idea on a number of levels, not least of which is the fact that biting kids will see you in prison – even if your defence consists of 'I was only showing them how painful it is, m'lud'.

In fact, in 2008 a mother was jailed for five months for doing just that.

So with that 'see how you like it' route out of the question, what can you do to make sure they know that this is serious stuff?

In terms of immediate action, you can tell them in a calm but stern manner that what they have just done is not acceptable. As long as you are absolutely prepared to carry it out at the very hint of a repeat offence you can tell your child you will take them home or up to their room if they do it again.

If they have indulged in a real spate of pushing and biting-type behaviour rather than the odd one-off incident, getting to the bottom of the root cause is the key. Are they feeling insecure about a new baby, or frustrated by recent change? If you can identify and address what's worrying them, you can often stem the flow of what's driving them to lash out at source.

Talking to them about how they are feeling has the added benefit of adding emotional language to their ever-growing vocabulary – which means eventually when they feel frustrated they may well tell you so rather than launching the next toddler that walks past them into space.

Words from your fellow fathers:

Jason, father of two: *I am definitely the bad cop, not intentionally I just follow how I was brought up.*

Oldest one is a Mummy's boy for sure, although number two seems to smile at me more so far.

There are naughty corners, steps and zones everywhere in our house and he is happy with them all. He would probably be happy in a dungeon. He does not understand the concept of punishment, or do we not know how to dish it out?

Rob, father of two: *Pure mental toughness is needed to avoid a meltdown.*

Try not to raise your voice at all. Kids at this stage tend to copy exactly what you do. Firm language without any stressful tones is the best way in my eyes.

Mark, father of one: *You have to back up each other whether right or* wrong (you can have those discussions afterwards on your own) as you can't have the little one playing you off against each other.

I'd also pick your battles, no point saying 'no' or being harsh if you don't really have to be. But when you mean it, follow through with it – or you're in trouble next time!

I always tend to kneel down to their height but can't help myself shouting sometimes.

Tom, father of two: *The worst tantrum I've witnessed involved noises that I can only describe as beyond feral. Generally over something so trivial.*

You find yourself sometimes coming up with ridiculous threats like 'if you don't behave, Christmas will be cancelled'. I did pretend to call Father Christmas once, and he was mortified – my son, not Santa.

Felt a little harsh but once you start, you've got to see it through of course, otherwise they realise you're crap at making up threats. Very clever, are children.

Simon, father of one: *My son is very easily distracted away from tantrums it seems. Especially by chocolate of any description.*

Marcus, father of four: *Our second was a biter. Would rather my child was bitten than was a biter, it's very hard to deal with.*

Stuart, father of two: *Our eldest was very much a biter (as was I as a child – drawing blood after biting my uncle's bottom after an excitable game of 'horse').*

On a few occasions she would latch onto my cheek with her teeth while I was play-fighting with her. Her younger sister is a pusher, which she finds hilarious.

I WANT MUMMY TO DO IT: SECOND-BEST SYNDROME

Life isn't fair – we all know that. It has the distinct habit of wedging the gusset of justice up the backside of hard luck and delivering something we didn't expect or deserve.

And so, brave father, it is my duty to tell you that although you may well have done everything that could have been reasonably asked or expected of you up to this point and then some – your child probably still favours their mummy and may even tell you so on a frequent and not so sensitive basis.

That's OK, though, isn't it? Mummies are soft, mummies understand and well, everyone loves their mum. And besides, we're grown men aren't we – it doesn't bother us one bit does it?

In public, no. In private? Well, maybe a little.

The odd 'I want Mummy to take me to bed' we can all handle – but if there's a noticeable and persistent desire to be with mum rather than dad it can really hurt, despite our male programming telling us to suck it up and make like it doesn't matter.

There could be two main factors responsible for these instances of mummy favouritism. The first is if you have already found yourself acting as the primary disciplinarian of the family. Playing the 'wait till your father gets home' role can be an effective deterrent for misbehaviour, but it can have the very real side effect of positioning you as the villain of the piece.

While being bad cop doesn't really mean much with a two-year-old, fast forward 18 months and you could find yourself in a place you neither expected nor enjoy. The temptation then is to redress the balance by sanctioning all sorts of stuff you wouldn't normally and generally acting the goat – all of which can lead to 'silly Daddy' syndrome.

Without wanting to disappear into the debate about the role men now often play in modern society, you can see plenty of 'silly Daddys' in action across a lot of children's TV. Up until relatively recently it was quite rare to see a father character being portrayed as anything other than either a well-meaning clumsy clot or parental law enforcer. What the sociological reason for this is is open to debate but the upshot doesn't make for the most rounded viewing.

Back in the real world, lurching from good cop to bad cop is a very tricky role to play and if you can, it's much preferable if you both take a hand in all areas of parenting so your child can form a balanced view of both of you.

Aside from defining your day-to-day role as a father, there's another more influential factor at play when it comes to why many a youngster favours Mummy – the fact that many of us fathers simply find it impossible to spend as much time as we need to with our children.

When you are trying your best to juggle work and home responsibilities, it can be hard to hear from your partner that the reason your child isn't as close to you as you'd like is because you don't spend enough quality time with them.

But it's probably true.

How precisely you are meant to rectify this sad situation is one of the modern father's main conundrums. Torn between a primeval instinct to provide and the desire to interact with our children we spread ourselves pretty thin, truth be told.

Would missing that late meeting really make that much of a difference to your job? It's hard for me to say without meeting your boss – but giving it a miss to play on the carpet with your nipper is definitely worth a go every now and then if you can.

The adage 'all things will pass' is also worth remembering if you are getting the cold shoulder from the little person you love most in the world. It may only be a matter of weeks before your child enters a stage where you give her exactly what she wants and needs at that point in her development and then mum is the one with the moist eyes and the hangdog expression.

What's more, as fortunes and affections swing back and forth you and your partner can at least console yourself with the knowledge that in a decade or so's time when you have a teenager on your hands neither of you will be flavour of the month.

Words from your fellow fathers:

Winston, father of two: My little girl used to tell me 'Don't want Daddy' and sometimes even 'Don't like Daddy' when she was around two. It upset me greatly as I would wonder what I had done to deserve it. My wife would dish out fearful bollockings to her for being mean to me, and it is surprising to realise how easily hurt I could be by a small child. I knew it was just a phase and it passed.

My son who is now nearly two has suddenly become protective of his mum and loves her in a different way from his sister. But he looks at me differently too and, poor boy, you can see a degree of hero worship. He'll grow out of it when he realises his dad's a dufus.

Chris, father of two: I'd come home from work all geed up to see my daughter, open the door and get blanked . . . it was crushing.

I understood it, but was crushing nonetheless. I do tend to be favoured when it comes to wrestle time and 'throw-your-kid-as-high-as-possible-in-the-air' time.

Oh and 'can I have a lolly' time – I'm a softer touch there.

Stuart, father of two: As Mummy was the worker in the family I *would routinely be dropped like a bucket of sick as soon as she got in from work and then at weekends Mummy would have a permanent little shadow.*

I do think absence makes the heart grow fonder, though, because when I have freelanced, when I got in from work I would be met with two very excitable children, very happy to see Daddy.

CANNING THE COT AND DITCHING THE DUMMY

Being two can hardly be classed as over the hill, but the difference between the toddler you know now and the newborn you began your fatherhood journey with is truly astonishing.

Walking, talking, laughing, joking – there's a whole range of complex activities that your little one can do without even thinking about it.

As she continues to learn, she also starts the process of shedding the things she needed to help her on her way from baby to mini person. The move from the cot to the bed is one of those significant little moments.

Even more visible a sign to the outside world that the baby days are being left behind is saying so long to the soother, for those still using them – and with medical advice suggesting that use much after three years old can interfere with tooth alignment, many parents use two as the point at which they try and pull the oral plug.

Moving to the big bed and ditching the dummy can be a natural and smooth progression which your child accepts with the wisdom of someone who's moved on these last 24 months.

Alternatively, they can kick off in a big way and bring sleepless nights temporarily back to your world.

You remember those, don't you?

The big bed

There's no hard and fast time when a child should move from a cot to a bed – although by the age of three most have jumped ship.

In many ways if she is comfortable and sleeps well in her cot only a fool would move her unnecessarily.

If, though, she is outgrowing her cot, arms and legs sticking out this way and that – or as my son did at just over two, clambering out of the bloody thing in the middle of the night and hopping down the landing in his sleep bag complete with chipped tooth and bumped head – you'll know it's time to make the move.

Another trigger is if there's another baby on the way and the current tenant of the cot needs to make way. If this is your reason, try to ensure that your toddler is well-settled in her new bed before the interloper arrives to avoid fanning the flames of disgruntlement.

Some children will adjust easily to a big bed, they'll love it even, thriving on the grown-upness, the space, the freedom – whereas others may not like it one little bit.

Chances are your firstborn will be the one most likely to kick up a stink because it may be one of a raft of changes to broadside her little life, like going to nursery or expecting a brother or sister. Later-born children also have the benefit of wanting to do exactly what their older siblings do too – and may well see cots as for babies.

If you are sensing unease, little touches like putting the bed in the same place as the cot was and transferring the same blanket across can really help.

As ever, getting them involved in picking the bed and the bedding is also a great idea – foster a sense of ownership of the move in them and you could be on to a winner.

No matter how prepared your child is to move to a bed, though, a guardrail is a must, without a support of some kind they can easily toss, turn, roll over and end up in a heap on the floor. Although you can buy beds with these built in, it's best to buy a separate one so you can take it on your travels with you and make any bed safe.

As for the bed itself, a lot of people go for the cot bed nowadays which via the magic of the Allen key sees a traditional cot transform into a cute little mini bed. The only drawback is that if you have a second child you need the cot back and either have to turf the toddler out (not great for sibling rivalry) or buy a whole new one.

Another possibility is visitations. Once they clock that they can get out of bed, their next move could well be the door and then your bed.

There's no way of combating this other than through patience and firm but gentle encouragement to stay in bed if she wakes up. Often this passes quickly but it can turn into an epidemic, five, six, seven times a night either going in after hearing her walking around or having to carry her back to her bed after she's snuck into yours again.

If this becomes the case, rather than contemplating locking them in, don't be shy of reaching the conclusion that you may have made the switch a touch too early and going back to the cot until they are ready.

Ditching the dummy

I know dummies get a bad press, but for their size and relative cost, they can deliver an extraordinary amount of contentment to small and big people alike.

If you used the little plastic wonder, there's a chance that for certain parts of the day or night it is still working its sleep-inducing magic and if that's the case you and your partner will have almost certainly had fitful conversations about how and when you pull the plug, as it were.

No one really likes how a dummy looks on a two-year-old and if it spends too long in the mouth of an awake child it can and does have a detrimental effect on tooth alignment and even speech development – but the peace and rest it brings is a hard thing to meddle with for all concerned.

But once you finally bite the bullet and decide that the time has come, there are some tried and tested ways to do it that can avoid the kind of bedtime Armageddon that your imagination can dream up.

The technique to avoid is stealthily stealing it and playing dumb as they become grief-stricken. Not only isn't that a very nice thing to do, it's not a very clever thing to do either, because the trauma that the sudden and unexplained disappearance can cause them dwarfs the removal of the thing itself.

No, the collective wisdom of those who have done it says that gradually decreasing the times it's used without so much as mention-ing your evil master plan is a sensible start. Once you've got dummy use down to, say, bedtime and the odd cold that crops up, you can move on to the end game.

When the big night arrives it's a good idea to have gotten rid of every dummy you have stashed away in the house and the car, because if things kick off in a big way you'll want temptation well out of your eyeline rather than winking at you from the changing table.

A visit from the dummy fairy remains a popular way to soften the blow, with a nice big-boy or -girl present left behind in its place. Some enlightened dentists – as opposed to the stupendously petrifying ones we used to go to as kids – can now even help you out too and the really cool ones sometimes have a place for youngsters to deposit their dummies in exchange for a sticker or toothbrush.

Times have changed.

Depending on your child, a little explanation and story like that might be all you need to smoothly say 'sayonara' to the soother and gently sneer at those who took great pleasure in telling you that you'd have a nightmare on your hands once they carried on using it past six months old.

Or you might find yourself in a situation where for three or four nights on the trot your house reverberates to the sound of an incandescent and terribly upset toddler. There's no easy fix for that as we all know, but if you see the dummy as having provided them comfort there's an argument to say that for a while you and your partner need to replace what's lost, so it's extra kisses and lashings of warm cuddles all round.

That and bribery, don't forget bribery.

CHECK ME OUT: YOUR CHILD'S HEALTH AND DEVELOPMENT AT TWO

Two-year checks for children are required by law for all children in England and are carried out by health visitors or other trained professionals. The two-year check is a developmental review that assesses a child's progress in areas such as communication, physical development and social skills. It is designed to identify any potential concerns early on and provide support and guidance to families.

The requirement for two-year checks was introduced in 2015 as part of the Children and Families Act. The act made it a statutory duty for local authorities in England to ensure that a developmental review is offered to every child aged two years old, or as soon as possible thereafter. In Scotland and Northern Ireland the checks are not mandatory but are recommended as good practice, likewise in Wales where a non-mandatory 30-month check is often carried out.

Here's what your child could be checked for:

Gross motor skills

Child can:
- walk and run without falling
- walk upstairs and downstairs holding on and using two feet per step
- throw a ball forward without falling over
- walk into a ball to kick it

Fine motor skills

Child can:

- build a tower of 5–6 bricks
- imitate a circular scribble and straight line
- turn the single pages of a book

Vision

Child:

- recognises pictures of animals and everyday objects e.g. cup, apple, banana in picture books
- has no squint.

Communication and hearing

Child can:

- name 3–5 pictures or objects
- use about 50 understandable words and understands more
- make little sentences of two words e.g. 'Mummy's keys'
- tell you what she needs
- carry out simple instructions.

Social skills and behaviour

Child:

- plays with toys meaningfully and in make-believe play
- has little idea of sharing but may be beginning to take turns
- plays alongside other children rather than with them
- is very possessive of own toys
- can drink from a cup and feed herself with a spoon
- is very curious and tries to investigate everything
- has no concept of danger

- has temper tantrums when frustrated but easily distracted
- may have toilet awareness e.g. know when wet or soiled.

Before you run screaming to the GP's surgery, as ever it's vital to remember that all children progress at different speeds in different aspects of their development. Some are great talkers and lousy runners and vice versa.

If you are worried about something specific it goes without saying, get it checked out. Eye tests are especially important; one survey found that 34% of parents with school-aged children (five to 16 years) have not had their child's eyes tested in the last five years, despite guidelines suggesting that children be taken for an eye examination by the age of three and every two years after that.

PROGRESS REPORT, 21–24 MONTHS

Your toddler

As we've seen, your toddler's personality and imagination are growing and developing at a fantastic rate at this age. With that growth comes the likelihood that they will begin to become scared of things.

It could be monsters, strangers, a character in a book they have been reading or the dark.

Listening to these fears, letting them know it's a natural thing to feel and even that you are sometimes scared of things will go a long way to helping them to learn how to deal with a feeling, let's be honest, that will be with them on occasion for the rest of their lives. When they are brave, tell them how proud you are of them and make sure they know that you will always be there to help make them feel even braver.

On a more physical level your child will start to favour either their right or left hand from this age onward. Up until now they will have been switching from one to another, trying them out, essentially.

The whole 'handedness' thing is still a bit of a mystery but what is known is that genetics plays a big part and around one person in 10 is left-handed. You'll soon know if your nipper is part of the lefty crowd.

As for walking – pah! Try climbing or even the odd run for size. She might be trying to kick a ball now, too, although not always with the desired result and the comedy routine that is missing the target, spinning round and landing on her bottom can be often enjoyed.

Jumping, which it turns out is anatomically really quite tricky to get to grips with, is still a little way off, though.

Put some music on and you might also be treated to a little dance too – more often than not an impossibly cute bobbing up and down number.

You and your partner

Here's a word you and your partner are about to hear a whole lot more of –

'Why?'

Be careful on that slide. Why?

Because you might fall off. Why?

Because it's a long way from the ground. Why?

Because you need the height differential to be able to slide down it. Why?

Because if it was flat you'd just lie there. Why?

Because gravity wouldn't be able to exert itself. Why?

I don't know, do I look like Isaac Newton? Ask Mummy.

They will want to know everything and in their eyes you know everything. So for the next wee while don't ever stray too far from Google.

What's also about to appear on your radar again is birthday time! While the second birthday isn't quite as much as a milestone as the first, the good thing is that while you still haven't reached the territory where 30 other parents abandon their children to your care for three hours while they go shopping – your toddler will love a bit of a get-together, even if they might not be fully aware why it's happening.

You don't have to blow a fortune on fancy stuff and grand themes; it'll still go way over their heads. No, a dressing-up box, plastic party horns, a story or two, a sandwich for them to throw and some cake for them to eat will do the trick and have them begging for more. Or a nap.

If anyone suggests party bags to you, tell them they are definitely on the agenda for next year. Definitely.

FANCY ANOTHER?

All two-year-olds are brilliant.

Yes, they can lose their rag, yes they rapidly begin to think they are invincible, and yes their running about and gung-ho chips are fully functioning while their danger one hasn't kicked in yet.

But they are still brilliant.

They want to know everything, to feel everything and to do everything. In their minds they are the kings and queens of the universe – no one has ever learnt more than they have as quickly as they have.

Imagine feeling like that! No wonder they go berserk when we stop them from opening a mere cupboard.

In keeping with this spirit of derring-do and the transition from baby to barrier-busting toddler, this age is often when children show signs of being ready to leave their nappy behind and join the adults in the toilet, if you see what I mean.

That's right, potty training has arrived – be afraid and on hand with some kitchen towel.

You'll also begin to notice that your little one becomes a much more social being once she turns two. Making friends is a big deal for all of us at any time of life, but these first forays into the world of other people are both interesting and sometimes heartbreaking for you to watch.

What's more, they also begin to gently reinforce that your position, your status, if you like, has changed forever – you're not just you anymore, you can be and will be often defined as someone's dad – a subtle but important change that will become more profound as your child gets older and as you do, too.

As other children arrive on the scene, either at nursery or on play dates, the odd concept of sharing begins to raise its head.

As British parents, sharing, or the lack of it from our children, is particularly hard to stomach given the mantra-like way we had it drummed into us as youngsters.

The sight of our children snatching a toy, reacting with fury and indignation when another child visiting the house dares to play with something that quite clearly belongs to the young master of the premises or – worst of the worst – when our own flesh and blood refuses to wait their turn for the slide and – I can barely even write it – pushes into a queue, all make us determined to get to work asap on bringing them into the 'after you, Claude' fold.

As we will see, though, explaining what sharing is and why it's important to a two-year-old for whom the universe was most definitely created for the sole purpose of spinning round and round them, is a very tricky thing to do indeed.

Finally in these six months the differences that your toddler's gender will make to their personality, development and outlook begin to make themselves known – with the nature and nurture debate at the centre of things as ever.

Perhaps the most profound of occurrences at this time is that thoughts, conversations and glances between you and your partner can all turn to the prospect of adding another member to your family.

With the average gap between children in the UK coming out at around 35 months, this is optimum 'let's start trying again' territory.

Are you ready?

POTTY TRAINING: KEEP CALM AND CARRY WIPES

It probably doesn't seem that long ago that you were fumbling around with your first nappy change, all poo-covered thumbs and smeared Sudocrem.

Soon the time to move from nappies to pants will be upon you and your toddler. As well as the practical side of things, this transition represents yet another giant leap towards independence.

Before we move into the soggy reality of it all, it's worth asking yourself one question – how many adults do you know who live their lives in giant disposables as a result of their parents having never mastered potty training?

Not many, I hope.

The reason why that's a pertinent point to focus on is that you might find yourself wondering if you and yours will ever crack it; if you will ever be able to travel anywhere again without a bin liner full of clean kids' underwear and a bottle of 1001 carpet cleaner.

But you will, don't worry, you will. Patience and good humour are as important in this little parenting challenge as they are in perhaps any other and besides, it's only poo and wee isn't it, you've practically got a PhD in the pair of them by now anyway.

When are they ready?

This is a key question: go too early and you could be in for a very long haul indeed, with your child forming a stubborn refusal to countenance attempting something that they have found incredibly difficult thus far.

The pressure not to go too late can often come in the form of two things – the first being that some or even all of your child's peers seem to have cracked it already.

The counter to this, as ever, is: 'So what?' And besides, if you have a son and the dry friends are girls there really is no point even wasting a second's worry on it, because, just for a change, girls tend to get potty training a lot easier than boys.

Poor us.

The other pressure point could well come in the form of a letter from the nursery you are hoping your nipper will attend when they are three. Nestled amongst all the info is often a list of 'things your child must be able to do'.

Just under the alarming-in-its-own-right 'taking off and putting on their own coat' you may well find 'be fully toilet-trained'.

Queue sirens, flashing lights and the purchasing of nine books and five different types of potty contraptions.

Take a breath, relax and have faith, you will get there, and a big part of making that happen is attempting to start the process when they are ready rather than when you need them to be ready.

Tragically, that point in time doesn't make itself known via a handwritten note or impassioned speech from your little one, but relies on you spotting some (but rarely all) of the following signs.

- She loves to play at pulling her nappy/pull-up/pants up and down. Who doesn't?

- She likes to follow you and/or your partner to the bathroom and even imitate what you do in there.
- She makes a discernible and often unmistakable physical demonstration when a bowel movement is being delivered – this can range from the classic poo face, to an attractive grunt, a giveaway squat or even a verbal warning to everyone within range.
- She uses words for stool and urine – hopefully not some of the more colourful ones.
- She seems to recognise the physical signals from within that means action is on its way and can tell you about it ahead of time – especially when you are on a packed bus.
- She actively dislikes the feeling of being in a dirty nappy. There's a theory that children are less likely to be driven to the potty for this reason now most of them are in ultra-absorbent disposables rather than soggy, heavy and uncomfortable towelling nappies. (I say 'theory' – it's what my Dad reckons).
- She has 'dry' periods of at least three or four hours which crucially indicates that the bladder muscles are up to the task of holding and storing urine.

Spot a handful of these and you are in business – but before we move on to what to do, it's worth looking at what not to do.

What doesn't work

So you think you've got the green light – time to put the foot down and zoom to a nappy-free world.

Not quite.

If toddlers feel undue pressure around potty-training it is the easiest thing in the world for them to clam up – literally. They will move through the stages of this in their own time and any attempt to give things a nudge can seriously backfire.

Likewise, when things don't go according to plan (and they won't, because they never do) getting frustrated or even angry is to be avoided at all costs, as is any semblance of punishment or rebuke for the many, many accidents you will be cleaning up.

Not only is punishment a complete waste of time, it will have a noticeably negative impact on what you are trying to achieve. Rather than looking forward to a trip to the toilet or the potty they will avoid it at all costs.

Keeping calm and carrying on is the way to go – and even if it's through gritted teeth trying to make – oh dear, never mind – your response of choice is a smart move. Not always easy, but smart.

Much like the world of breastfeeding, you will also find advice on how you can and should approach potty training coming from every corner. If you manage to avoid someone telling you that you are waiting too long or being too soft you will be doing well.

Practices, conventions and techniques have changed on this as on many other fronts – using children as chimney sweeps or to pull coal wagons underground springs to mind – so if you can, smile sweetly and move on. Either that or launch into one and make yourself feel a bit better.

What works

Didn't they do well?

Children love praise.

What am I saying? We all love praise, it's just that children haven't been taught to be coy about showing the fact yet. You'll be amazed what praising the very arse off every little bit of progress and celebrating the merest sniff of success can do.

And I mean really celebrate, go mad, do a little dance around the front room, the works.

As ever, though, if you really do go too far they can be so overwhelmed by your extraordinary reaction that the thought of failure and letting you down can produce such a build-up of pressure that they will wet themselves.

We tread a fine line as parents, don't we?

Accidents happen

Has there ever been anyone on the planet who has learnt to drive a manual car without stalling it at least once?

I very much doubt it.

You'll have puddles, you'll have poo parcels, you may even have a trail of both up your cream stair carpet.

C'est la wee.

Open door policy

Toddlers learn by copying, so encourage them to watch. It's probably best that boys watch you and girls watch mum so as not to confuse, but the more they see you both in action the more they will want to do it.

Show-stopping pants and knickers

Take your little one shopping and let them pick whatever underwear they like – children's underwear I mean.

Whatever your views on marketing to kids, whatever your principles on television consumption, if purchasing a pack of Iggle

Piggle pants or Upsy Daisy knickers will help you motor through potty training just swallow hard and get them bought.

Make a plan

Defeating the nappy enemy requires some serious military co-ordination. If your youngster is at nursery or with a childminder you'll need them to be on the same page to stand a chance.

Once she has her über underwear you'll need to decide if you are going to set periods of the day in both or go headlong into permanent pant mode and to hell with the consequences and the upholstery. The training pants you'll see in the supermarket get the thumbs-down from many experts because essentially they are still nappies and won't feel wet.

In the early potty training skirmishes, it's actually a good idea to plan in some time when they can get naked (the reason many parents choose to tackle potty training in the summer months). This means there's no barrier whatsoever between your toddler's hindquarters and the floor, but it's a great way for them to really start to learn what it feels like when they need to go.

You will rapidly become an expert in spotting the slightest twitch which signifies they need to go too – the clutch, the hop and, if you're not quick enough, the squat.

There are lots of little ways you can make the whole thing a little more fun. Stack her favourite books next to the potty or toilet or turn to the popular sticker method which sees every success rewarded with another of the adhesive little beauties stuck to a progress chart.

Imagine how much simpler the world would be if adults loved stickers as much as kids did.

If they lose their lustre, you may just have to resort to unadulterated bribery, which normally operates on a sliding scale something like this – raisins, apricots, Percy Pigs, muffin, small toy, large toy, university tuition fees.

Kit

Potties have come a long way.

Some of the ones on the market nowadays look more like Captain Kirk's seat on the bridge than a plastic toilet. As with the pants, if you can engineer it so that your tot feels like they own and love their new grown-up gadget, getting them to sit on it will be a whole lot easier.

Although many toddlers are scared of falling into the cavernous toilet, some refuse to demean themselves and sit on a potty and want to do what you do where you do it. If that's the case then an adapter seat is a good buy and can transform the big porcelain hole into a comfy seat perfect for a little bottom. They even manage to retain a smell of wee after only a couple of uses so you can find them in the dark. What will they think of next?

If your child point-blank refuses to sit on either the potty or the training seat avoid a stand-off at all costs – act like it's no big deal but keep the potty out and keep talking about it. They will have a go eventually, especially if they see their favourite cuddly toy casually having a wee in it from time to time without so much as a by-your-leave.

Once you've got them sitting down don't rush them, quite the opposite in fact, keep them entertained – the more time they spend on there at this stage the more used to the whole strange affair they will become.

If you have a boy, it makes a lot of sense to start them off by sitting down to do both number ones and twos. We all partake in the luxury of a sit-down wee every now and then, especially when we become knackered dads, so why should we keep it from them? Besides, it's a more straightforward way to learn the basics before they have to master the stand-up aim – and we all know how tricky that is.

If you have a girl, try to teach her the front-to-back wipe from a pretty early stage. If this feels too early for her to grasp, then a pat dry technique is a good halfway house.

Into the night

Once you've cracked it and your days have become a dry paradise you can start to tackle night-times. Don't be tempted to go too early on this though; much better to really make sure the day is nailed.

Once you think the coast is clear, start keeping an eye on nappies in the mornings and if they are consistently dry put a wipe-clean mattress cover under her sheet and give it a whirl without. If after a few nights it's obvious their bladder isn't ready to hold tight until the morning, go back to the nappies in a very easy come, easy go way and let her know that you'll try the no-nappy night-time game again soon.

Never restrict drinks, but steer away from giving her a massive drink before bed, to give her a fighting chance. You can even wake her up for a 'sleep wee' when you go to bed, too, if she's a solid sleeper and you know she'll go straight back off again. Staying dry through the night is a tough trick to perfect, so don't worry if you continue to get the odd accident for a good few months or even years after you think you are home and, well, dry.

Words from your fellow fathers:

Chris, father of two: *We are still going . . . our daughter is now three-and-three-quarters as she likes to tell us repeatedly. Pity her pooing isn't as good as her fractions.*

To be fair, she's good during the day, but still wearing nappies at night. There's the odd accident and mopping of floors, but very rarely and usually when she's been distracted.

The car seat gets a belting when she's fallen asleep for a while. Bless easy-wash covers.

Tom, father of two: *Potty training was pretty good, some spectacular accidents. The sticker chart did well, with stickers on anything vaguely acceptable as a toilet (except the cat litter).*

My personal horror experience was naturally centred around a poorly tummy, where it just started to slide down her leg. We were in a playground area, Mummy was talking to another mum, and our daughter was very politely trying to communicate there was an issue, sadly for me I spotted it so whisked her to an area to deal with her.

Shit was everywhere, ran out of wipes (of course), flies having a field day, park toilet locked (naturally, what use is that on a Saturday?), it was minging.

Rob, father of two: *Multiple accidents for at least two months for us. Poos on the landing. Poos in the bedroom. Poos on the toilet seat!*

Winston, father of two: *One thing you find out when you have kids – they can do massive turds.*

MAKING FRIENDS

For quite a long while, small children just ignore each other.

You arrange playdates, you throw birthday parties, you assemble in the park and each time they manoeuvre round each other like embarrassed guests at a gathering no one wants to be at.

Occasionally they will notice or even acknowledge each other, usually with a hand to the face or a tug of wispy hair – but generally they just aren't that bothered to react – even violently.

Then one day, often after they've got walking really nailed down, they suddenly begin to become social animals. They click with a little pal and before very long they are laughing and chasing and asking when they will see them again.

It's a lovely thing and yet another major physiological and sociological milestone in your child's development from vulnerable babe to proper little person.

In these early exchanges it's more often than not a beautifully simple relationship or two your little one will strike up with a handful of their peers. It revolves around playing and chasing and giggling. The first signs of little in-jokes are sometimes also spied as they seemingly talk semi-gobbledygook to their new mates but end up laughing like drains at whatever it is they have jointly made up.

It's hard to overplay how significant these first fledgling independent interactions are. They represent your child formalising her sense of herself and defining and moulding who she is by the way she interacts with other people.

As sweet and lovely as these early stages are, rest assured the complexities that we all know exist as adults around interpersonal relationships and the fact that hell, on occasion, can indeed be other people, do rear their head in the not-too-distant future for your child.

As time goes on, you'll witness them being rejected and even ridiculed by older kids, having their innocent little overtures and ideas rebuffed and eventually rattling round the school playground on their own on that daunting first morning.

It's hard to describe what all these things do to you as a parent and a father – but suffice to say it's a feeling you won't forget in a hurry. You are essentially witnessing your child learning for the first time that the world and the people in it aren't quite as benevolent, friendly and straightforward as the closeted and loving little environment that they have spent their lives thus far inhabiting.

It really is the first time the fig leaf has fallen away.

On the flip side, they are also becoming alive to the possibility that fun and laughter and excitement can be had in great quantities thanks to the other people they know around them.

Although you're a few months off that yet, now is when that process begins and it's important to clock it – as it is to clock that these social changes in your child's make-up also has a subtle but lifelong significance for you and your partner.

Occupation: Daddy

So your child has embarked on her lifelong journey of meeting people – which means you are about to spend the best part of 20 years getting to know other people's children, too.

You'll have your favourites, you'll have ones you can't bear, you'll have ones that make you even more proud of your own children and ones that make you worry about them in comparison.

At this early stage, just a month or two either way age-wise can make a huge difference in the dynamic of a fledgling little friendship. In fact you can quite often see a look of total hero worship on your toddler's face for someone six months older and a look of absolute disdain for some poor mite who is the same distance back.

It's just as easy for parents to make judgements, too – seeing some kids as good influences and some as bad. If your child goes to a nursery or playgroup you'll soon be having all sorts of names thrown at you too, rafts of Jacks and Olivias will enter your world as your increasingly chatty little one tells you about her friends.

Where there are other people's children there are other people. Again you'll no doubt take to and take against these new additions to your life as you see fit, but new additions some of them certainly will be as your child spends years in their children's class at school.

And that's what's so important about the start of this little social dance for your tot. It marks the beginning of their interaction with others and the slow start of the process where you are defined by your children and not the other way around.

Think of your friends, some of whom you'll have known for years and years no doubt and the memorable times you've had together.

Now think of their parents, the people who made you vast amounts of dinner, who gave you lifts, who let you have wine like an adult, or who bollocked you for smoking in the garden.

That's you, now, that is.

To every child and parent who comes through your door, from the toddlers now to the teenagers down the line, first and foremost you'll be someone's dad.

What kind of dad is up to you: cool dad, funny dad, angry dad, hide-behind-the-curtains-and-scare-the-pants-off-them dad – the choice is yours – but you will always be a dad now to a whole raft of new people in your life.

Don't let it scare or depress you. The other part of your life, the 'you' part, isn't over, it's not gone for good, although it might feel like it at times. It's merely taken a back seat for a while, so you can focus on someone else.

And what's fascinating is that it's through being there for someone other than yourself, through being seen as someone else's father for a while, that you really find out who you are.

The weird world of sharing

The advent of friends also brings your child into contact with a new, strange and frustratingly counterintuitive skill they need to master – sharing.

Now none of us is born with the ability to share – and why would we be?

On a strictly Darwinian level, sharing is for losers. In fact, up until very recently it's been thought that we humans were the only ones in the entire animal kingdom who exhibited this frankly whacko altruistic behaviour.

A recent study showed that our closest cousins, chimpanzees, are capable of sharing, too. Although what scientists didn't discover is whether adult chimps cover their eyes in horror and squeal a thousand apologies when their hairy little offspring snatches a banana off a neighbour's infant.

That's the problem, you see, it's us parents who have the big problem with it – especially British parents. I mean, what's more un-British than not waiting your turn? The only thing I can think our children could do that would induce more cringes in us is if they asked every visitor to our house exactly how much they earned – including bonuses – and how they voted in the last general election.

So how should we deal with it?

First, try and disconnect your embarrassment bone. All

two- and three-year-olds think they own the world and especially the stuff in their own toy box, so they are acting perfectly within type – hitting a behavioural milestone, in fact, by understanding the concept of possession.

'Mine' and 'no' register among the first few words of almost every toddler and for good reason, so don't fret.

The next most important thing to clock is that the journey to help them understand the importance of sharing is a very long one. A quick chat won't do it and you'll think the penny has dropped many a time only to be confronted by a very unsavoury scene over a small red ball.

Practising taking turns during games and play is a good idea, especially if you build in the learning that just because you temporarily give up things, it doesn't mean you'll never see them again.

As with potty training, telling your child off for not being a benevolent being is a waste of time at best and counterproductive at worst.

She's not Mahatma Gandhi, it's OK if she wants to keep back her favourite toy and just because there's another parent there to witness it doesn't mean that you are compelled to make an example of her. Rather, when she does share something let her know that you think she's just done a very great thing indeed.

When she gets a bit older, it can be well worth exploring the emotional side of how she feels when someone else plays with her stuff. Talk about how it can make her feel sad and let her know that you understand. Be careful this exercise doesn't boomerang back on you, though, otherwise the next time someone borrows your pen at work you might find yourself pulling everything off your desk in a rage against the injustice of it all and giving the water cooler a series of violent kicks.

As ever, a big part of learning will come through seeing what you do. So when you give her some of your drink, let her know you are sharing with her, or don't just tell her a story or a secret, share it with her instead – that way she will come across this odd little concept often and realise that it isn't just her that has her civil liberties infringed, it happens to all of us.

> ### Words from your fellow fathers:
>
> **Chris, father of two:** *Sharing still depends on the mood of my eldest. Sometimes she's the UN peace-keeping force. Other times she's out to conquer the world and own everything.*
>
> *In general a good sharer, especially with other kids at playschool, not so much with her sister.*
>
> **Winston, father of two:** *There is the middle-class dance parents do when they make their child give everything they are holding, even their dearest toy, to the toddler who is visiting. 'No Jacob, let Tabitha play with Mr Snuffy.'*
>
> *Sometimes it might be best to let them work it out for themselves.*
>
> **Marcus, father of four:** *Four children in a very short period of time solved any sharing problems.*

BOYS AND GIRLS

As your toddler has begun to grow and develop you'll have noticed that she has left the homogenised and limited repartee of the baby behind her and started to exhibit and exhort herself as an individual.

Oh yes, you'll have noticed that all right by now.

Many factors help to shape your child's character – genetics, environment, diet, all play their part.

But as she grows, it's obvious that one factor in particular shows its hand more than most – gender.

As little boys swoop around the garden arms outstretched in jet mode and become obsessive about steam trains that even their grandparents struggle to remember first-hand, you begin to ask yourself, have we made this happen or is it just in them?

Then, in some ways even more starkly, given the changing role of the modern women, when your little girl loves nothing more than putting her soft toys to bed and vacuuming with her replica appliance you (and especially your partner, perhaps) will be amazed at how conformist these little people seem to be to the old-school gender stereotypes that have been far from pushed on them.

This in itself is a generalisation. Plenty of boys love doing 'girl' things and vice versa, but the fact remains that there's more to this nature and nurture debate than just making sure you miss out the sexist bits in any Enid Blyton you read to them.

So other than the obvious ones, what are the actual differences that are playing out in front of you and what's going on in their little hearts, bodies and minds?

The physical side

Although boys and girls grow at roughly the same rate up until early adolescence when girls spurt first, only for boys to catch up and often pass them a year or two later, there are significant differences in the way their motor skills develop.

For boys, the macro or gross skills such as balancing, jumping and running often kick in slightly earlier, while girls' fine skills such as writing develop sooner. This is one of the reasons why girls often speed ahead in early education (often never to be caught up, if the stats are to be believed).

When boys take physical risks, the pleasure centre of their brains lights up like a Christmas tree and they get a thrill, which explains why if you're a parent of a little man you will be kept very busy as they impulsively explore and push boundaries.

The stereotypical story goes that little boys are harder when they are young, crashing, bashing and breaking everything in their path, while girls sit and colour in for hours on end. Then, when the teenage years come around boys become straightforward and easier but girls are transformed into mega-stroppy handfuls.

There's even a term coined on Mumsnet, SMOGs – Smug Mothers of Girls – to neatly encapsulate those for whom the early years of parenting apparently breeze by in a whirr of pink princesses and peaceful play. A counterinsurgency group DMOBs – Defensive Mums of Boys – has even sprung up.

I'll leave you to decide what you make of this war of the young roses being played out online, but you can't help feeling that if someone were to actually state that all small girls should be quiet and timid while all small boys fearless and inquisitive they would rightly get shot down as displaying gender prejudice of the worst kind.

Communication

Verbally, most girls get the gift of the gab earlier than boys, and boys use fewer words on average. Girls have also been seen to be better at clocking non-verbal signals like tone of voice and expression, which play a huge part in them being overall better early communicators than their male peers. Pointing out the emotions felt by characters in books and indeed felt by themselves is a good idea no matter what the sex of your child, but for boys in particular it's a great way of helping them to kickstart that part of their make-up.

Pink brain, blue brain?

As we've mentioned, discourage gender stereotypes though you might, some will still sprout and flourish before your eyes – for instance boys love guns, they just bloody love them, you can banish them from your house if you like but the TV remote, the clothes pegs, the fingers on his hand mean that you can't ban them completely.

Why is that – do boys and girls have different brains? Scientists suspect that might be the case.

There might be, for instance, a part of a boy's brain that makes moving objects, like wheels and balls, utterly fascinating and beguiling and another part of a girl's grey matter that drives them toward pushing a plastic baby round the living room in a toy pram for hours and hours on end, to nurture.

It's often postulated by armchair anthropologists that this is a throwback to our savannah days, when survival depended on men stalking the moving beasts of the plain and women keeping those same beasts away from the children.

They could be right.

Research into the enduring mystery of the 'blue for a boy and pink for a girl' world in which we live recently found that women do seem to be hardwired to preferring the pinks and lilac end of the colour spectrum because in our hunter-gatherer days the ability to tell an edible ripe berry from a potentially poisonous one relied on the ability to grade those types of hues.

What's for certain is that some areas of the brain grow faster in females than in males – and vice versa – and that this process begins from birth.

Research has shown that in girls, the language and emotion parts of the brain are bigger, as is the area that connects the left and right lobes, we males on the other hand have been found to have a slightly bigger deeper emotion centre which looks after things like fear. Brilliant.

Let's not get too fatalistic about this whole boy-brain-girl-brain thing, though.

It's worth remembering as a parent that the old adage that your brain is a muscle that must be exercised like any other turns out to be very true indeed, especially in the young. Key areas can expand or shrink depending on how they are used – so despite the odd bit of predetermined hard wiring there's plenty of room for them being what they want and thinking what they want.

AREN'T BABIES BRILLIANT? THINKING ABOUT TRYING FOR THE NEXT ONE?

The sleep deprivation has passed, kind of, the muslins are all but packed away and the carry cot is full of toys.

You need another baby!

Well, you might do. Although two children remains the most common family size in the UK, the number of only children is on the rise. In 1972, 18% of the nation's children had the toybox all to themselves, while the latest 2020 ONS figures show that around 38% of all the UK's children are living without siblings.

The reason for that seems to be multilayered, with finance and the number of couples already feeling like they are stretching themselves very thin indeed as they both juggle full-time jobs and a child, both being cited.

We all know the lazy stereotypes bandied around about only children – spoilt, bossy oddballs who struggle their entire lives to form well-balanced relationships because they could always watch what they wanted on the telly.

As ever with these kinds of myths, it's possible to trace it back to a single point, in this case according to Susan Newman, a social psychologist and author of *Parenting an Only Child*, to the late 1800s when G. Stanley Hall, known as the founder of child psychology, labelled being an only child 'a disease in itself'.

Newman adds that there:

'. . . have been hundreds and hundreds of research studies that show that only children are no different from their peers.'

As well as the effect of keeping it to just the one has on the child itself, there's also the emotional pull felt by mums and dads alike. Put simply, many of us just want to do it all again. Despite the undoubted difficulties, the chronic sleep deprivation and the loss of great swathes of our former lives – despite how we may moan about it on occasion – being a parent is an experience like no other and to many the thought of only feeling that the once is inconceivable.

Call it greedy breeding if you like, and many do in the world of diminishing resources on which we find ourselves spinning, but for millions of us it's an innate drive that doesn't have an off switch.

There is no absolute guarantee that just because you and your partner have conceived once, you will definitely be able to do it again. Secondary infertility, as it's called, is thought by some experts to be on the increase and even more common than primary infertility – with the later age that couples are choosing to start their families pointed to as part of the cause.

But if you've both decided that you do want another and if you are lucky enough to be able to conceive another you've got two key questions to answer: Can we afford it? And what is the best age gap to leave between our children?

Finance

I hope you're sitting down.

A report by the Centre for Economics and Business Research (CEBR) in 2021 estimated that the average cost of raising a child in the UK from birth to age 21 is around £185,000.

Just take a moment if you need one.

Now it's all very well and good to say that vulgar and coldly pragmatic factors like cost shouldn't come into such an emotional and profound decision like having another baby or not, but at that kind of money you'd be impetuous, love-flooded fools not to at least give it some serious thought – or just absolutely loaded.

There are savings to be made and compromises to be struck, but even if you make your brood make do with a satsuma at Christmas and have them run everywhere to save on petrol, you're still looking at hundreds of thousands of pounds that you'll need to find over the next two decades.

Like most couples who have more than one child, you'll probably do the sums, scratch your head and think, 'we'll manage'. Your next decision is what you see as the optimal age difference between your offspring.

Mind the gap

According to the Office for National Statistics, the average interval between births in England and Wales is 35 months – which as it happens is just about exactly the gap that research has suggested is best for both children and parents.

In truth there are pros and cons to whatever age gap you choose, although medical opinion is pretty undivided on the fact that waiting at least 18 months before having your next one allows the mother's body to recover from the battering it has just been through and also reduces the risk of the next baby being premature or underweight.

In terms of reducing the threat of sibling rivalry there's no doubt that having your second before your first is two years old can have a positive effect, primarily because the older child hasn't really developed a fully rounded sense of identity yet so is less likely to feel full rounded jealousy.

But having two babies in the house, neither really capable of entertaining themselves, or potentially sleeping through the night and both still in nappies must be incredibly hard work. For a while you'd essentially have twins (if your second actually turned out to be twins, life, as you know it, would be over). As time goes on, because they are close in age they stand more of a chance of playing well together earlier. So you take your choice.

Sibling rivalry can be at its most intense when the age gap between children is around the two-year mark. Frustrated and short of fuse anyway, the arrival of an interloper who halves the attention they receive at best can go down very badly indeed. Again, though, once you've got through the tough few years you could well have a couple of lifelong playmates on your hands.

With a gap of three years or above, the chances of sibling rivalry slackens off again with the emotional maturity of the older sibling helping them to cope with the new arrival and often enjoy it.

There's also a sense with a 36-month gap that you've somehow had the time to enjoy the first child properly and give them the attention they need. It also gives both parents a taste of their old life back; work, friends, sleep, all make a gentle return.

For some this is a good thing, for others it's a tease, a nostalgic dream sequence that will soon be snuffed out as they are plunged back into newborn babydom.

While there's no hard and fast answer to the best gap to choose, the fact that for once research and actual activity chime may well point to the fact that a two-to-three-year gap feels best all round. Given that your partner was probably capable of conceiving just a handful of months after the birth of your first child you may well be reading this expecting your second already.

Good luck.

Words from your fellow fathers:

Chris, father of two: *We were both up for number two and we started trying fairly soon after. Unfortunately we lost two pregnancies both at about three months. Possibly the most traumatic, emotional time of my life to date. I could see it nearly destroyed my wife and it's been a long road back – all that hope, that happiness at finding out you're pregnant, all destroyed in an instant, and then back on the same rollercoaster.*

I remember the second one I was super positive, and thought I had a gut feeling that it'd be fine. Maybe I just didn't want to consider the alternative.

But my wife is a vet, and as the doctor waved the ultrasound around, she could 'read' what was on the screen whereas I couldn't. She knew before the doctor even said anything. It was devastating.

The only thing that brought us all back was try number three that came through to become our beautiful daughter – and that three-month check was as nervous as I've ever been.

Mark, father of one: *Our second is due soon – we pretty much had to forget how tiring it all was and look back with rose-tinted glasses to build up the courage, but we're getting old and we didn't want to wait too long or we would never do it.*

Tom, father of two: *We were both equally up for having our second.*

The only disappointment was how quickly it happened vs the first. It was a bit like when you play a child at pool, you quickly find yourself with all your stripes down, and desperately want to play it out so the child can eventually win.

Then, while snookered beyond belief, you manage to pot the black.

PROGRESS REPORT, 25–30 MONTHS

Your toddler

Your child's Tellytubby-like shape that you have become so used to seeing wibbling and wobbling around your house may well begin to change now.

As well as the lengthening of her arms and legs as she grows, the sheer amount of calories burnt on a daily basis as she gets up to all sorts will mean that some of her puppy fat will disappear before your eyes.

What with tantrums, exploration and the fact that every single day brings something new and wondrous to their little lives you will have a very tired soldier on your hands come the end of the day.

Hopefully you've managed to cling on to the lunchtime nap which will help get her through the day, but even with that, she needs to kip and kip long of a night-time. If for whatever reason she has a broken or shortened night you will know about it in a big way the next day.

All of which means, despite swearing years ago that you'd never do it when you were on the receiving end, you will slowly but surely turn into a 'time for bed' parent.

It comes to us all.

You and your partner

Leaving aside the 'let's have another one' debate and the fact that the ever-present exhaustion has not abated, this is often a period to be savoured for both of you.

Forget the much-mentioned tantrums, you've got an endlessly inquisitive, impossibly cute and relentlessly enthusiastic ray of sunshine in your house for the most part.

You'll be truly amazed how quickly the time will come when you are waving your baby goodbye at the school gate for the first time, with a lump in your throat and enough mixed emotions in your head and heart to make you dizzy.

Cliché though it is, you'll never get these moments back, so when you find yourself debating whether to leave early or take a cheeky half day, do it, it's only work after all. Soaking up every minute you can of your two-year-old is a better use of your time in so many ways.

BYE BYE, BABY

So we have nearly reached the end of our journey from newborn to nursery.

The helpless little baby you gingerly brought home nearly three years ago – yes three years ago – is now a fully-fledged member of your family and imagining life without her is nigh on impossible.

As well as having opinions and questions – lots of questions – she will also be developing a lovely little sense of humour. As well as being a joy to behold, not to mention the beginnings of a captive and receptive audience to your jokes, humour is an important part of your toddler's development and brings with it all sorts of benefits and learnings – as if just having a laugh wasn't good enough in itself.

Slightly less funny is having a fussy eater on your hands as many parents do. A baby who throws everything hither and thither is one thing, a headstrong three-year-old who refuses to eat 99% of what is put in front of her is quite another and can cause real worry and stress.

If you've decided to double the size of your family and a new arrival is on the way you might also be anxious about how child number two will be received by current king of the hill number one. It can be a tricky one, but the good news is there are some practical things you can do to lessen the impact and even turn it into something they genuinely look forward to, rather than resent the very mention of.

Quite often this age can be a time of big change for your toddler, not just because of the arrival of a brother or sister, but also because that big event coincides with another – starting nursery. With all three- and four-year-olds entitled to 15 hours of free nursery education for 38 weeks of the year, many a little one makes their first foray into structured childcare – some even putting on a uniform to do it, which will make you proud and sad in equal measure.

If watching your child playing at nursery for the first time doesn't make the point perfectly you'll realise you really are saying goodbye to your baby when they turn three.

Group hug.

KNOCK KNOCK: HUMOUR AND YOUR CHILD

Making a baby smile is one of life's little joys and, when you stop to think about it, they learn to express their pleasure at an astonishingly early stage in their development.

Making a noise or pulling a face to generate a gummy grin soon moves on to games such as peek-a-boo that mildly shock, but because the surprise comes from a trusted source like you or your partner the incongruity tickles them pink.

It's that ability to first recognise and then compute that something unusual or out of the ordinary has just happened that comes to the fore as they move into toddlerhood.

First it's often based around physicality. Daddy with Nana's glasses on! Why, that is hilarious. Mummy pretending to drop a toy on the floor? Priceless.

It may not be award-winning comedy but it's far from a simple process you're witnessing when your toddler gets things like that and falls about. First she needs to know what's normal before they can spot what's not.

Then research has shown that before she cracks up she needs to be able to tell that the action is a deliberate mistake or exaggeration. It is essentially a very early introduction to the notion that an action can have more than one meaning – which is a complex concept indeed for someone who still can't wipe their own bottom properly.

Once her vocabulary gets that bit more wide-ranging, she will start reacting to words that pop up in the wrong place, or seem to.

'The juice is in the bottom of the bag' could, on any given day, reduce a three-year-old to pant-wetting hysterics. Not only does that represent the continuation for another generation of the fine and longstanding obsession we have in this country with toilet humour, it is also wordplay, pure and simple.

As well as being just lovely to be around, this blossoming sense of humour really is something to be encouraged because it brings with it some tangible benefits.

As well as helping her to see things from different perspectives and beyond their face value, she also develops the confidence to respond spontaneously to situations.

You'll probably have noticed that toddlers often take themselves and their problems really quite seriously. Intense, some might call them on occasion. Well, as their sense of humour starts to really come together at this age it can be a real ally. Making a toddler laugh as she teeters on the precipice of a major meltdown can have miraculous effects.

As she grows up, a well-developed sense of humour, as we all know, is a fantastic thing to have in her arsenal – from making her generally happier to being better able to handle the slings and arrows of outrageous fortune that life launches at her.

As well as the obvious benefits, medical evidence of the physical and mental pluses laughter brings continues to mount. From stimulating your major organs and muscle groups thanks to your increased intake of oxygen-rich air to pacifying your stress response, laughter, if not the best medicine, is certainly right up there with penicillin and chocolate.

So what can you do to help your child grow up loving to laugh? Well, being funny yourself is a good start. No pressure, of course.

You don't have to be that funny, it is small children we are talking about. As audiences go, they are on your side as you are already one of the two funniest people they have ever met – but just remember to be a bit silly and laugh out loud, even when you are having the week from hell.

Also, making a point of recognising and encouraging your child's early attempts at humour is a great idea. As a man you will know for a fact that there are very few feelings on the planet with the ability to make you feel as good about yourself as having someone laugh at your jokes.

You can also help to create a humour-rich environment by getting really involved in the books they read, there are some seriously funny children's titles out there. If you are stuck, check out the inspired nonsense that comedy legend Spike Milligan wrote for his kids – it will have you all laughing out loud.

The only pitfall to look out for on this front is that learning when humour isn't appropriate is actually quite tricky – or at least, I find it tricky. So when they put the whoopy cushion under your aunty with the heart condition, or decide to end everything they say, all day, with the word poo, go easy on them, it's just a joke!

Fussy eaters

Fussy eating isn't funny.

If you've got a picky toddler at your dinner table every day you'll know that it can be a hugely stressful and upsetting situation to tackle.

It must be something to do with the very basic need we have as parents to make sure our offspring are well fed, but watching them refuse one thing after another can get to you in a way few other things do – to the extent that some parents actively dread mealtimes and the futile battle of the bowl they must once again wage.

As soon as the little person in the highchair gets wind that you are getting vexed about the whole thing, she will clamp her lips together tighter than ever and wave dish after dish away like a disgusted food critic.

The trick, hard though it may be for you and your partner to pull off, is to breathe deeply, pull a smile from somewhere and take the heat out of the situation. As dire as it may feel this, like so many other things you think will be lifelong afflictions, will pass in the fullness of time.

Part of the problem is often the empty plate syndrome. We parents love nothing more than to see every speck of grub devoured, but we often don't give enough thought to the size of the stomach we are trying to fill or the portion size that would accomplish it.

The result is a toddler confronted with a relative mountain of food and a parent disheartened that they've not finished it.

If your child keeps their mouth shut halfway through a meal, shakes their head, says no, pushes the spoon away, squirrels food in their mouth and refuses to swallow it, tries desperately to get out of the highchair or begins to gag or retch – guess what? They have probably had enough.

As obvious as that sounds, it's amazing how easy it is for a parent to ignore signs that from an adult would be as conclusive as can be and put them down to mischief or misguidedness just because they come from an infant.

Aside from keeping an eye out for them just being full, there are things you can do to encourage your toddler to broaden their horizons a little and take the brave step away from yoghurt and toast towards a world of nutritious and exciting eating possibilities.

Like almost everything in their lives, when you place a new food in front of a toddler they are almost certainly seeing and smelling it for the first time. While some youngsters barely let it hit the plate before devouring it, others sniff, prod and poke at it as if they are expecting it to come alive and run off at any moment.

They need time to learn that the food you put in front of them is safe and enjoyable – some do this in a split second, others take months and even years. Be careful not to fall into the trap of thinking a certain food is off limits just because they have refused it a couple of times. Bring it out a few weeks later with a flourish and she might just tuck in.

Arranging a daily routine for meals and eating together as a family or occasionally with her little friends can be a good idea too. Once she sees how much everyone else loves sprouts, she could well be encouraged to try them herself, maybe.

Making finger foods part of mealtimes can make a difference, as can putting a sheet down and letting her make as much mess as she likes. If you put her in the bath and told her to sit perfectly still while she was washed she would probably start to refuse to do that too. Make it fun.

Talking of which, when you have a bit of time, take her shopping, get her to choose her food and then ask her to help you make it. It's not just bosses who need to feel ownership of things. If your child thinks she has been part of the decision-making process around mealtimes, she is much more likely to end up with food in her mouth than on the floor.

Praise, as ever, is your best friend. Treat the digesting of one pea like a major lottery win and adorn your toddler with kisses and stickers and resist the temptation to end the moment on a downer by then loading up the fork with 35 more of the green demons.

A little pitfall to be aware of, and one that I must have stumbled into hundreds of times before I cottoned on, is to give a drink before or with her meal. Several glugs later I'd have an empty glass and a little boy who was full of liquid.

If things get really bad and you or your partner start to actually make a reserve meal for when the first is refused, you need to rein things back. Once your toddler realises all they need to do to have their food replaced is turn their nose up, you will soon be running a Yo! Sushi carousel for one very picky customer.

Likewise, the old threat of withholding the pudding if the savoury isn't eaten has always struck me as a sure-fire way for kids to begin life thinking that anything that isn't sweet is inferior. Don't be afraid to try them on things you are convinced they won't like, or because you don't like them and don't be afraid to do a bit of rebranding.

Fried calamari? Never.

Octopus chips? Gimme, gimme, gimme.

Finally, don't feel guilty or down if one mealtime turns into a nightmare. Go again next time full of enthusiasm and optimism. They can smell a doom-laden situation a mile off, these three-year-olds.

If things continue to be difficult and you become seriously worried about how much she is taking in, or if you suspect she has lost any weight, make a list of all the food and drink that has passed her lips over the course of a week and go and chat to your GP.

Chances are the problem isn't anywhere near as grave as you thought and the doctor will helpfully tell you that you've got a fussy eater on your hands.

Thanks, Doc.

Words from your fellow fathers:

Simon, father of one: *Our boy isn't a bad eater at all – he eats the same as us where practical. I was very keen to get him eating grown-up stuff such as olives, garlic, etc. Don't know why, all he really likes is garden peas!*

Jason, father of two: *Our eldest was good in the early years and respected his Irish and Sri Lankan roots by gobbling potatoes and rice.*

At three he eats sausages, olives and not much else.

Tom, father of two: *I made several vats of things, 20 ice cube trays' worth. I was a bit gutted at the rejection of my 'cod, spinach and potato'*

> *number, particularly so as it became my work lunches for a few times. Man,*
> *was it plain.*

GETTING READY FOR YOUR NEW BABY

Bringing a new baby back to your home, a home which is now your toddler's personal castle, can be very tricky.

It doesn't have to be a nightmare and you could be pleasantly amazed by how loving and accepting your eldest child is, but there's always a chance that every cuddle will turn into a vice-like bear hug and every seemingly gentle stroke into a poorly disguised poke.

It's understandable, though, isn't it?

You've poured affection and attention into your eldest in quite staggering amounts, you've told them that they are the most beautiful thing in the whole wide world on a daily basis and you've fallen in love with them hook, line and sinker.

Then along comes another one and halves it all. Although it probably doesn't feel like half to them, no matter how many 'proud brother or sister' balloons you give them – it must be a very strange thing for them to get their head around.

You can help them, though. There are ways and means of softening the blow and even getting them excited. First, don't be tempted to tell them you are expecting a brother or sister too early. Nine months is an eternity for a toddler and the more time you give them to mature and grow the better chance you have of them computing the news that bit better.

Once you do spill the beans and tell her that there is a baby growing inside Mummy's tummy, be aware how utterly mind-blowing and bizarre the news must sound to them.

A baby, one of those things in the pushchairs, growing in Mummy's tummy, GROWING IN A TUMMY?!

Not only will they struggle with the biology of it all – and I'm not sure I fully understand it – they will have no idea of the changes a second baby will bring to their lives.

And neither will you.

Tell them that the baby can hear them, which after a few months is true, and encourage them to talk to their brother or sister and even get some photos out of them when they were tiny so they can visualise this new thing in their lives.

It's tempting to talk about the new baby being a playmate for them, which will indeed get them excited, until they are presented with the non-talking, non-moving, non-anything bundle in a few months' time and quite simply think it's rubbish.

As the birth approaches, there are some good children's books that address this issue out there. Getting your toddler involved in the preparations can be a smart move, too, and make them feel really involved and grown-up.

Letting them choose a present for their brother or sister is a similarly bond-inducing exercise and if when they first meet the baby the little mite has also remembered to bring a present for them, well that would be just fantastic and start everyone on a good footing.

The first meeting between the two is much discussed and probably over-analysed. There's one school of thought that says never let your toddler catch first sight of their new sibling when it's in Mummy's arms. Legend has it that this will leave an indelible imprint on them from which they will never recover.

What's for sure is that if your partner has been away from your older child for a few days in hospital she will want to hug her to within an inch of her life once they are reunited so for that reason alone it's probably best if the baby is in the cot rather than her arms.

A word to the wise, if your older tot is still in a cot at home, a cot that you need for the new one on the way, it's best to make the move to the big bed before the baby is anywhere near the point where she will essentially turf their older sibling out on their ear.

Once the baby is born, it's inevitable they will get a lot of attention. Everyone loves a baby, and the cooing and fussing can be hard for your toddler to stomach so be alive to it. If necessary, ask relatives who come to visit to make a fuss of both of them – any of them who have had children themselves will almost certainly know the score on this having lived it themselves.

While any contact your toddler has with the newborn will need to be strictly and closely supervised, it's important not to appear hugely over-protective of the baby. Up until now the only person they have seen you care that much about is them so try and be sensitive to how you come across.

Watching a toddler 'hold' a newborn, even with you in ultra-close attendance, can be one of life's more nerve-wracking experiences, but if you ban all contact between the two it is very hard for any kind of relationship, no matter how fledgling, to develop between them.

Having said that you should never leave the two of them alone together, no matter how mature or pleased with the baby they seem to be.

With your partner having just given birth and concentrating on feeding and bonding with her new child you have an important role to play. Some fathers see what was a quite frosty, mummy-focused infant suddenly become dad's best friend and some long-lasting bonds can be formed in this early spell.

Making some special time to be with your toddler on her own, just playing and talking and listening, can really work wonders. It gives your partner a break to get to grips with early motherhood again, and it can strengthen and deepen your relationship with your child at a time when they need it most.

The tricky thing is that even with paternity leave, time will be at a premium for you because you, my friend, will have another baby in the house!

What's having two like?

We are all men of the world so I'll give it to you straight. It's very hard indeed.

As a couple you become pulled in either one of two directions – neither of which is towards each other. Sleep deprivation returns like a long-lost friend, except this time rather than being able to catch a few zzzzzs when the baby dozes through most of the day, you'll have a toddler with 10 hours of sleep in them demanding you build that obstacle course you promised.

And that's just you. Your partner will be seriously under the cosh and needs all the help she can get. All the preparation tips you hear but never do before your first baby are now essential – freeze lots of meals, never turn down help and let the finer points of housework go hang for a few weeks.

Speaking as one of seven children I literally have no clue how my parents kept us and themselves alive. None.

All I can imagine is that there were a spate of mild winters, they had the capacity to survive on the equivalent of one night's sleep spread across the entire year (a gift they have not passed on to me) or that somehow the 60s and 70s and 80s existed across a different time dimension that meant children spent the first decade of their lives in a kind of sedentary stasis – growing but never moving or talking.

Either that or previous generations were just hard and we patently aren't.

Of course, you will survive the arrival of your second, you learn to cope and turn it into a new version of normality just as you did when your first one arrived and catapulted your world upside down.

What's on your side this time is that you've already been there once. You'll both be less panicky and more measured as you recognise scenarios that sent you off the deep end first time round but are met with no more than a knowing smile now.

You'll still be beyond knackered, though.

Words from your fellow fathers:

Winston, father of two: *The age gap of around two-and-a-half years, so far, works very well, in that the older child is mature enough to accept another child and understand, while the younger one is close enough in age to be of interest to the first.*

To walk in a room and hear them giggling together is a thing of joy. It is normally because one is sat on the other, squashing them.

Jason, father of two: *No real jealousy between the boys, just mummy envy from me, she was in demand.*

Tom, father of two: *I wanted a third, she didn't. The business has now officially ceased trading. I'm cool with that.*

SAYING GOODBYE TO YOUR BABY

So here we are, at the end of our story.

Everyone involved in our little journey from newborn to nursery has come a very long way since the nervous drive home from the hospital.

Your baby started out as an utterly dependent being who looked and acted, let's be honest, so undercooked that she felt like she could have done with another six months in the oven-like womb to warm through thoroughly.

But once she got her bearings, found out where the milk was coming from and got on with the business of growing, she has transformed at an astonishing rate into the bobbydazzler you see before you.

Your partner has seen herself transformed too; a whole new way to be and feel has buried itself deep in her psyche and the emotions, impulses and beliefs that motherhood has instilled in her will be with her forever.

And you?

You have become a father, not just a 'new dad' or a mother's helper, but a father. There's a long way to go and many more moments of joy and pain to experience, but by the time your child reaches three you have at least begun to understand just what a responsibility and a blessing it is to have someone call you Daddy.

All right, so you can't go out and enjoy yourself as often, or put as much into your job as you used to, but the truth is your children will give you more enjoyment than you know what to do with in the coming years if you let them.

As for work, this is the hardest, most important project you'll ever take on – anything else is primarily just paying the bills.

The third year of your child's life can bring with it a change in tone and environment for many parents, with nursery entering the picture. While it's not exactly packing the kids off to boarding school there's no doubt that when your baby starts their first day on the long educational road – even when this first step is a very gentle one – you will feel the sands of time passing incredibly quickly as they come home with tales of best friends and songs sung, of fallings out and races won.

The little one you've carried around, cuddled and wiped the bottom of will be making a big move towards independence and while you'll no doubt feel pleased and proud at the progress they make, it hurts a little bit too as they need you that little bit less.

But let's not get too tearful. We've got years of being there for them ahead of us so let's resolve to enjoy and savour as much of it as we possibly can. Let's also give ourselves and our partners the credit we deserve and not, in this age of the micro-manager, fret about every decision we make or judgement we might get wrong.

It's worth remembering that not so very long ago, life used to be about survival and that while the luxury of time we have been given can bring with it a host of benefits, we can also think, ponder and analyse ourselves to a standstill.

You are right in the thick of the best, most important thing you'll ever do, enjoy it.

So here's to fathers' intuition and the trusting of it – and here's to you and your family.

Final words from your fellow fathers:

Colin, father of two: *We recently took our daughter for her first day at nursery – I was in BITS. Cried, no, sobbed all the way to work.*

Ben, father of two: *The best thing about being a father is looking at your growing family and thinking how wonderful it is to love and be loved.*

This feeling is increased tenfold if your children are all asleep.

Chris, father of two: *The best part of it all is cuddles and laughter with your kids. Just having them there in your life – it is indescribable how such small simple things that they do, or say, or the way they look at you, can cast so much sunshine in your life. They enable you to truly feel love. And they turn grown men into sops.*

Jason, father of two: *My eldest son says the best thing about being a dad is being able to play on the computers.*

I say it's the best thing that happened to me.

PROGRESS REPORT, 31–36 MONTHS

Your toddler

It's tempting, especially if a second baby has arrived, to expect your three-year-old to never put a foot wrong. Compared with the newborn she will seem like a fully grown adult, but they are still tiny little things.

In fact, your toddler becomes a bit of a sensitive soul at this stage and is quite aware of other people's moods and emotional states and might be curious as to why Mummy is sad or why Daddy is cross.

Being as open and honest as you can is almost always the best bet – although explaining that the panicked look on your face is due to the fact that as a family you are very close to the breadline and unless you find a bag of used tenners in the street soon you will have to sell the dog, is probably worth giving a miss.

Encouraging her to feel comfortable talking about her feelings and fostering the sense that it's completely normal to have different emotions is a great habit to get into – and might even teach you a thing or two.

With nursery round the corner your child will come into contact with all sorts of new feelings and situations as she becomes even more of a social being. Helping her to be attuned and at home to her own emotions as well as those of others is a real gift you can help to give her.

Also on the cerebral front your house might get a visit from an imaginary friend at this age.

If an invisible playmate does turn up, don't panic and call in the shrinks, it's not only normal, it's actually very creative.

Often it is also a way children make distinctions between good and bad, by using their friend as the one who is responsible for naughty things that she may have done herself or for playing out scenarios to see what would happen without having to do it for real.

They sound good these imaginary friends, don't they? We should all have one.

Try not to make a big deal of her friend either by bursting her imaginary bubble or, conversely, by embracing them too wholeheartedly and losing your marbles.

You and your partner

Now that your baby is all grown-up and reaching her third birthday, she now officially becomes your best mate.

She will still have her moments but all in all it's astonishing just how grown-up three-year-olds are nowadays. Whether it's a good or a bad thing is a moot point but I'm pretty sure we weren't up to, or in to, half as much as they are when we were infants.

You'll find yourself having proper conversations with them now and you will definitely be able to see traits from both you and your partner coming through loud and clear – most of them good, some of them making you realise that you need to be very careful what you do and say in front of them.

Outbursts in the car, arguments at home, they are all fair game and hearing your toddler repeat something you'd really rather they didn't is one of life's low points.

That little pitfall aside, you begin to get a real glimpse of the person you have helped to create at this age and just how much enjoyment, love, pride and friendship you can benefit from as they continue to grow.

You and your partner have put an awful lot into getting your baby this far and you should be proud. From now on in your child will be increasingly paying you back for your efforts with interest. The things she says, the things she does, the hugs she gives and the privilege of being able to see a unique little person developing at such close quarters will bring so much to your life that the memories of the sleepless nights will fade away to nothing as your heart is filled with pride and love for the special little person you have both brought into being.

Good work.

INDEX

alcohol 53–4

antenatal classes 49–50, 116–20

assisted deliveries 191–3

au pairs 326

baby baths 96–7

baby blues 269–70

baby bouncers 316–17

back pain 146–7

baby and parent progress
  0-3 months 275–6
  4-6 months 292–4
  7-9 months 310–13
  10-12 months 333–5
  13-16 months 363–5
  17-20 months 389–92
  21-24 months 419–21

25-30 months 447–8

31-36 months 464–6

baby walkers 316–17

babymoon 72–5

bath time 262

bed linen 39

beds 412–14

being told of pregnancy 7, 8–9, 20–1

birth choices 120–3

birth plans 149–52

birth process
  assisted deliveries 191–3
  description of labour 179–85
  final push 190–1, 194
  first stage of labour 173–5
  maternal bonding 195
  pain relief 183–4, 185–8

birth process (*cont.*)
placenta delivery 195–6
second stage of labour 175–6
stories of 197–209
third stage of labour 176
transition stage 173, 174,
189–90
umbilical cord 195
birth units 121–3
birthdays 330–2
birthing partners 123, 177–8
biting 405–7
bleeding
after birth 267
during pregnancy 21
books 348–50
bottle-feeding 247–8
brain development 337–9, 441–2
Braxton Hicks 89–90, 170
breastfeeding 239–47, 268
bruises 377–8
buggies 92–6
bump size 86–8
burns 381–2

caesarean section (C-section)
193–4, 268–9
castor oil 212
cat litter 39

changing mats 97
childcare 322–9
childcare vouchers 329
childminders 323–4
choking 378–9
clothes 98
colds 263–4
communication 137–8
conception 2–5
constipation 26–7
controlled crying 283–5
cot death 254–6
cots 96, 412
cravings 76–8
crawling 299–302
crying 258–9, 283–5
curry 212
cuts 377–8

dehydration 380
dental work 58
digital devices 357–61
doulas 123, 177–8
Down's syndrome 44–6
dummies 280–2, 412, 414,
415–16
dying hair 57

ectopic pregnancies 15–17

Entonox 185
epidurals 187–8
exercise 54–6
exhaustion 28–9, 39

family for childcare 327
fathers of fathers-to-be 105–8
fathers in history 126–7
fathers as second-best 409–12
fearfulness 385–9
finances 83, 91–2, 444
first aid 376–82
first stage of labour 173–5
flexible working 327–9
food and drink
    during pregnancy 52–3, 76–8,
        84
    fussy eating 453–7
    weaning 296–9
friendships 432–8
fussy eating 453–7

gas and air 185
gender
    of baby 70–1
    brain development 441–2
    communication skills 440–1
    developmental differences
        439–40

roles at home 128–31, 135–7,
    287–90
getting to hospital 156–7
growth of new-born babies
    248–50

haemorrhoids 165
heartburn 27–8
heat stroke 379–80
hitting 405–7
holidays 366–76
home births 120–1
homeopathy 212–13
hormonal changes in fathers-to-be
    60–4
hospital bags 152–6
humour 450–3

importance of fathers 109–10
inducing labour 213–15

journal keeping 66

kicking 405–7

labour
    description of 179–85
    first stage 173–5
    inducing 213–15

labour (*cont.*)
pain relief 183–4, 185–8
second stage 175–6
third stage 187
transition stage 173, 174,
189–90
language and literacy development
339–43, 348–51
lifting and carrying 66, 268–9
love for children 383–5

massage 83
maternal bonding 131–4, 195
maternity leave 101, 160–1
meal preparation 172
membrane rupturing 214
midwives 177
miscarriages 9–14
mobile phones 59
morning sickness 22–5
Moses baskets 96
movement of unborn baby 79–81,
90–1
muslins 97–8
must-dos during pregnancy
month 1 20–1
month 2 39
month 3 49–50
month 4 66

month 5 83–4
month 6 112–14
month 7 146–7
month 8 165–6
month 9 171–3

name choosing 101–5
nannies 325–6
nappies 97
nappy bins 98–9
nappy changing 260–1
National Childbirth Trust (NCT)
49–50, 117–20
nesting 158–60
NHS antenatal classes 116–17
nuchal translucency scan 44–6
nurseries 324–5

overdue births 209–15

pain relief 183–4, 185–8
painting and decorating 58–9
parenting styles 320–1
parties 331–2
paternity leave 100–1
pelvic floor exercises 113–14
pethidine 186
physical recovery after birth
266–7

piles 165

pineapple 212

placenta delivery 195–6

play 344–7

poisons 379

postnatal depression 270–4

potty training 424–32

pregnancy progress

    month 1 17–19

    month 2 37–8

    month 3 47–9

    month 4 64–5

    month 5 81–2

    month 6 111–12

    month 7 143–6

    month 8 161–4

    month 9 169–71

pregnancy tests 5–6

premature births 140–3

Prostaglandin 213–14

pushing 405–7

raspberry leaf tea 165–6

relationships

    after birth 124–5, 138–9,
        305–6

    and gender roles 289–90

relaxation 172

runny nose 26

scans 41–6, 68–72

seat belt extensions 146

second child 422–4, 442–7,
    457–62

second stage of labour 175–6

separation anxiety 319–21

sex

    after birth 307–10

    during pregnancy 31–7, 114,
        211

sharing 436–8

sleep

    0–3 months 134–5, 252–4

    4–6 months 278–80, 282–3

smacking 403–4

smiling 261

sore breasts 26

stretch marks 113

Syntocinon 214

talking to unborn baby 88–9

teething 302–3

television 353–7

telling people about birth 171

telling people about pregnancy 8,
    20, 46–7

TENS machine 183–4

terrible twos 394–408

third stage of labour 176

toys 345–7

transition stage 173, 174,
189–90

travel cots 264–5

treats 49, 146, 165

two-year checks 417–19

umbilical cord 195

urinating 49

walking
baby 315–17
during pregnancy 146–7

waxing 57–8

weaning 296–9

wedge pillows 112–13

wind 78–9

yoga classes 66